GW00808277

The **Guardian**

History of the Open Golf Championship

The **Guardian**

History of the Open Golf Championship

edited by
John Samuel

Fourth Estate · *London*

First published in Great Britain in 1992 by
Fourth Estate Limited
289 Westbourne Grove
London W11 2QA

A catalogue record for this book is available from
the British Library

ISBN 1–85702–037–5

Typeset and originated by
August Filmsetting, Haydock, St Helens
Printed in Great Britain by
The Bath Press Ltd
Book design by Peter McClure

CONTENTS

Foreword by Peter Alliss 1
Introduction 3

1920 Deal 9
1921 St Andrews 12
1922 Sandwich 15
1923 Troon 18
1924 Hoylake 21
1925 Prestwick 24
1926 Lytham St Annes 27
1927 St Andrews 31
1928 Sandwich 33
1929 Gullane 36

1930 Hoylake 38
1931 Carnoustie 41
1932 Sandwich 44
1933 St Andrews 46
1934 Sandwich 50
1935 Muirfield 53
1936 Hoylake 55
1937 Carnoustie 58
1938 Sandwich 61
1939 St Andrews 65

1946 St Andrews 67
1947 Hoylake 69
1948 Muirfield 71
1949 Sandwich 73

1950 Troon 76
1951 Portrush 78
1952 Lytham St Annes 80
1953 Carnoustie 82
1954 Birkdale 84
1955 St Andrews 87
1956 Hoylake 89
1957 St Andrews 91
1958 Lytham St Annes 94
1959 Muirfield 97

1960 St Andrews 99
1961 Birkdale 101
1962 Troon 103
1963 Lytham St Annes 106
1964 St Andrews 108
1965 Birkdale 110
1966 Muirfield 112
1967 Hoylake 115
1968 Carnoustie 117
1969 Lytham St Annes 119

1970 St Andrews 121
1971 Birkdale 124
1972 Muirfield 126
1973 Troon 128
1974 Lytham St Annes 130
1975 Carnoustie 132
1976 Birkdale 135
1977 Turnberry 138
1978 St Andrews 140
1979 Lytham St Annes 143

1980 Muirfield 145
1981 St George's 149
1982 Troon 151
1983 Birkdale 154
1984 St Andrews 157
1985 St George's 160
1986 Turnberry 164
1987 Muirfield 167
1988 Lytham St Annes 170
1989 Troon 175

1990 St Andrews 179
1991 Birkdale 183
1992 Muirfield 186

Picture credits 189
Index 191

FOREWORD
By Peter Alliss

Cricket, boxing and golf, three very different sports, have provided some fine writing over the years. Boxing is without doubt the most brutal of all sports, so why should it be able to conjure up such magical prose? Cricket... the sound of leather on willow... the strange complexities of the game... the settings... the characters – ah, the characters!

And then golf, perhaps the most curious of games. A good walk spoilt, say some. But then, in the words of Henry Longhurst, 'One of its great joys is that it takes us to so many glorious places.'

I turned to professional golf in the autumn of 1946. I had played in the Boys' Championship at Bruntsfield on the outskirts of Edinburgh and was beaten in the semi-finals by a chap called Donald Dunsdon. I came home disappointed, as the writers of the day had decided I was going to be the champion. And why not? Was I not Percy Alliss's son? Well, it wasn't to be, and upon my return father decided that as I wasn't going to be Lord Chancellor, the Governor of the Bank of England, an opera singer, or a leading accountant, I should join him as his assistant.

One of my first professional outings was to Manchester – to be precise the Mere Golf & Country Club on the south side of the city. It was the third of three tournaments to which I, as a seventeen-year-old, had been despatched by my father. My brother Alec was chaperon. We started at the *Yorkshire Evening Post* Tournament in Leeds, where I failed to qualify for the final two rounds. Disappointment... But our heads were still relatively high as we moved to St Andrews where I managed to qualify for the final thirty-six holes by the skin of my teeth and came away with a cheque for £5! Well, it was a start. Then it was off by train to Manchester and Mere, where I finished fifth and won £57.10*s*. So our three-week trip had not cost Dad a penny; in fact we came home with money in our pockets.

It was not a profit in real terms but I was on my way. I tell you this because my memories of playing that delightful course are very clear. It was here for the first time that I saw someone reading the *Manchester Guardian*.

His name was Fred Wormold, and we went on to become great friends. It was he who introduced me to the joys of reading a 'posh paper'. Perhaps they did not consider it a posh paper at the time – it was really a large provincial – but one thing it certainly provided was good writing. I shall always be grateful to Fred because it took me away from the tabloids of the day.

It was to be a number of years before I was to meet, know and recognise the writers. In my early days they were simply 'Our Golf Correspondent'. In fact the *Guardian* has been blessed with three splendid 'name' writers over the last forty years or so – Pat Ward-Thomas, Peter Dobereiner and Dai Davies.

Pat Ward-Thomas was a sharp-featured man with a slightly nervous air. When things went wrong his temper was amazing. It was a strange temper, rather like the weather on the north face of the Eiger. One minute all would be sunny, then, as something disturbed him, a glorious fit of rage. Oh, it was a wonder to see! Reading glasses were his speciality. He had a habit of pushing them on to the top of his head, then forgetting where they were – a cause of great anguish. Once he lost a pair for several hours. After struggling all day and borrowing various colleagues' spy glasses, he found them lying on the front seat of his car. With perhaps twenty or thirty strangers around, he opened the door, saw them there and shouted at the top of his voice: 'There you are, you little bastards!' Startled faces all around...

Pat Ward-Thomas was a lovely writer, a man who became very friendly with the great stars of the day. He loved telling us how he had been on a trip in Arnold Palmer's aeroplane, or how he'd visited Augusta for the first time. Truly a joy to read.

Peter Dobereiner is a very different kettle of fish – a tall, rather doleful-looking man, reminiscent of a loveable basset hound with a slow, loping walk, he has the keenest of minds and a wonderful sense of the ridiculous. That's the greatest asset one can possess, no matter what one's profession – to see the nonsense of it, to prick the pomposity.

After all, golf is only a game. Dobereiner managed to bring a new dimension to golf writing and I'm not absolutely certain he was in immediate favour with 'them'. He may actually have been the first golf writer to put a swear word into print. He has a way with words, a way of describing things. He goes on flights of fancy. He introduces readers to overseas players. He loves not only the ridiculous, but also the wild colonial boys and their weird and wonderful 'goings on'.

Dobereiner in the *Guardian* was always interesting, informative and a good read. Now, holding that venerable seat, we have David (Dai) Davies, who is indeed a formidable figure. His physical shape has changed a little over the years. Someone once remarked of Bobby Locke that he was getting slightly portly. No, said Locke, the only trouble was that his chest had dropped slightly! Now this may or may not be a sign of good living, but certainly Dai Davies provides good writing. Again, he is a man who looks for stories and happenings that are slightly out of the normal. Perhaps more than any other personality he is in the Pat Ward-Thomas mould. He can get monumentally cross about a variety of subjects. He's affectionately known in the trade as Captain Grumpy. When you see him on one of his tirades he looks good for promotion.

Cricket, boxing, golf: they have all had the benefit of writers who could write, people who have the ability to make us think, smile, and actually feel as if we were there. The game of golf and the *Guardian* have both been blessed with their writers, and long may that continue.

INTRODUCTION
John Samuel

Peter Dobereiner, one of the *Guardian*'s eminent golf writers over the years, referred once to the immense value of a golf book. 'What you do is balance it on top of your head and then swing a club as hard as you can. Once you have mastered the art of taking a full, vicious swing without dislodging the book, you can play golf.'

He was referring, of course, to books which tell you how to cure a hook or a slice and this is not intentionally one such. It is a last-day record of the Open Championship, as reported in the pages of the *Guardian*, from 1920 when the Royal and Ancient Golf Club took over to the present day. The prehistory of the Open is a romance of its own. On 17 October 1860, Willie Park, Sr of Musselburgh won a leather belt presented by the Earl of Eglinton at the Prestwick club on the west coast of Scotland scoring 174 over three 12-hole rounds. It was not strictly 'open'. There were only eight players, all professionals, but the barred amateurs all made such representations to the club that they were admitted the following year and ever since the championship has been 'open'.

Using a gutty ball, Young Tom Morris won the belt outright with three successive victories from 1868 to 1870. In 1871, for the only time, there was no trophy, but Prestwick then associated the Royal and Ancient and the Honorable Company of Edinburgh Golfers in the purchase of a silver claret jug to be awarded to the winner annually (he takes a replica home, the original being retained at St Andrews).

The venues spread over the years, and in 1894 J.H. Taylor, then of Winchester, became the first English winner at the first English host club, St George's, Sandwich. The triumvirate of Taylor, Harry Vardon and James Braid created a new era for golf with sixteen victories until Vardon's sixth and last in 1914. Just before the outbreak of the First World War, a letter to the magazine *Country Life* was instrumental in the R and A taking over the running of the Championship. It was from a golf course architect, W. Herbert Fowler, who urged the R and A that having given the world the Rules of Golf in 1888 it should wake up to its responsibilities and assert its authority and position to run the Open and Amateur Championships with a committee of, say, thirty members.

Wake up the R and A eventually did, the committee came into being in 1919, and, as 'A.L.L.' of the *Guardian* was pleased to report, George Duncan of Deal in 1920 became the first modern champion with a four-round score of 303 and first prize of £100.

'A.L.L.' was Arthur Leonard Lee, a respected general reporter and sports writer from Leicester, and a considerable games player himself, who eventually became sports editor of the *Guardian*, doubling it with golf writing before ill health forced his retirement in 1932.

David Ayerst, historian of the *Guardian*'s early and mid years, remarks that the 'M.G.' of the interwar period much prided itself on its sports reporting. 'A paper that had had A.N. Monkhouse writing on golf and which still regularly sent Neville Cardus to cricket matches set an exacting standard.' Evelyn Montague, an Oxford athletics blue and steeplechase bronze medallist at the 1924 Paris Olympic Games, looked after the sports pages until his brother Larry took over in 1934.

The inter-war years were times of major social and political change and golf reflected it. America's invasion of the Open began in 1921 when Jock Hutchison, a Chicago professional of Scottish origin, beat the Oxford amateur, Roger Wethered, by nine strokes in a two-round play-off. The following year 'A.L.L.' was reporting that the prestige of British golf had never had such a blow. Americans took three of the first four places.

Moreover . . . 'Hagen, whose age is 30, won the American championship in 1914, and after that became associated with a financial firm in Wall Street, so that when he competed for the Open title at Deal and St Andrews his temperament was more that of a holiday-maker than of a prospective champion.'

On the course he had a style dangerous to copy. 'His address is made with the hands in front of the ball, his weight is nearly all on the left foot, and at the moment of hitting he is so much on his toes that he always seems in danger of tumbling.'

For eleven long years, from Arthur Havers' victory in 1923 until Henry Cotton's triumph at Sandwich in 1934, 'A.L.L.' reported on a stream of American successes, Walter Hagen the king succeeded by Bobby Jones the omnipotent. Each placed a different mark on the British game. Hagen did so insouciantly, his butler serving him a champagne picnic from a hired Rolls. Jones, the amateur, victorious in 1926, 1927 and, most gloriously, in 1930 as part two of the Grand Slam, had a gentlemanly grace deeply admired in the members' club rooms.

Correspondents often took it upon themselves to defend the game's codes. 'A.L.L.', finding some comfort in the 1925 victory at Prestwick of a Cornish-American, Jim Barnes, offered a tart tailpiece: 'It is time Scotsmen realised that golf courses are not airing grounds for dogs, but it is probably too much to expect that they will themselves refrain from scampering over the links like sheep. To-day there must have been over [sic] 20,000 spectators, and there were occasions on which the players were left such narrow lanes to play along that some of them could not see the flag.'

Tommy Armour, a Scottish-American, won in 1931, but Cotton earned a large measure of 'A.L.L.' obloquy. Losing seven strokes to Armour during the day he 'threw the championship away by erratic short play . . . standing for long periods with his club motionless behind the ball.' All was forgiven in 1934.

On the final day 'cars clustered in the parking places like great shining beetles. Cinema cameramen mounted their talkie machines on the tops of their vans, and laid long, wriggling cables across the tee.' Cotton equalled Sarazen's record in winning with a total of 283, and 'A.L.L.''s only regret was that the trophy would return not to England but to the Waterloo club in Brussels.

The American tide receded with victories to Perry in 1935, Padgham in 1936, Cotton in 1937 ('By superb pitching and putting beating the Americans at their own game'), R.A. Whitcombe in 1938, and Burton in 1939. 'Burton won the Championships for himself but upheld the dignity of British golf for us all,' the *Guardian* wrote. Left with a four to beat J. Bulla of America at St Andrews' eighteenth, Burton 'took out his driver and lashed an enormous shot up the very middle of the fairway. The crowd cheered as though the championship was already won, but as he had done throughout the round, Burton sauntered along with a cigarette on his lips and an expression of complete unconcern on his face . . . he made no bones about chipping well past the hole to be certain of a four.' Hagen's point was finally being made. You could get away with insouciance providing you were a winner.

The same score, 290, again at St Andrews, was enough for Sam Snead to take the replica claret jug back to America in the first post-war Open. *Guardian* reports were trimmed to half the length in deference to newsprint shortages. F. Daly (initials were standard practice) won at Hoylake in 1947 but another era was beginning – that of the South African A.D. Locke and Australian P.W. Thomson. Locke won a play-off with H. Bradshaw at Sandwich in 1948 ('a triumph of style and grace'), and followed up in 1949 with victory by two strokes from R. de Vicenzo of Argentina at Troon. Max Faulkner in 1951 broke Locke's sequence of three wins but, at Carnoustie in 1953, B. Hogan won 'one of the finest open golf championships ever played'. And for the first time the writer thus moved said so under his own name, Pat Ward-Thomas. Over the previous four years he had written as 'Our Golf Correspondent'. Finally he had got his *Guardian* colours.

Pat Ward-Thomas

'The still, grey afternoon was fraught with the presence of great deeds . . .' Such was the style. Ward-Thomas, a bomber pilot shot down in 1940, had spent five years in prisoner-of-war camps. In the famous Wooden Horse camp of Sagan, he was the first 'Open' golf champion, one of the mad Englishmen who diverted the guards – not a Langer amongst them – by playing endlessly out of sand bunkers with home-made clubs and balls.

The route by which he joined the *Guardian* was almost circuitous. From his POW camp he had sent Henry Longhurst a carefully edited version of golfing life at Sagan. Longhurst introduced him to Henry Cotton who wrote about it in his golf columns. In the early post-war years Ward-Thomas began to contribute soccer and golf reports to *The People* as an aside to his work in the historical branch of the RAF. Introduced by a colleague, Ward-Thomas sent Larry Montague, still sports editor of the *Guardian*, a very personal account of the 1949 Ryder Cup match won by the Americans at Ganton. Ward-Thomas, frustrated at so little space in *The People*, had written it simply to get it off his chest and had consigned it to a back drawer. Montague said: 'This is the way I want golf in the *Guardian* to be written.' So it was for twenty-eight memorable years.

This was Ward-Thomas on Hogan: 'Imagine him as he scrutinises a long difficult stroke, with arms quietly folded, an inscrutable quarter smile on his lips, for all the world like a gambler watching the wheel spin. And then the cigarette is tossed away, the club taken with abrupt decision, the glorious swing flashes and a long iron pierces the wind like an arrow. That was Hogan. We shall never see his like again.'

Locke was to return for a fourth title in 1957, Thomson celebrated his fifth in 1958, from among Palmer, Nicklaus and Lema, and so did Ward-Thomas in prose. It was, he said, 'the supreme performance of his golfing lifetime... It was a surpassing triumph for one of the purest swings that golf has ever known, a technique that has few peers in British conditions, a remarkable golfing intelligence, an assurance and composure of manner that have become such a familiar part of the golfing scene in this land for a decade or more.'

By 1961, though, Ward-Thomas was heralding another hero, one who remained especially close to his heart to the last. The long period of wartime strain and rehabilitation was over, as Ward-Thomas would understand more than most. Palmer's presence and victory at Royal Birkdale reaffirmed British status as the creators of the game, its character shaken by the laden westerlies of the Scottish and Lancashire coasts, in the bump and run of a links pitched shot, and in the wholly unAmerican surrounds of Victorian clubhouse architecture. Palmer, so rugged, so vulnerable, caught Ward-Thomas's attention like no other. At Royal Birkdale he wrote: 'There was an inevitability about the sight of his strong, hard figure bent low over the ball, with knees locked together, arms close to the body and firm, low stroke. This putting, and his formidably powerful, controlled striking, suggested a ruthless progress to victory, but it was far from being so.' Palmer won by only one stroke from Dai Rees.

Nicklaus and Watson, who were to follow Palmer in their support of the Open, commended themselves to Ward-Thomas for their manners and decorum as for their flair with wood or iron. Turnberry in 1977 was Ward-Thomas's last Open as the *Guardian*'s correspondent and Watson, he believed, was heir to the kingdom.

Alistair Cooke wrote on Ward-Thomas's retirement:

> There were two things about his golf reports that set him apart from all the others. He tramped the courses when most were settled in the press building scanning the big scoreboard and – on the basis of a figure change – tapping out 'he fired a birdie on the ninth'.
>
> And he loved the landscape, all the landscapes of golf, from the ocean beauties of California's Pebble Beach to the Siberian wastes of Rye, from the pine and undulations of Swinley Forest to the yawning bunkers of Pine Valley and the cathedral aisles of Augusta. He knew the terrain, and made you know it, and how it shaped its peculiar form of golf, of every county of England and Scotland.
>
> When others settled for 'this magnificent course', he pictured the beeches and copses, distinguished an upland from a weald, weighed the comparative hazards of a cypress tree or a swale. Nobody has ever conveyed so easily the sense of being in Wiltshire or County Down or Fife or Arizona.

Ward-Thomas was that rare figure, a hero at his own fireside. The *Guardian* printers' golf society lovingly encased the Arnold Palmer putter which Ward-Thomas, as their president, gave them for annual competition. On his death in 1980, it needed a good deal of tact to have them typeset the tribute, temperamental warts and all, of his successor, Peter Dobereiner.

Dobereiner was launched into Jack Nicklaus's third Open victory at St Andrews in 1978 and Severiano Ballesteros's triumph at Lytham the following year. His racy, prolific pen could have as much fun with the word 'deem' (How often do you deem? Why does golf literature teem with deems?) as it could with Ballesteros's first Open victory: 'He kicked down the doors, elbowed the mighty Jack Nicklaus, Hale Irwin and Tom Watson aside, and plonked himself down in the seat of honour. The dust of that brutal assault has not yet settled. Debris continues to fall. It will take a while for the spectators of the violence to recover; we are dazed, like witnesses to a nearby explosion... not a scratch on us, but the medics know that we are candidates for a cup of sweet, strong tea and a quiet lie down.'

For the *Guardian* they were heady days with Ward-Thomas still strolling the course, his eye swift as ever for changing mood and landscape. His death in 1982 left a major gap, and so did the retirement of Dobereiner to concentrate on his *Observer* column and other golfing interests.

David Davies, a golf and rugby playing Welshman long ensconced in Midlands journalism, arrived

Peter Dobereiner

from the *Birmingham Post* and soon was lauding the first British win since Tony Jacklin in 1969. 'Sandy Lyle won the 1985 Open Championship at Royal St George's and in so doing proved wrong one of the oldest of all sporting adages. Nice guys can, and just did, win.' The Shropshire lad he had seen develop from boyhood had plucked the finest fruit from the tree. Nick Faldo three times, Greg Norman, Ballesteros, Mark Calcavecchia, and Ian Baker-Finch are the more recent beneficiaries of the Open Championship. In the short term Faldo's 1992 title was worth £95,000. In the age of television and sponsorship it is worth ten and twenty times more.

Davies surveys the modern scene with a wry humour and realism. In 1991: 'It was Tony O'Reilly, the Irish rugby wing, who missed the tackle and complained, "Horrocks went one way, Taylor went the other, and I was left holding the hyphen." Yesterday no one saw which way Baker-Finch went after his superb start.' The Australian of course won the 1991 Open by two shots. In 1992: 'With a monumental display of courage and determination Nick Faldo recovered from being two behind with four to play and won the Open. As he sank the final put, a one-foot tap-in, the Faldo façade of icy control finally cracked. His tears were plentiful as he celebrated reaching a plateau in the game no other modern British player has achieved.'

Ward-Thomas, Dobereiner and Davies have commented on major changes, especially in the thirty-two years since Arnold Palmer came to the Centenary Open of 1960 to finish runner-up to Kel Nagle. Prize money then was £7,000 with Nagle receiving £1,250. At the 1992 Open it was £950,000 in total.

Colour television has introduced a huge new public. Only fourteen seaside links have ever been used for the Open as opposed to the forty and more for the American Open, few of them links in the British sense. They have to house crowds of up to 40,000 a day with appropriate viewing, parking, accommodation and access, not to mention the vast tented village reflecting the game's commercial commitments and responsibilities. Great courses like Carnoustie have been lost because they cannot keep up.

The Press area is a village in itself. In one huge marquee a giant scoreboard sets out pars, birdies and bogeys by each of the golfers. This opens out on to the interview tent, where every newsworthy golfer

David Davies

talks to the press, and closed-circuit TV room. Pressmen may follow matches but on a strictly controlled basis of armband allocations vetted by a golf writers' association almost unionistic in its membership rules and styles.

Year by year deadline pressures grow. Most national newspapers send a posse of reporters to assist their senior correspondent. On the final day of the Lytham St Annes Open of 1952, Bobby Locke strolled down to the hotel garage to find it locked and bolted. It did not open until nine o'clock, thirty-five minutes after his tee-off time. Worse, his clubs were in the car. A passing milkman saved his day, and indeed his Open title. The obliging milkman took him on his float to get the keys from the garageman, whom he happened to know, and Locke holed a birdie twenty-foot putt on the first hole to steady himself for the winning round.

In the old days news stories such as this rarely made the papers. Most correspondents, as Ward-Thomas noted in his autobiography, *Not Only Golf* (Hodder and Stoughton), did not readily mix and chat with professionals. Partly this was a fear of having their judgements clouded, partly because the correspondents themselves were a part of the game's conscious or unconscious snobberies. Today the press posse would have lassooed Locke's story in an instant.

The R and A are a private club running a genuine world championship in a major sport. It is a tribute to their flexibility of mind, as well as their organisational skill, that they continue to do so with worldwide approbation.

John Samuel was sports editor of the Guardian *from 1968 to 1986.*

Acknowledgements: for their help in compiling this unique record, I would like to thank Helen Martin and her staff at the *Guardian* Library, R.A.L. Burnet at the Royal and Ancient Golf Club, Jean Ward-Thomas, my wife Mary, Giles O'Bryen at Fourth Estate, Peter Alliss and contributors who to a man offered consent and good wishes to the venture.

John Samuel
July, 1992

G. DUNCAN OPEN GOLF CHAMPION

A day of surprises at Deal

The fight for the Open Championship of golf, which last night seemed almost certain to go in favour of Abe Mitchell, has gone to George Duncan after a day so full of changes that it has hardly been possible to keep pace with them. Duncan, one of those who started his first round of the day before nine o'clock, played such wonderful golf that his score of 71 established a new record for the links since the alterations were made. All the time Duncan was playing in this style, Mitchell, who had a lead over him of thirteen strokes, was waiting, and before he set off he knew what Duncan had done. The waiting, and that knowledge, probably upset him. At any rate he started to play badly and never really recovered, and an 84 brought him back exactly level with Duncan.

The poorness of Mitchell's golf can be judged from the fact that nearly half of the players who started before him had scores of under eighty. More than an hour before it became known that Mitchell was almost certain to lose all his lead, Herd and Barnes (who were tying for second place on Wednesday night) had finished in 77 each, and for a long time it seemed that these two would start the fourth round with a lead of one stroke. Then L. Holland, of the Northampton County Club, who had been in the seventh place, upset all calculations by equalling Duncan's record of 71, a performance which gave him the leadership.

The position when the deciding round began was:

Holland	229
Barnes	230
Herd	230
Duncan	231
Mitchell	231
Wingate	231
Ray	233

With confidence in Mitchell gone, Duncan was regarded as the most likely to keep the title from going to America, and when he went out in 35 and finished in 72 everybody hailed him as the winner. Not far behind him, Barnes had made a moderate start, but Herd was progressing steadily, giving nothing away and yet making no brilliant shots that meant the gaining of strokes. His total for fifteen holes was sixty and seemed likely to tie with Duncan. At the sixteenth, however, he pushed his drive into a bunker, and when he got out had to play off a downhill lie. He took a risk in selecting a brassie, and smothering the ball with the stroke sent it into another bunker. The hole cost him seven, and although he registered fours for the last two, his chance had gone. Barnes failed to recover from his poor start, and a 79 left him six strokes behind Duncan.

Before these events were complete Mitchell had gone off again, and although he got a three at the fourth, after being in a bunker his start was not encouraging, and as at the thirteenth he was three over fours it was realised that his task was beyond him. The glorious prospects with which he had commenced the day had faded away, and all attention was turned to Holland as the only man remaining who could deprive Duncan of the honour. He had gone out in 36, which meant that he was still in the running. Thirty-seven back would leave him at the head. But at the tenth he fluffed his pitch, and at the eleventh and twelfth he failed to get to the green in two. The three holes cost him fifteen, and so his chance faded too.

Duncan has thus come into his own as the result of two magnificent rounds after one of the most disappointing days of his life. It cannot be said that the play at this meeting has suggested any player as a really tip-top champion, but Duncan's play since he left the army has put him at the head of affairs and at last his friends are content. Manchester golfers, especially, will be delighted because for a time Duncan was in their midst as professional at Timperley. Born at Aberdeen in 1883, he has finished third, fourth, fifth, and three times eighth in the championship contests, so that the honour has not come to him out of turn.

Duncan's first round was made up as follows:

Out:	3	4	3	3	5	3	4	3	5	–33
In:	4	4	5	4	3	4	4	4	6	–38
										71

Of such a round there is little to be said. He was rarely off the most promising line to the hole, and he holed only one putt that could be called long. That was at the third, where he got down from four yards. At the sixth he was almost dead from his run-up, and the only poor shot of the outward half was at the ninth, where he pushed his second out a little.

At the sixteenth he was short with his second, but nearly holed his mashie shot, and at the hole where he had his only six he was the victim of an unfortunate incident. Just as he was driving, a spectator crossed the course, and a steward, seeing the danger, which Duncan could not, shouted 'Fore'. Duncan's club was swinging on to the ball and the shout caused the hands to be brought in suddenly. The ball went into the rough, and as the lie was not very bad Duncan tried to play the next with a wooden club. He sent the ball about fifteen yards and was beyond the green with his third.

George Duncan, thirteen strokes behind Abe Mitchell after three rounds, on his way to victory by two strokes from Sandy Herd. Mitchell's collapse to fourth place rebounded for years.

In his second round he had no six, and after a five at the third, through pitching over the green, he registered a two by holing a four-yard putt. Out in 35, he knew, of course, that his opportunity of atoning for many disappointing years had arrived. This time he did not 'crack', and for the next six holes he was one under fours. A five at the sixteenth was good. At the next he sank a four-yard putt, and a complete round of 73 left his competitors with very severe tasks.

Mitchell's collapse in the morning was astonishing. A score of something like 78 would have created no surprise, but an 84 was not reckoned as within the bounds of probability. His first mistake was on the first green, where he made a magnificent approach over a hummock, and when little more than a yard from the hole knocked his ball half-way. That was one stroke gone, and at the second another went, because he pulled his drive into the rough and did not get out with sufficient strength to reach the green. At the third he was even worse, for he pushed out his drive, had to be content with chipping back on to the course, and missed the putt. A four at the short hole was followed by an eight at the fifth, where he was bunkered a hundred yards from the tee. He took two to get out, played his fourth from the rough on one side to the rough on the other, and was over the grass with his fifth.

Twenty-eight for five holes meant that all his advantage had disappeared, but on the next tee he had a long wait, and instead of making him worse it marked the beginning of an improvement. At the eighth, where yesterday he had a one and the two players in front of him as well as his partner had twos, he registered a two. At the ninth he putted badly, and a six made his total 44, so that compared with their earlier scores at that point he was level with Barnes and two strokes ahead of Duncan. After that a vist to the rough caused him to take six for the eleventh, and pulled putts lost him other strokes.

At the thirteenth, however, he played a magnificent stroke from a bad lie. The hole is 430 yards, and when any ordinary man would have thought about using a mashie, Mitchell, probably on the principle that desperate diseases demand desperate remedies, chose a brassie and banged the ball to the green, so that a four went on his card. Such a stroke ought to have been a prelude to a brilliant spell, but the brilliance did not come, and his afternoon round was only good enough to put him in fourth place – the position he filled in 1914, when he first appeared in this competition.

Barnes in the morning went out in 37, with a five at the third, where he was short with his second, as the only flaw. Coming back he was one over fours to the fifteenth. That gave him an excellent chance, but at the sixteenth he was bunkered, and although he played out well he missed an easy putt and took six for the only time on the round. At the next he missed another putt, and at the last he muffed his drive, but holed out from 15 yards for a four and a total of 77. In the afternoon he was not so steady in any department and finished sixth, a long way ahead of Hagen, who had found Deal a much more difficult course than he imagined.

Holland's first round figures are interesting, if only for comparison with Duncan's. They were:

Out:	3	4	4	4	5	3	4	3	4–34
In:	3	5	5	4	4	4	5	4	3–37
									71

Duncan's 143 for the final two rounds, played on the same day, was not beaten until 1935. Total prize money was £225 of which he took a £25 golf medal and £75 in cash.

He was never off the course or in a bunker, and the only blemishes were the fours at the two short holes. At the tenth he holed a three-yard putt, and at the last he got down a four-yarder. Holland's age is not quite 33, and as he has frequently done well in stroke competitions he is likely to be heard of again. A well-built man, he plays with a swing something like that of Vardon, and is very interesting to watch.

Herd, second for the fourth time, was, as usual, a fine example of steadiness, and Ray, in finishing third, only fulfilled the expectations of those who appreciate his great hitting powers and accuracy on the greens. Wingate would probably have done better had he not been Duncan's partner to-day. He was fighting hard all the time, and was without experience of playing before such a large crowd. At any rate the contest has pushed the men who have had a monopoly in the championship for over twenty years into the background. The day of the younger men has come.

A.L.L.

The scores

303: G. Duncan (Hanger Hill), winner of the Championship Gold Medal, value £25, and £75 in cash, 80, 80, 71, 72

305: A. Herd (Coombe Hill) 72, 81, 77, 85

306: E. Ray (Oxhey) 72, 83, 78, 73

307: A. Mitchell (North Foreland) 74, 73, 84, 76

308: L. Holland (Northamptonshire) 80, 78, 71, 79

309: J. Barnes (Sunset Hill, USA) 79, 74, 77, 79

313: S. Wingate (Ravensworth) 81, 74, 76, 82; A.G. Havers (West Lancashire) 80, 78, 81, 74

315: W. H. Horne (unattached) 80, 81, 73, 81; G.R. Buckle (Edgbaston) 80, 80, 77, 78; A. Compston (Comberton) 83, 75, 78, 79

1921

St Andrews, 27th June

ANOTHER CHAMPIONSHIP FOR AMERICA

Hutchison beats the Oxford amateur

J. Hutchison (USA)	74 and 76 = 150
R.M. Wethered (R & A)	77 and 82 = 159

As was expected the play-off for the Open Golf Championship between R.H. Wethered, the ex-captain of Oxford, and Jock Hutchison, a professional at Chicago, who was formerly a caddie at St Andrews, has been won by the American, whose scores for the two rounds were 74 and 76 against 77 and 82. Hutchison has played splendid golf throughout the week, but it is admitted on every hand that he was lucky to have the opportunity of playing off for the title to-day. The registration of a one at a short hole on Thursday ought to dispel any doubt about the American's luck, and on the other hand the fact that Wethered incurred a penalty stroke by stepping on his ball, and also had a simple chance of a four at the last hole in his fourth round spoilt by a spectator shouting as he was hitting the ball, makes it clear that the younger player was unfortunate not to have had the cup in his keeping on Friday evening.

To-day the amateur has been well beaten, but he made a splendid fight until Hutchison began a spell of brilliant play in the second round. He made one big mistake. He achieved his distinction of playing four rounds in a lower score than St Andrews had ever known by using an old-fashioned wooden putter with which he rarely slipped a stroke, but instead of trusting it again he reverted to a steel club and continued to use it although early in each round it was evident that there was lacking the delicacy and accuracy of touch which makes for success. Five or six times in the morning round he hit holes without getting the ball to drop, and at three of the first four holes in the afternoon he had the same depressing experience. After that Hutchison quickly increased what had up to then been only an insecure lead by means of play which no man could have beaten. A

Triumphant return of the caddie – Jock Hutchison

man who registers a three at the longest hole (533 yards), and has the same figure put on his card for other holes of 345 yards, 139 yards, and 273 yards before the turn is unbeatable, and Wethered, recognising the uselessness of further strain, fell into slack ways, although at the end he regained three strokes.

The inability of the amateur to sink his putts early in each round had a great influence on the play, but in my opinion the fortunes of the game at the fifteenth in the morning had a greater effect. By beautiful iron play Wethered had reduced his arrears from four strokes to two, and at this hole a topped second by Hutchison escaped the punishment it deserved from rough grass and bunkers. Hutchison made the most of his luck by playing a magnificent third to within three inches of the hole, so that, instead of falling behind as he might easily have done, he retained his lead.

Hutchison undoubtedly gained a considerable advantage by using ribbed clubs, which are to be illegal in future. With these he was able to play to the greens and to get back-spin on the ball without having to resort to the methods required with an ordinary club. The effect of the spin imparted by the ribbed clubs was very curious. The ball when it reached the green made one bounce forward in the ordinary way and then stopped almost dead. The British methods adopted by Wethered did not have anything like the same success; he tried his utmost to get the ball to stop quickly, but with the greens very hard the spin he obtained was not sufficient to prevent his ball travelling yards beyond Hutchison's even when it dropped on nearly the same spot.

The only features of the play at the first two holes were that Wethered narrowly missed a three at one and that Hutchison recovered well from an over-strong second at the other. Hutchison gained two strokes at the third, for he made a beautiful pitch, whereas Wethered failed to get the required 'cut' and then hit the hole with his fourth. Wethered, however, immediately rubbed off his arrears, and as he again went over the hole he very nearly took the lead. Hutchison made a short drive into the rough, went only a few yards with his next, and playing again from the rough found a bunker, so that he did well to escape with a six. They remained level for two holes, at one of which Wethered left his ball on the lip while at the other Hutchison missed from little over a yard. Then came four threes to Hutchison against four fours. At the seventh Wethered holed from 18 yards when appearing likely to suffer badly from the effects of a bad drive, and Hutchison got down from eight yards. The eighth was a bad hole for Wethered, as he had the inside position from the tee but dropped a stroke through not hitting his first putt firmly. At the ninth both putted from eight feet and the American was successful. The scores to the turn were:

Hutchison:	4	5	3	6	5	4	3	3	3–36
Wethered:	4	5	5	4	5	4	4	4	4–39

At the tenth Hutchison hit the hole with a 40-yards pitched shot, and both missed chances on the next green. Wethered got a stroke back at the thirteenth through Hutchison pulling his approach, and still further reduced his deficiency at the long fourteenth where he was well on in two to three,

The crowd watch Duncan on the 18th.

son having made only a moderate drive. Hutchison was very lucky at the fifteenth. He half-topped his second but the ball went through some rough grass, missed two bunkers, and finished near to the green. A pitch-and-run then sent the ball dead. At the sixteenth, however, he took three putts, but Wethered, now only one stroke to the bad, pulled his drive at the Road hole, and did well to get a five by a curly run-in over the bank and a good putt. Hutchison also made the tricky approach successfully, and at the last hole he became three to the good, Wethered's second being so strong that it reached the bank at the back of the green. The scores for the return half were:

Hutchison:	3	4	4	5	5	4	5	4	4–38:	Total 74
Wethered:	4	4	4	4	4	4	4	5	5–38:	Total 77

Hutchison pulled his first drive in the afternoon, and, using a wooden club for his second, so narrowly missed the burn that the ball stopped only 18 inches beyond. Wethered went very close indeed to starting with two threes, and soon afterwards was in a hopeless position. He was bunkered at the fourth and required three putts; at the fifth (533 yards) Hutchison gained two more strokes by holing a chip of 30 yards, and at the sixth the American was down with his first putt from four yards. At the next Wethered had three putts and Hutchison succeeded from two yards, while at the eighth and ninth Wethered lipped the hole with his second strokes. The scores then were:

Hutchison:	4	5	4	4	3	3	4	3	3–33
Wethered:	4	5	4	6	5	4	5	3	3–39

At the eleventh Hutchison went in to the Shell bunker, and, trying to play back, moved the ball a few inches, and was then able to play on to the green. Wethered tried too boldly for a two, and gained only one stroke, which he threw away by pulling his next drive into such a bad place that he took four to get on. He then had three putts. The amateur was bunkered at the fourteenth, and was beaten by the two strokes taken in getting clear. Hutchison was then leading by 12, but he dropped one at the sixteenth by pushing out his second close to the railway, another at the seventeenth by pulling his drive into a bunker, and a third at the last by missing a two-feet putt. The scores at the last nine holes were:

Hutchison:	4	5	5	4	5	4	5	6	5–43
Wethered:	4	4	7	4	7	4	4	5	4–43

When most of the Americans began their homeward journey in the evening a band was playing 'Will ye no come back again?' They will be here again next year, perhaps in stronger force than ever, and in the meantime we must be content with the efforts Duncan and Mitchell will make to avenge this week's defeat during their trip to America.

A.L.L.

The scores

296: R.H. Wethered (R & A) 78, 75, 72, 71; Hutchison (USA) 72, 75, 79, 70

298: Kerrigan (USA) 74, 80, 72, 72

299: Havers (West Lancs) 76, 74, 77, 72

301: Duncan (Hanger Hill) 74, 75, 78, 74

302: Williamson (Notts) 79, 71, 74, 78; Herd (Coombe Hill) 75, 74, 73, 80; Leach (Northwood) 78, 75, 76, 73; Kirkwood (Australia) 76, 74, 73, 79; Massy (Nivelle) 74, 75, 74, 79; Barnes (USA) 74, 74, 74, 80; Hagen (USA) 74, 79, 72, 77

1922

Sandwich, 24th June

OPEN GOLF TITLE GOES WEST AGAIN

Hagen's Brilliance

The fears that our golfers would be unequal to the task of preventing the Open Championship going overseas for the second year in succession have been justified to-day, when the Americans secured three of the first four places. The prestige of British golf has never had such a blow, but it must be admitted that our visitors have secured their honours by splendid golf and without more than an ordinary share of good fortune. The only satisfaction Britain can gather from the competition is that George Duncan, by a phenomenal round of 69 when almost every hope had been abandoned, tied for second place, and with a bolder stroke at the last green would have enforced a play-off.

The new champion is Walter Hagen, and with Duncan and Barnes tieing for second place the fourth position was filled by Jock Hutchison, the winner at St Andrews twelve months ago. Next came. C.A. Whitcombe, a young player who has never before distinguished himself in a national competition. It was a fine performance by Whitcombe to finish only three strokes behind the leader, but even greater praise must be given to J.H. Taylor, who won his first championship 28 years ago and yet finished only four strokes behind the winner. To-day's golf has been played in stormy weather, but, except that Hagen and Hutchison had completed their morning round before the clouds first spilled some of their contents, the conditions have been fairly even.

Hagen, whose age is 30, won the American championship in 1914, and after that became associated with a financial firm in Wall Street, so that when he competed for the open title at Deal and St Andrews his temperament was more that of a holiday-maker than of a prospective champion. He has given up his career in business in order to devote himself entirely to golf, and on his third visit here has proved himself a great player. He has a style entirely his own, and one which it would be dangerous to copy. His address is made with the hands in front of the ball, his weight is nearly all on the left foot, and at the moment of hitting he is so much on his toes that he always seems in danger of tumbling. In spite of that he sends the ball great distances, and on the greens he is a master. How nerveless he is can be judged from the fact that during his last round he had a man signalling to him the score made at each hole by Hutchison.

The insouciant Walter Hagen gave up a Wall Street banking career to become the first of America's native-born Open champions in 1922. Duncan failed to catch him with a putt that finished two inches short of the hole.

Play in the third round lasted from 8.30 to three o'clock, and at the end of it Hutchison, who was the first man to start, led the field. The only feature of his outward half in 34 was an excellent three at the third, and afterwards his adventurous hole was the fourteenth, where he topped his second and struck an iron post with his third. The ball rebounded about 80 yards and nearly went out of bounds. Two mashie shots put him on the green, and he was down in six. He also failed to get the par figure at the short hole, where not more than a third of the players found the green, but he finished in 73. Hagen, who was one of the second couple and who led Hutchison by four strokes on Thursday night, lost half that advantage during the first half of the round, and that although he holed putts of four and 15 yards and also a pitch of 15 yard at the ninth. He finished weakly with two sixes, being badly bunkered at the seventeenth and missing his drive to the last. A little later, Walton, of Lytham and St Annes, who missed four or five putts he ought to have holed, came in with 77, which temporarily gave him third place four strokes behind Hutchison and two behind Hagen.

J.H. Taylor, who began the day two behind Hagen and two ahead of Hutchison, knew when he drove off what he had to do to beat last year's champion, and for a time all went well with him. He did the eighth in two, which gave him an average of four under fours. Then his troubles began. At the ninth he pushed out his second and was short with his mashie shot, so that the hole cost him six. This disappointing play occurred at the beginning of the first storm and worse was to follow, for Taylor took three putts on each of the next five greens, in addition to socketing his mashie shot to the fourteenth. He holed a seven-yard putt at the fifteenth and another of eight yards at the seventeenth, but after a moderate drive to the last he was unlucky to be put off when playing his second by a man passing behind him.

Ten minutes later Gassiat, the Frenchman, finished in 74, which made him level with Taylor. Gassiat played with admirable steadiness. He was one of the few men who had threes at the short holes. He finished with two fives, but that was not exceptional: a five at the second hole was a much worse blot. He lost two strokes on the round by using iron instead of wood for his seconds, but no one beat him in accuracy of running-up or putting.

Hagen: 'a style dangerous to copy . . . and a temperament more that of a holiday-maker than a prospective champion.'

Barnes beat the other Americans at the short holes by registering threes, but sixes at the fourth and fourteenth spoiled his card, and he finished level with Hagen and C.A. Whitcombe, of Marlborough, for fourth place. Whitcombe's score of 72 was the best of the championship up to that point, and it was remarkable because only twice did he exceed five for a hole. The fourth, where the garden fence just beyond the green was responsible for much trouble, cost him seven, and the five he had at the fourteenth was really good going considering how often the out-of-bounds fence, the hillocks, and the 'canal' had caused sevens and even nines to be registered there. Attention was then turned to Roger Wethered, but it was soon realised that his case was hopeless. He had to play through the first two storms, and as soon as the handles of his clubs became wet he began to drop strokes. That spoiled his chance of completing the first nine under fours, and when he registered nine at the fourteenth, where he was twice out of bounds, his last hope vanished.

As Duncan failed, the position when the fourth and last round returns began to come in was that no British players, except Taylor, Whitcombe, and Walton, had a reasonable prospect of preventing the championship from again going overseas, and the difficulty of their task was immediately rendered immense by Hutchison finishing in 76. He had gone out in 36, with a seven for the fourth, when he incurred the stroke and distance penalty for sending his second out of bounds, and was short with his fourth. When Hutchison finished, Hagen was approaching the seventeenth. He knew that two fives would give him the leadership, and he made a magnificent iron shot to the seventeenth which gave him a four. At the last he took three putts, but his aggregate of 300 made it almost impossible for his rivals to dispossess him of the honour. Throughout the round he hit magnificent seconds, and the best of all was at the seventh (484 yards) where his brassie shot sent the ball dead. His only slips on the greens were at the sixteenth, where he had a good chance of a two, and the last.

Barnes had to struggle nearly all the way round, knowing that he required an average of fours to tie. He fought as though he had no nerves, and although he had six at the third through getting into a bunker he reached the turn in 36. Five at the twelfth was moderate, but a brilliant four at the fourteenth put him right, and on the last tee he had four to tie. His second, played rather quickly, went to the right of the green, and another shot played snatchily sent him fourteen yards past the hole. He had to hole the next or acknowledge defeat, and sent it two yards short. Taylor also struggled magnificently after taking six for the first, but at the turn he had only 34 to tie, and it was not surprising that he failed. He had threes at the fifteenth and sixteenth, and would have had a chance had he not missed a five yards putt at the seventeenth by a fraction of an inch. After that, a visit to a bunker at the last was important only because it deprived him of the honour of tieing for third or fourth place.

Gassiat had fallen behind in the race before he reached the seventeenth, where a pulled shot caused a seven to go on his card, and as Whitcombe had also failed to produce his best – he missed five reasonable putts – all the interest that remained was in Duncan, who had to do something more sensational than he did at St Andrews. Duncan, the last man out, wanted 68 to tie, and he played as only Duncan can. His figures were:

Out:	4	4	4	4	3	3	3	4	5–34
In:	4	4	4	3	5	4	2	4	5–35

He missed a short putt at the eight, and when his task seemed impossible he recovered with a spoon shot to the sixteenth, which gave him a two. Then a brilliant four left him four to tie. His brassie shot to the last was pulled a little and finished at the foot of a slight slope 20 yards from the pin. Duncan seemed cool enough, but his chip was weakly hit, and his only chance was a seven yards putt. His line was true, but the ball stopped two inches short, and the championship was America's without a play-off.

A.L.L.

The scores

300: W. Hagen (USA) 76, 73, 79, 72

301: Duncan (Hanger Hill) 76, 75, 81, 69

301: Barnes (USA) 75, 76, 77, 73

302: Hutchison (USA) 79, 74, 73, 76

303: Whitcombe (Dorchester) 77, 79, 72, 75

304: Taylor (Mid-Surrey) 73, 78, 76, 77

306: Gassiat (Chantilly) 75, 78, 74, 79

307: Vardon (South Herts) 79, 79, 74, 75; Walton (Lytham & St Annes) 75, 78, 77, 77

308: Alliss (Clyne) 75, 78, 78, 77

1923

AFTER TWO YEARS

British Golf Open Championship comes home again

Roles were reversed in 1923. Arthur Havers of Coombe Hill won by a shot from Hagen, bunkered beside the last green.

The British Golf Open Championship was won back from America yesterday by A.G. Havers, Coombe Hill, Surrey, until recently the West Lancashire club's professional. His score was one stroke better than that of Walter Hagen, USA, who himself defeated George Duncan at Sandwich last year by one stroke. The trophy had been in American hands for two years.

The contest has been a thrilling one, and Hagen, last year's champion, was beaten by the single stroke he lost to Havers in the two rounds played on Thursday. Hagen made a great fight, and it was not until he found a bunker against the last green that his chance disappeared.

Havers, who was 23 last Sunday, began to play golf when he was about 11, and at 14 he established a record for the Royal Norwich links which only he himself has since beaten. When 16 he entered for the Open Championship, and although that was his first appearance in an open competition he qualified in rounds which were played on the Troon Old and Municipal Courses. Three years ago he tied for seventh place in the Championship, and a year later he finished fourth.

Last year he made the cup presented by the *Manchester Guardian* for the Northern Championship his own property by winning it twice in succession, but since then he has been disappointing in play with wooden clubs. That trouble was not overcome until Wednesday, when S. Wingate went out with him for an hour and corrected his faults. To-day Havers has driven splendidly, and at the ninth this afternoon must have sent the ball quite 300 yards from the tee.

Havers is 6ft 2in in height, and the golfing temperament seems to have been born in him. He makes mistakes, of course, and near the middle of his fourth round he seemed to be throwing his chance away. The slips, however, did not upset him, and playing confidently home against a wind stronger than in any other part of the afternoon he returned in 38 for a 76, which following three rounds of 73 each, left Hagen and Whitcombe very hard tasks to beat him.

Hagen just failed, but as was the case last year the players from overseas occupied three of the first four places. Tom Fernie, who was fifth, spoilt his prospects with 18 on Thursday afternoon. Duncan was consistent but nothing more, and Mitchell earned only a moderate place because his spells of brilliance were very short.

When the last round started there were two Americans and an Australian in the first five, and it soon became known that Macdonald Smith was almost sure not to be the winner. Smith went to America from Carnoustie about 16 years ago, and was in the army during the war. He gave up golf for a time, but as he finished but one stroke behind Hagen he is a player deserving of great respect. A little more steadiness or luck in his last round and he would amost certainly have beaten the field.

The next man to go out was Kirkwood, who had an erratic homeward journey. At the fourteenth he was bunkered twice, at the next he missed a short putt, and at the sixteenth he drove into the rough, got into the burn, and registered seven.

Havers, who had started half an hour behind Kirkwood, made no mistake until he took three at the seventh, but that was the beginning of a bad spell, for a putt hung on the lip of the sixth hole, and he was bunkered at the next green. Then he missed a yard putt at the ninth, only to be encouraged by holing out from eight yards at the eleventh. Then everything went well until he pulled his second to the last hole and was bunkered. He got well out, but missed the four.

Meanwhile Hagen had taken 28 for seven holes, but the short eighth proved his undoing. He was bunkered from the tee, and played out into another one, with the result that he took five. He had to return in 36 to tie, and immediately made his task more difficult by taking three putts at the tenth. After that he played magnificent golf, only to find that he had to play the last two in one under par to insure a play-off.

The seventeenth produced the regulation 3, and everything depended on his second shot to the last. He was well placed, but cut with his iron a little too much, and the cross wind carried the ball into a bunker level with the flag. His shot out was four yards short, and although he holed the putt he knew that he was losing by the margin he had over Duncan twelve months ago. He had many sympathisers, but he was lucky to have the chance of doing so well, as he would not have qualified had one of the last men in on Tuesday holed an easy putt on the last green.

After Hagen's defeat only Whitcombe had a chance to beat Havers, and even before the Bath player reached the turn that had disappeared.

Havers receives his victory medal, the last by a British player for eleven years so it turned out. Havers, just twenty-three, played in his first Open at Muirfield as a sixteen-year-old.

Whitcombe cracked badly, but was unlucky on the greens. Robert Scott, of Glasgow, finished as the leading amateur twelve strokes behind Havers, but Tolley earned much applause by driving to the first green, 350 yards away, and using only one putt. Barber, who recently went to Alderley Edge from Oldham, distinguished himself with a 71 in the morning, a score which included 8 for the tenth (420 yards). The first few hours were perfect, for there was hardly a breath of wind and the light was good.

The sensations began early, Macdonald Smith, one of the third couple to start, breaking the record established by Whitcombe on Thursday morning by one stroke. His figures were:

Out:	3	3	4	5	2	5	4	3	4	– 33
In:	4	5	4	3	3	4	5	4	4	– 36
										69

At the first two holes he took full advantage of pitches which gave him the chance to save two strokes, and at the third he holed from two yards, whilst at the fourth his ball hit the hole without dropping. At the fifth he succeeded with a twelve-yard putt, at the next he made amends for weakness following the drive by using only one stroke on the green, and at the eighth his tee shot nearly hit the flag. He made no slips until he was playing the 15th where he was bunkered, but avoided a six by holding a five-yards putt. He also dropped a stroke at the 17th. His iron play throughout was beautifully crisp and accurate in direction, and the other feature of his play was the regularity with which he sent his approach putts close to the holes. He was lucky in starting early, as a breeze after midday made the links a stroke or two more difficult.

The next news was that Duncan was failing to find the luck needed to give him a chance. His long putts always went past, and 35 out did not do justice to his play. There was always hope, however, until he reached the 15th, where he missed his second shot, sent the next into a bunker from which he reached another beyond the green, with the result that he registered a 7.

Robert Scott, who had been fifth, fell out through returning 79, and Scottish hopes were dashed by Lockhart taking 76. He required 5 at the eighth, which has aptly been described as the 'postage stamp' hole, and at the 11th he pulled into a bad place in the whins and took 7.

Not far behing Lockhart was Kirkwood who, after taking three putts on the first green, settled down to sound golf which gave him an average of four for the first nine. After the eleventh he had three 3s in succession, one being earned by a twelve-yards putt. His second to the 16th was bunkered, but he made a magnificent pitch out, and from four yards was unlucky not to register four, the ball stopping on the lip of the hole. That left him requiring two 3s to beat Macdonald Smith's record, and it was only a slightly pulled putt of five feet on the home green that robbed him of the distinction.

While Kirkwood was doing this Havers was struggling against the effects of weak putting on two greens, where his partner's success would have placed him in an excellent position. A bunker at the seventh caused the loss of another stroke, and at the eighth three putts handicapped him further. Out in 37, he made a great effort to retrieve himself, and succeeded in coming back in 36 despite one failure from 18 inches. His 5 at the 16th was good considering that he was bunkered behind the green, and at the 17th he was unlucky with a putt that hit the hole.

Walton, of Lytham and St Annes, was not quite as good as usual, and with Ray failing all attention was given to Whitcombe, who delighted his friends by going out in 34, with his only 5 at the long sixth. Coming back, however, he got into five bunkers, and twice took three putts. Mitchell, too, had 34 for the first nine, but destroyed his chance by finishing with 5, 5, 4, and 5.

Hagen, who had gone out in 35, took 6 at the 10th, where he was in the sand from his drive and then went into the whins. He dropped another stroke at the 15th through a bad iron shot, and still another by finding a bunker at the 17th, so that when the third round was completed he was fourth, a stroke behind Kirkwood and Whitcombe, and two behind Havers, with Macdonald Smith fifth, and Fernie, Lockhart, Brews, and Watt all on the 225 mark.

A.L.L.

The scores

295: A.G. Havers (Coombe Hill) 73, 73, 73, 76

296: W. Hagen (USA) 76, 71, 74, 75

297: Macdonald Smith (USA) 80, 73, 69, 75

298: J. Kirkwood (Australia) 72, 79, 69, 78

300: T.R. Fernie (Turnberry) 73, 78, 74, 75

302: G. Duncan (Hanger Hill) 79, 75, 74, 74; C.A. Whitcombe (Lansdowne) 70, 76, 74, 82

303: H.C. Jolly (Foxgrove) 79, 75, 75, 74; J. Mackenzie (Ilkley) 76, 78, 74, 75; Abe Mitchell (North Foreland) 77, 77, 72, 77

1924

Hoylake, 28th June

AMERICA REGAINS THE OPEN GOLF TITLE

Hagen again

The Open Championship has gone to America for the third time in four years, for Walter Hagen, the winner at Sandwich two years ago and the runner-up at Troon last year, has again proved a great figure-producer at a pinch, and has beaten E.R. Whitcombe by one stroke.

It was a great struggle and an exciting one, for Hoylake, always a great test, took its toll of the aspirants and one after another fell out. Duncan made mistakes when his prospects were brightest; Taylor fell away in a manner that was not surprising considering that he was a champion about thirty years ago; Frank Ball fell just short of the standard demanded; and another American, Macdonald Smith, who was first a Scotsman, cracked when almost within sight of victory.

The position when Hagen went out, the latest starter of those who had a chance, was uncertain, as Whitcombe was about an hour in front of him. Whitcombe finished with 302, and Hagen, who had gone out in 41, required 36 for the homeward half to beat him.

Hagen's start had been anything but impressive. He pulled his first drive, pulled his second, and registered six. Another six came at the third, one of the most difficult holes on the links to-day, and he dropped another stroke at the fifth through bunkering his second. At the eighth he had an adventurous six for crookedness, and bunkers caused him to take five to reach the green. He was lucky to get down in six as the putt was one of eight yards.

Up to the turn, and, indeed, to the fourteenth, he rarely reached a green in the proper number, and only his deadly chipping saved him by giving him a chance to get down in one putt. That he frequently succeeded with one showed that he has nerves of steel, and although Hagen's golf is open to criticism he is far above his rivals in producing figures when they are required. He seemed certain to drop a stroke at the short thirteenth, but he pitched so well from a bunker that he got down in three. From the fourteenth his golf was great, but when he required to play the last three holes in thirteen the task was reckoned beyond him. He was just off the sixteenth green in two, and using his putter took three more to get down. As the seventeenth, with its well-guarded green lying close to the road (which is out of bounds), is full of danger, all that seemed reasonable to expect was a tie. But Hagen went out to the right from the tee and left himself the clearest approach that is possible here. His second shot was one of the best played in the championship, and gave him a putt of about four yards for a three. He missed it narrowly, and everything depended on the last hole.

He banged the drive straight down the middle and was left an ordinary pitch over the cross bunker. Probably remembering how he failed to make a tie twelve months ago through playing a poor second to the last hole, he now made very careful preparations. He made several trial swings, wiped his hands on the grass, and then made more trial swings. When he hit the ball he sent it past the flag and about 2ft over the green. The grass there was only short, and his clip back finished five or six feet from the hole. He made up his mind quickly, and as the ball fell to give him victory by one stroke he tossed his putter joyfully to his caddie.

Hagen began his golf education as a caddie, and is now a freelance of about 32 years of age. His feat of winning the open championship twice in three years and finishing second in the intervening competition must be regarded as the greatest in professional golf, for there are now more really good players than ever before. Once again Hagen has shown that concentration counts, and that a man who refuses to smoke during a round has an advantage over his rivals who cannot keep their pipes or cigarettes for other times.

In the morning little attention was paid to anybody but the leaders, and even the fact that Mitchell and Massy made no return aroused no interest. Duncan, as on Thursday, was an early starter and apart from a five at the third – a reasonable score there against the wind – he was all fours and threes to the eighth, so that his position was full of promise. At the ninth, however, he was on the edge of a bunker from the tee, and from a bad stance he failed to lift the ball sufficiently to clear the bank beyond the bunker. The ball came back, and when he missed a five-feet putt he made his score seven. He recovered from that by playing the next four in one over threes, but the fourteenth pulled him back. He was bunkered beyond the green, and although he was about three yards from the pin in three he took three more to get down.

Duncan had shown that he realised all that depended on him by frequently inspecting the lines of approaches, and he did this at the seventeenth, where a fine shot from the rough gave him a fair chance of four. The inspection, however, was useless as he did not hit the ball hard enough and a pull resulted. Still a total of 74 left him well in the running.

Hagen's progress was so smooth that there was nothing to describe. He took three putts at the second, but apart from that it was a case of reaching the greens in the proper number and using two putts. He was out in 37, and made no change in his schedule until the sixteenth, where he drove into the rough and after getting well out found a bunker. That meant the only six on his card.

Meanwhile J.H. Taylor was arousing great enthusiasm by wonderfully steady progress. Twice in playing the first four he holed putts of three yards, and he made no mistake until the sixth. He was thirty yards beyond Ray with his drive, but pulled his second and took five. He was unlucky to be bunkered at the eighth, but got a five through his trusty mashie. He showed signs of faltering at the ninth and tenth, but was well in the running until he left the fourteenth tee. There he began to stray from the line, and six went on his card for the hole at which in 1913 he made sure of the championship by getting a three. Thenceforward he was uncertain, and 79 was a disappointing return.

Macdonald Smith started moderately with 5, 4, and 6, but he was out in 39 and back in 38, figures which mean very little room for deviation from the mechanical golf the Americans play.

The disqualification of C.A. Whitcombe, who played a ball from the rough at the fourteenth and found when he had holed out that it was not his own, was of little importance, as it was on his brother, E.R., that British hopes rested. The hopes were blighted somewhat by a score of 77. Blots were made on his card by bad drives at the sixth and seventeenth, the taking of three putts at the eleventh, and inaccuracies with his seconds at the holes running round the paddock.

The position at the end of the third round was that E.R. Whitcombe and Hagen tied for first place three strokes better than Duncan, Frank Ball, and Macdonald Smith, with Taylor a stroke further behind.

Again a great crowd followed Duncan, in the belief that he might produce one of his electric rounds. Three fives made only a moderate beginning, but 22 for the next six gave him a great chance. Then he began to make serious errors. At the tenth he pulled his second, and showed his disgust by waving his club angrily in the air. Five there was followed by a similar score at the short eleventh, where a strong cross-wind caused trouble to many. Duncan allowed for the wind which, however, declined to act at that moment, and the ball fell in a bad position to the left of the green. His second was a failure, and again he revealed his annoyance by banging his club into the sand, an action which those who did not know the ball had gone to the left thought was another stroke. At the twelfth he took three putts, and when he registered seven at the fifteenth his chance had disappeared completely. He sliced into a bunker and got out into the rough, so that 'the subsequent proceedings interested him no more'.

Macdonald Smith made an excellent start, which included a twelve yards' putt for two at the fourth. Twice in playing the first five he hit the holes without getting the ball to drop. He played fourteen holes in 57, and then began to go wrong, for he was bunkered at the fifteenth and bunkered and out of bounds at the sixteenth, whilst at the next his ball rested against the wire. Even at the eighteenth, with the wind rather

Hagen's second victory is rewarded with a kiss. His nerve held for a one-shot advantage over Ernest Whitcombe.

helpful, he pushed out his drive, and at the end his total was 304. He had thrown his chance away by what is unusual with an American – a weak finish.

Frank Ball, a member of the Hoylake family to which the Heaton Park professional belongs, went well in his fourth round until he reached the eighth. There the tension seemed to tell, and two weak shots spoilt his card. Then he took six at the tenth, hooking his iron shot into brambles, where nearly five minutes were used in searching for the ball. He made so sure of getting out that he went over the green into another bad place. At the thirteenth he holed a five-yarder for a two, but at the next three he suffered through shortness, and at the seventeenth he missed from about a yard. He finished gloriously with a three by holing out from eight yards, but had no more satisfaction than that gained from tieing with Macdonald Smith.

Meanwhile Whitcombe had seemed to leave Hagen a fairly easy progress to the title by taking 43 to go out. He was bunkered at the first and second, and at the ninth he went into some long rough, from which he played out into a bunker. He reached the green in four, and increased his misery by taking three putts.

His return half was great, the figures being: 4, 3, 4, 3, 4, 4, 5, 4, 4–35. The only error in this was a putt above the ordinary allowance at the sixteenth. Whitcombe's 78 placed him two strokes ahead of Ball and Macdonald Smith, and of those who were still playing only Hagen had a chance to beat him. Whitcombe had more than an hour to wait, and then he knew himself beaten by one stroke.

A.L.L.

The scores

301: W. Hagen (USA) 77, 73, 74, 77

302: E.R. Whitcombe (Came Down) 77, 70, 77, 78

304: Macdonald Smith (USA) 76, 74, 77, 77; F. Ball (Langley Park) 78, 75, 74, 77

307: J.H. Taylor (Mid-Surrey) 75, 74, 79, 79

308: G. Duncan (Hanger Hill) 74, 79, 74, 81; A. Boomer (St Cloud, Paris) 75, 78, 76, 79; L. Holland (Northampton) 74, 78, 78, 78

309: J.M. Barnes (USA) 78, 77, 79, 75; J.G. Sherlock (Hunstanton) 76, 75, 78, 80

1925

Prestwick, 26th June

BARNES WINS OPEN GOLF CHAMPIONSHIP

Title goes to US for the fourth time since the war

The Open Championship was won to-day by Jim Barnes, the Cornish American, with a total of 300. Such a result as this seemed unlikely on Thursday evening, when Macdonald Smith, the Carnoustie man who went to America years ago, led Barnes by two strokes and Compston by six strokes, and it was still less likely when Macdonald Smith increased his lead to five strokes over Barnes in the third round.

Never since Ray won at Muirfield had a player possessed a better chance than that of Smith when he began his last round, knowing that a score of 78 would give him the title; but after playing the first two holes in correct figures he frittered away his advantage at hole after hole. He reached the turn in 42, and, requiring an average of fours for the homeward journey, made his task almost impossible by dropping three strokes before he reached the thirteenth tee. A six at the fifteenth shattered his last chance, and when he made his last drive the only open question was whether he would equal Ray and Compston, who were tieing for second place. He finished in 82, and had to be content with fourth place. A more complete collapse than this has never been known in a fourth round, but Mitchell threw away an even greater lead in the third round at Deal five years ago.

Barnes was born at Lelant, and was a caddie there until 1905, when, still in his teens, he determined to try his fortune in America. He won the Open Championship there four years ago, and first came to try for our title after the war. He was sixth in 1920, tied for seventh place in 1921, tied for second place the following year, and last year was sixth again. He said when he failed first that he would continue to come every year until he succeeded, and this afternoon, when another American seemed almost certain to give him another disappointing experience in his sixth attempt, he sat for hours in the professional's shop hearing fragments of news that raised his hopes. When Macdonald Smith came over the hills the last time rumours were confirmed, but Barnes remained in the shop until it was certain that the championship was his. A quiet man of under forty and well over six feet in height, Barnes is a freelance professional in New York, and his success this week is sure to do much towards making him wealthy.

Barnes was the first man out in the morning. He dropped a stroke at the short second through being too strong at the tee and with his return, and he lost another at the next, where he was bunkered behind the green. At the fourth he drove into the burn, at the eighth he missed a reasonable putt, and at the ninth he drove into the sandhills, so that he did well to reach the turn in 40. Going to the tenth his second was in the rough, and the hole cost him six. Then a two yards' putt gave him a two, which restored his confidence and enabled him to record good figures to the fifteenth, where he was bunkered. He beat the par score for the next, but at the Alps he was through the green, and at the last he used two strokes in a bunker near the green. When he first tried to get out he was lucky to escape a penalty, as the ball rebounded off the bank and missed him by about an inch. He finished in 79, and knew that Compston, who was immediately behind, was threatening to depose him.

Compston, as a matter of fact, had wiped out Thursday's difference between them by playing the first three holes in three, two, and five, by holing putts of three and two yards. His first slip came at the sixth, his shot to the green going over, and a putt of less than two yards being missed. A six was registered at the eighth, where he found a bunker with his second and did not get out cleanly enough to reach the green. Still, as he was out in 36 he was level on aggregate with Barnes, and he seemed certain to take second place until he lost a smoothness of swing that had characterised his putting, and began to snatch at the ball. This was first noticeable at the twelfth, where he missed from about the same distance. Each of those holes cost him a stroke more than they should have done, and he dropped another at the fourteenth, a drive into the marsh preventing him from reaching the green in two. He finished with four fours, and was level with Barnes for second place.

Barnes and Compston started their final round before Smith and Mitchell finished their third, so that they were in doubt about what they had to do. Barnes began with a five through getting against the wall, but picked up strokes at the fifth and sixth and was going splendidly until the eighth, where he pushed out his drive and was short of the green in three. That meant a six, and, turning with 36, he immediately handicapped himself by taking three putts. He registered four at the remaining eight holes, losing a stroke at the short eleventh through being too strong, and saving one which appeared to be lost at the seventeenth by holing a difficult downhill putt of over two yards.

Compston followed Barnes's example in having five at the first, his fault occurring on the green, but a two yards' putt for a two at the second gave him the better aggregate. Disaster befell him at the Cardinal, his second going into the burn, but a three at the sixth – the result of a successful four yards' putt – gave him his chance again, only to take sixteen for the next three holes, where visits to the rough were responsible for all his trouble.

Out in 39, he refused to acknowledge defeat, and a beautiful pitch from the rough at the tenth left him a yard putt for four. He accepted the chance but lost a stroke at the thirteenth through putting too strongly from the edge of the green, and when he reached the last tee it was necessary to get a two in order to tie with Barnes. His drive finished about ten yards past the flag, and when a brave attempt to hole the putt failed, the North Manchester man knew that whatever happened to Macdonald Smith he himself could not be champion this year.

Macdonald Smith played perfect golf at the first two holes in the morning, but at the third a moderate drive left him so far from the Cardinal bunker that he elected to play quietly out of the rough. The wisdom of this policy was justified by what followed, for his fourth finished five feet from the hole, and his first putt went down. There was a curious incident connected with this hole. At the fifth he was short with a chip from the edge of the green and took four, but he recovered that stroke by holing out from five yards at the next. He cut his second to the seventh into the rough, but he holed a put of ten feet for the correct figure. He reached the eighth green with two magnificent shots with wooden clubs, but was lucky at the ninth, the ball missing a bunker by an inch or two. That good luck was balanced by his first putt hitting the hole without dropping, but as he began the homeward journey with a score of 36 he was in a very comfortable position.

Jim Barnes, the Cornish American – playing a chip on the 17th – wins Prestwick's last Open. Macdonald Smith, a Carnoustie-born American, threw away a third-round lead of five strokes to finish fourth.

The sensational incident of the round came at the twelfth. His approach sent the ball over the green about twenty yards from the flag, and from there he took four, first missing a putt of under two yards and then one of fifteen inches. His only lapse after that was the taking of three putts from about two yards at the fifteenth.

In the late afternoon his trouble began at the third, where he was through with his third and short with his next. He was bunkered at the fouth and fifth and missed an easy putt after getting out of a bunker at the seventh. He got a lucky four at the ninth and turned with a total of 42. He took five for the short hole through getting into a bunker, and six for the fifteenth, rendering almost perfect play at the last holes useless.

When Compston failed the only British hopes rested on Ray and Mitchell. Ray made a great effort until he reached the ninth green. There he took four to get down from about twenty yards, but that mistake made him fight harder than ever, and he played the last nine holes in 33, with four threes on his card. His total of 73 was the best of the day, but it did no more than leave him level with Compston.

Mitchell handicapped himself by losing strokes on the first two greens, but he got one back with a splendid pitch shot at the fourth. The ball touched the hole and stopped four inches away. After that his chance gradually disappeared. On nearly every green his first putt hit the hole without dropping, and Tom Fernie, who finished a stroke ahead of him, had the same sort of bad luck.

Apart from Compston, who greatly enhanced his reputation by scoring 76 in his first round and 75's in the others, Mitchell and Fernie played best of all the Britons, but in the two days neither holed a long putt except on very rare occasions. The eclipse of other men who are reckoned high in the British ranks was complete. Duncan took 46 for the first nine holes in his final round, and C. Whitcombe retired in the morning after a disconcerting experience with two dogs on a tee. It is time Scotsmen realised that golf courses are not airing grounds for dogs, but it is probably too much to expect that they will themselves refrain from scampering over the links like sheep. To-day there must have been over 20,000 spectators, and there were occasions on which the players were left such narrow lanes to play along that some of them could not see the flags.

A.L.L.

The scores

300: Jim Barnes (USA) 70, 77, 79, 74

301: A. Compston (N M/c) 75, 76, 75, 75; E. Ray (Oxhey) 77, 76, 75, 73

303: Macdonald Smith (USA) 76, 69, 76, 82

305: Abe Mitchell (unat) 77, 76, 75, 77

310: W.H. Davies (Prenton) 76, 76, 80, 78; Percy Allis (Wanstead) 77, 80, 77, 76; J.W. Caudin (Alwoodley) 78, 81, 77, 74; S. Wingate (T'lenewsam) 74, 78, 80, 78; J.H. Taylor (Mid-Surrey) 74, 79, 80, 77

1926

AMERICA TAKES OPEN GOLF TITLE AGAIN

Invaders capture first four places

The British Open Championship has for the fifth time in six years been won by an American, but the competition of the Royal Lytham and St Annes links has provided one variation, as it has given the title to an amateur for the first time since H.H. Hilton won it twenty-nine years ago.

The new winner is Robert Tyre ('Bobby') Jones, who although only twenty-five years of age, has twice been the American amateur champion and has twice tied for the American open title and won it once in the replays. This is only his second visit to Britain. On the first occasion five years ago he was beaten in the fourth round of the amateur championship and tore up his card in the third round of the Open. At Muirfield recently he was beaten by Jamieson, but in the Walker Cup contest he gave Tolley the biggest thrashing of his career, and this week he has played great golf, with 74 as his worst round. Jones has a reputation for fine iron play, beautiful putting, and a habit of registering level fours for each round. But there was some excuse for a slight falling below his standard this afternoon, as he was playing with Watrous and knew that, accidents apart, one of them would be champion.

Watrous is only twenty-six, so that we saw two young players struggling for the greatest honour in golf. Jones had to beat Watrous by three strokes in that round and he could not have succeeded had the professional not developed a tendency to take three putts towards the end. Jones himself used thirty-nine putts on the round – more than he has taken in seven national competitions except one.

After Jones had finished two strokes ahead of Watrous all attention was turned to Hagen, who was in his favourite position, that of knowing exactly what he had to do to win. Hagen started his last round before Jones finished his, but he soon knew that he required a 71, and when he reached the turn in 36, having dropped strokes at the eighth and ninth, his position was almost hopeless. He went on registering scratch scores until he came to the short fifteenth. There his tee shot found sand and he missed a three. That left him no hope, and at the last hole he needed a two to tie. He gave his second a chance, but the ball rolled into the bunker behind the green, and the six that followed did no more than prevent him from taking the third place unchallenged. As it was, he tied for that position with Von Elm, an American amateur.

Hagen must regret as much as Mitchell that they played their match last week. They have not given of their best at St Annes, although Mitchell showed signs of recovering to-day when he followed a seventy-two with a seventy-one. Those two rounds allowed Mitchell to tie with Barber, of Buxton, for the leadership of the British players, but as he finished eight strokes behind Jones the distinction is only a moral one. Barber spoilt his chance by taking seventy-eight in the morning, and after going out in the afternoon in thirty-four he missed his chance of beating Mitchell by taking five for the last when needing four for a seventy. Barber has done well, but for the rest of the Britons there is little to say. They have proved themselves unable to hold their American rivals, and until they learn the art of recovering from bad positions and not allowing the loss of a stroke to upset their play we shall have to reconcile ourselves to the ignominious position of arranging competitions for Americans to win. In this championship four Americans have finished at the top, and then after Mitchell and Barber come three Americans and an Argentine. Truly the British rout is complete.

But if the Americans have proved their superiority in play Lancashire has shown that it can run in a big competition in excellent style. To-day there have been ten thousand or more spectators, but the control has been excellent.

The morning's play brought a change of leadership, Watrous jumping from fourth place to the first, two strokes ahead of 'Bobby' Jones, with whom he was playing. Hagen remained third, but Melhorn by taking 79 dropped from second to equal fifth with Von Elm. Watrous secured the lead with a round of 69, made up as follows:

Out:	4	4	4	4	3	4	4	4	2–33
In:	4	5	4	5	3	4	4	4	3–36

His play was so perfect that it may be described as uneventful. His two was the result of a ten-foot putt and the slip that cost him a stroke at the thirteenth was a drive into the rough. He recovered that stroke by holing from ten yards on the next green, was a little unlucky at the fifteenth, and finished by holing a three-yarder on the home green. His putting throughout has been splendid, and several times he deserved better figures.

Jones was not quite as machine-like as usual and it was noticeable that many of his approach putts were short. This, a rare fault with Jones, caused an American friend to say to him that he had never seen a hole move to meet a ball, whilst a little later Jones said, 'I'm sticking to my guns but they won't shoot.' He registered his first six since he crossed the Atlantic by bunkering his second at the fourth and playing an explosion shot so forcibly that the ball went over the green. He lost another stroke through being bunkered at the ninth and at the fourteenth he was bunkered again. This latter misfortune, however, caused him to give a sample of the play by which Americans beat us. He was very short out, but then played a fine running shot and holed a three-yarder for the par score.

Melhorn fell below his best and sent two balls out of bounds at the eighth, but Hagen, apart from slight mistakes at the third and fourth, played excellently to reach the turn in 35. Coming back against the wind he lost some of his accuracy with his irons, and after looking certain to finish in 75 played a perfect shot to the last green, where a five-foot putt for three gave him 74.

The position at the end of the third round was that America filled the first six places and that J.H. Taylor led all the Britons. Taylor's position must have made some of the younger men wonder what was wrong with their golfing education, for Taylor, now fifty-five years of age, won his first championship before some of those who ought to have distinguished themselves this week were born. Taylor went out in 33 although he dropped a stroke at the third, and finished in 71, which with a little better luck on the greens might have been 67. His only mistakes were at the thirteenth, where he failed to reach the green in two and missed a five-foot putt, and at the last where he was bunkered at the side of the green. His play made one wish we could meet the American challenge with Taylor, Vardon, and Braid twenty years younger than they are now.

H.A. Gaudin had the remarkable experience of reaching the turn in 32, which included a six at the second, but his 71 left him no chance of troubling the leaders. Barber, of Buxton, played the first nine in one under fours, but after passing the twelfth he fell off, and 7, 5, and 5 for the last three spoilt his prospects. Duncan again failed, but Mitchell played more like the real Mitchell than we have seen this week in registering 72. Coming back he dropped strokes at the tenth, thirteenth, and seventeenth, but he had a great four at the long eleventh.

The amateur Robert Tyre ('Bobby') Jones at twenty-five wins the first of his three Opens in a spectacular head-to-head with fellow American Al Watrous. With his opponent on the 17th green, Jones's shot of 180 yards from a sandy lie to four yards was historic. Watrous three-putted and Jones, effectively, was home.

The spectators had a treat in the afternoon such as rarely occurs in a stroke competition, for Watrous and Jones went off together, knowing that one or the other had a great chance of winning the championship. The spectators probably numbered about 4,000, and their behaviour was excellent. Once or twice the players had to wait until movement behind them ceased, but they were given a fair field. The only untoward incident was when Watrous was driving from the eleventh tee. Just as he was making his downward swing a round of applause near an adjacent green from people who could not see what the Americans were doing undoubtedly affected his shot.

Jones started knowing that in order to win he had to gain three strokes on his partner, and his first success came at the third, where Watrous bunkered his second. Jones lost a great chance of going ahead at the short fifth, for Watrous played over the green from a bunker, was short back, and took five. Jones, however, required three putts, and the two were level. Watrous went ahead again at the seventh, where a much longer iron shot than Jones had to play reached the green after narrowly missing a bunker, which Jones found. Then at the ninth Jones again took three putts, and Watrous, who played finely from the bank at the back of the green, began the homeward journey still in possession of his two strokes lead.

He immediately lost one stroke by driving to the foot of a high mound, but although his poor drive at the eleventh, made in the circumstances already referred to, caused him to take six, Jones obliged with a similar number through missing a three-foot putt. Jones was in sand from the thirteenth tee, and became two strokes behind again, but then Watrous seemed to 'break'; at any rate his putting, which had previously been excellent, deserted him, and on three greens he used nine strokes. The decisive stroke of the game came at the seventeenth, where Jones drove into sand about 180 yards from the green. Jones thought a long time before he played, and then sent the ball four yards from the pin. At the last Watrous went from one bunker to another and finished the round in 78, so that his aggregate was two strokes worse than Jones's.

Compston suffered his second disqualification on this course after playing the third round. When playing from a bunker near the twelfth he sent the ball into a plantation, and said he preferred to play from there, although his marker warned him that he was out of bounds. He did play, and at the end he paid the penalty.

A.L.L.

The scores

291: Mr R.T. Jones (USA) 72, 72, 73, 74

293: A. Watrous (USA) 71, 75, 69, 78

295: Mr G. von Elm (USA) 75, 72, 76, 72; Walter Hagen (USA) 68, 77, 74, 76

299: Abe Mitchell (unattached) 78, 78, 72, 71; Tom Barber (Cavendish-Buxton) 77, 73, 78, 71

301: Fred McLeod (USA) 71, 75, 76, 79

303: Joseph Jurado (Argentine) 77, 76, 74, 76; W. Melhorn (USA) 70, 74, 79, 80; Emmet French (USA) 76, 75, 74, 78

1927

St Andrews, 16th July

RECORD VICTORY IN THE GOLF 'OPEN'

R.T. Jones's triumph

The Open Championship Cup is to go to America again, as R.T. Jones has followed his success at St Annes with a record-breaking success. His total score of 285 – made up of rounds of 68, 72, 73, and 72 – is six strokes lower than any Open Championship total in Britain, and is three better than the best recorded in America.

No championship field has ever been spreadeagled as this has been, and that although the scoring all round has been phenomenally low. Several men have finished with scores good enough to win in an ordinary year, but the decreased totals must be attributed to the conditions that have prevailed and not to an improvement of form. St Andrews has never provided an easier test, and this record of 'Bobby' Jones is likely to stand for many a year.

At twenty-six he has already won six championships, and there seems no reason why he should not go on winning. H.H. Hilton is the only other amateur who has won our Open title twice, and Jones is good enough to go on teaching our professionals the art of real putting and hitting perfect long shots, even when pressed by a crowd of 15,000 spectators.

The third round, which is considered the severest test in a championship competition, was not very exciting, because Jones, who started in the first hour, recorded 73, a score which left his rivals very little chance of catching him. Instead of being caught he increased his lead from two strokes to four, because Kirkwood, the Australian-American, and the two British young men who were nearest to him on Thursday evening all fell back. His nearest opponent at the end of the round was Fred Robson, and it was doubted whether he had the physique to do more than hold his own in the afternoon.

Robson had a brilliant round of 69, made up of 35 and 34, and the only incidents were on the greens. He took three putts at the first and missed from a yard at the fifteenth, but against those errors he had the satisfaction of holing two of four yards and one of six yards. His iron play was excellent, and he played the famous Road hole with a perfection rarely equalled this week. A long drive induced him to take the risk of trying to get on in two, and a splendid hit avoided all the traps that abound there and gave him an easy four.

Kirkwood had a curious round, with a five at the second his only slip on the outward half. Coming back he did not have a four on his card except for the last hole. He had three 'birdies' by means of putts of four or five yards, but took five for the short eleventh, where he used two strokes in a bunker. He was bunkered also at the thirteenth, and four holes farther on he missed from eighteen inches, so that, all things considered, he did well to finish in 75.

Hodson, the Welsh champion, who was second on Thursday night, cracked badly on the narrow part of the links, where all the long holes are. He had three fives in succession there going out, and coming back his errant ways with his wooden clubs became even worse, so that 27 were taken for five consecutive holes. Cotton dropped out of the running because he fell into the habit, painfully apparent among our golfers this week, of not giving the hole a chance. Holes never move forward to meet the ball, and we shall never regain our supremacy until our players realise that a putt of six inches is as easy from the farther side as one that has finished short. Cotton's worst spell came soon after the turn, when he took 16 for three holes through missing a very short putt and using two strokes in a bunker.

Boomer, who moved up the list, had three poor holes, and at one of them he missed a yard putt after 'fluffing' a mashie shot. He was bunkered at the third and was very unlucky at the fourteenth, where a magnificent iron shot from a difficult position 'kicked' into a pot bunker. C.A. Whitcombe improved with a 71, and would have had a wonderful round had he not left about half a dozen putts half an inch or so short of the holes, whilst Perkins, the English native champion, made himself the leading amateur by finishing in 70. Perkins started with two fives, but afterwards only once went above four. He had three at five holes for which the regulation score is four.

Jones's morning round was almost uneventful. He went out in 38, after taking three putts at the fourth and three from twelve yards at the ninth. Coming back, it was noticeable that his approach putts were firmer than before, and his only slip was at the twelfth, a hole which has given him trouble all this week.

It soon became evident when the final round began that Jones was to retain his championship. Boomer only three times deviated from fours in the round, having a two at the eighth and fives at the thirteenth and fourteenth. Robson was quickly dropping strokes that left him no chance, and as Jones reached the turn in 37 it was reckoned that he could take forty for the return half and yet win. He started that return with three threes, or two under par, played the middle holes perfectly in fours, and had fives at the sixteenth and seventeenth. At the sixteenth he pulled his drive and sliced his next so badly that he nearly went on to the railway. At the Road hole he missed a very short putt, but a four at the last gave him a homeward score of 35.

The scene whilst he was playing his last three strokes was remarkable. After the drives the spectators rushed madly towards the green, and it took ten minutes for a lane to be cleared along which he could play his pitch. The ball finished in the hollow which lost Wethered an Open Championship, and again the crowd dashed forward. Jones and Seymour had considerable difficulty in getting through, but Jones was unperturbed and laid a difficult putt dead. There was a great cheer when he holed out, and when Seymour had followed suit thousands rushed across the green. Jones was lifted shoulder-high, and, submitting to continuous pats on the back and innumberable handshakes, was carried to his hotel.

After Jones had disappeared from view there was little interest in the rest of the play. A seventy by Havers merely emphasised the poorness of his earlier play, and the fact that Robson played the last 13 holes in 51 proved that the dropping of four strokes whilst playing the first five only increased Jones's winning lead. Rodgers, of St Annes, finished at the head of Manchester district players, Hallam, of Chorlton, spoiling a day of good play by taking a seven and a six when coming home in the afternoon.

A.L.L.

Jones again. His 285 was six strokes lower than any British Open total and three better than the best recorded in America. Conditions, said A.L.L., 'were at their easiest.' For the first time the championship was extended to three days with the leading hundred required to qualify over two rounds.

The scores

*Amateur

285: *R.T. Jones (Atlanta, USA) 68, 72, 73, 72

291: A. Boomer (St Cloud, Paris) 76, 70, 73, 72; F. Robson (Cooden Beach) 76, 72, 69, 74

293: J. Kirkwood (Radium Springs, USA) 72, 72, 75, 74; E.R. Whitcombe (Meyrick Park, Bournemouth) 74, 73, 73, 73

296: C.A. Whitcombe (Crews Hill) 74, 76, 71, 75

297: B. Hodson (Newport Mon) 72, 70, 81, 74; A.G. Havers (Coombe Hill) 80, 74, 73, 70

298: T.H. Cotton (Langley Park) 73, 72, 77, 76

300: P.H. Rodgers (St Annes Old) 76, 73, 74, 77; R. Vickers (Heswall) 75, 75, 77, 73; *T.P. Perkins (Castle Bromwich) 76, 78, 70, 76; T. Williamson (Notts) 75, 76, 78, 71; P. Alliss (Berlin) 73, 74, 73, 80; A. Herd (Moor Park) 76, 75 78, 71; *W.B. Torrance (Edinburgh Burgess) 72, 80, 74, 74

Jones takes the championship cup and gold medal; Boomer and Robson each win £62. 10s; Kirkwood and E.R. Whitcombe £20 each; C.A. Whitcombe £15; Hodson, Havers, and Cotton £10 each, and Rodgers, Vickers, Williamson, Alliss, and Herd £3 each.

1928

BRITISH GOLFERS FAIL AGAIN

Hagen wins the Open Championship for the third time

The Open Golf Championship has gone to the United States of America for the seventh time in eight years. Walter Hagen, who won in 1922 and in 1924, has won again with rounds of 75, 73, 72, and 72, which left him two strokes ahead of Sarazen, another American, and three ahead of Compston.

Hagen has thus restored the prestige he lost when Compston thrashed him a fortnight ago, and it may be said that his putting in the third round did the trick. Although he started that round with three putts, he used only 15 going out and 16 coming back. On five consecutive greens he used only six putts.

Only five men finished under 300, but Davies and Taggart did well for Cheshire, and T.P. Perkins again led the amateurs. Taggart's performance was excellent for one little more than a boy, and it is to the youngsters we must look if we are to regain our laurels. The old hands have failed and will not be trusted again.

Asked afterwards what he considered his most important shot, Hagen said it was at the fifteenth hole in the fourth round. He under-clubbed himself and found a bunker in front of the green. He was lying well and knew he had to take a risk. His shot out was successful, and as he holed out for four from seven feet he felt that victory was near. He had never played in a championship with less confidence in himself, and he was surprised that he had been able to go on as well as he did.

Jurado was the first of the leaders to go off in the morning, and those who thought he would 'crack' saw nothing then to justify their belief. He went out soundly in 37, and showed the wisdom of a real golfer at the tenth, where his drive was bunkered. Many men would have tried to reach the green, but Jurado cut his loss and made certain of a five.

His evenness continued to the thirteenth, where he was extraordinarily lucky. He pulled with his brassy shot and the ball finished in an unplayable position against a fence and a wooden bench. At first it was said that he would have to play the penalty, but immediately the captain-elect of the Royal and Ancient Club was called up he pointed out that there was a local rule dealing with the situation, and under that Jurado dropped the ball within two club lengths of the seat, made a perfect chip, and got his four.

After a four-year gap Hagen has them on the run again.

He dropped a stroke at the fourteenth, but at the next, 457 yards, he played a wonderful second which Braid, his partner, said he would never have attempted. There is a cross bunker in front of the green, but Jurado cleared it and had an easy four. The last hole was his worst. He was bunkered against the green, and after playing out cleverly he hit the hole with a six-yard putt and missed the short return.

Hagen started curiously. For the first time in the competition he got on the first green in two, but the effect was spoilt by his taking three putts. At the third, where he had never before had a three, he registered that figure by chipping perfectly from the back of the green. At the fourth he played a champion's shot. He pulled his drive into a bunker, but

A contemporary illustrator sees golf as a costume drama.

with a mashie iron he hit the ball over about 160 yards of very rough country to the foot of the green. At the sixth he holed a seven-yarder for a two, and at the next he got down from eight yards.

He was 33 at the turn, so that with 27 holes still to be played he was one stroke ahead of Jurado. He made a beautiful pitch at the twelfth, when the small patch of land he had to reach was hidden from view, but he dropped strokes at the eleventh, fourteenth, and fifteenth, one of them through lifting his head. He had a two at the sixteenth, however, and the rest he played in the correct figures.

Compston had missed a great chance of taking the lead. He began with a three, but at the second he bunkered his drive, and, using a straight-faced iron in an attempt to reach the green, used three strokes in the hazard, so that seven went down against him. Threes at the third and fifth put him right, but at the short hole he underclubbed himself and took three putts. He reached the turn in 36 and, playing soundly afterwards, was helped by a two at the sixteenth, where his putt was eight yards downhill.

Sarazen handicapped himself by getting into a bunker at the first and missing a four-foot putt for a five. He missed from two yards at the fourth, but he thoroughly deserved his 34 to the turn. After that he went on smoothly to a 73, with successful putts of ten and fifteen feet the only incidents.

Duncan and Mitchell fell completely out of the running, and of Mitchell it must be written now that, almost invincible on inland courses, he is unable to master seaside links. Alliss went out in 35, but had four fives and a six coming back. Robson was more consistent in registering 73, and Taggart, out in 37, spoilt his homeward half with a six at the fifteenth.

The position when the last round started was:

Hagen, 220; Jurado and Sarazen, 221; Compston, 222; Burns, Melhorn, and Robson, 225; Alliss, 226; Taggart and Williamson, 227.

Of those who finished early Alliss did the best. He had seven fours and two threes going out, but he played the eleventh badly in six and dropped another stroke at the seventeenth. Immediately behind him Jurado was frittering away whatever chance the morning's play had left him. The Argentine champion developed a habit of pulling his seconds, and as his putting deserted him his plight became hopeless. He failed to stay the course on the most strenuous day of all, but he had impressed some of our best judges, and after the third round J.H. Taylor said that stroke for stroke he was the best golfer in the field.

Melhorn went out in 35, but lost all hope at the twelfth, where he played a terrible shot off the socket of his niblick, took three in a bunker, and registered seven. A good 72 by Boomer was of no importance because Hagen, who was in the next couple behind him, was making his position almost impregnable.

Hagen had started with three fours, and the missing of a yard putt at the third seemed to shake his confidence. From the fourth to the eighth, where he holed from six feet for a two, he was evidently worried on the greens. At the seventh he topped his drive and was short in three, whilst he was decidedly lucky at the ninth, his ball running along a path between bunkers to a position that enabled him to chip 'dead'. Out in 36 he settled down, but still deliberated so long about his putts that he held up the players who were following. He missed a short putt at the seventeenth, but his total of 292 seemed good enough.

Joshua Crane, an American amateur, with his one-handed, eighteen-inch putter. It did not bring him notable success.

Compston had played the first three holes well, but after that he did some pulling, and although he holed from seven yards for a two at the eighth his putting had not the accuracy to give him a real chance. He was left to play the last nine in 33 to tie, and a succession of fours made the task beyond him. He fought bravely, but that awful seven in the morning had ruined him. When Compston finished only Sarazen remained with a chance, and an outside one at that. A six at the seventh smashed his hopes, and fives in the middle of the homeward journey completed the wreck.

A.L.L.

The scores

292: W. Hagen (USA) 75, 73, 72, 72

294: G. Sarazen (USA) 72, 76, 73, 73

295: A. Compston (unattached) 75, 74, 73, 73

298: P. Alliss (Berlin) 75, 76, 75, 72; F. Robson (Cooden Beach) 79, 73, 73, 73

301: J. Jurado (Argentina) 74, 71, 76, 80; A. Boomer (France) 79, 73, 77, 72; J. Barnes (USA) 81, 73, 76, 71

302: W. Melhorn (USA) 71, 78, 76, 77

1929

Gullane, 11th May

HAGEN STILL THE KING OF GOLF

Americans sweep the deck

Walter Hagen to-day retained the Open Championship he won last year, and as he was the winner also in 1922 and 1924 he equalled the record of Vardon and Braid of gaining the title four times in eight years. His supremacy has been even greater than that of those great masters, for he did not come over for two of the competitions played since he had his first success, and in the other years he finished second and equal third.

Hagen is the Ol' Man River of golf. He may seem out of form a little before a championship competition, as he did at Moortown a fortnight ago, but when a title is at stake he registers par figures in long rows, occasionally gains a stroke by getting down with a single putt, and whenever he causes astonishment by having a poor hole he usually does something extraordinarily good.

At the age of 37 Hagen has finished six ahead of Farrell, the American champion, and eight in front of Mitchell and Alliss, who led the British players. He has made nearly all our men look very ordinary. On the greens he is a king and his rivals merely commoners, for in strenuous play three putts on a green are rare with him, whilst they handicap themselves by taking threes thrice or more in every round. To-day he began his third round in the competition two strokes behind his fellow-American Diegel and two ahead of Mitchell, and by making only two slips on the greens against their many slips on the greens he made his position impregnable, the leading totals when the last round began being:

Hagen	217
Alliss	221
Mitchell and Diegel	222
Farrel	223
Cruickshank	225

The weather to-day was thought to be in favour of Mitchell and Alliss, as a westerly wind often had the force of nearly a gale, but at the only moment in which Mitchell seemed likely to offer a serious challenge he threw away his chance by taking four putts from eight yards.

The strength of the wind may be judged from the fact that only eighteen of sixty-four players had scores of under 80 in the morning round. After one pitch by Hagen the ball was carried three yards back by backspin or the wind when it fell on the green, and many players nearly incurred penalty strokes by the ball's oscillating when they were preparing to putt. Hagen called attention to one incident of that sort, and the question of a penalty was left to the authorities in the clubhouse, who decided that there was no evidence that the ball moved.

Hagen's was the eighth American success since the war. There has not been a British victory since 1923, and there is no sign of a break. The only thing certain is that we are being fairly and squarely beaten.

The draw gave Mitchell and Alliss the advantage of playing together, and Mitchell pleased by getting to the eighth tee with an average of fours. He had a single putt at the second, and fives at the fifth and sixth were explained by a bunkered drive and two poor shots when the wind was blowing furiously. Then he played two holes badly, being bunkered at one and taking three putts at each. At the next three holes he picked up a stroke, playing a putt of eight feet and a long chip perfectly, but his putting at the short thirteenth was tragic. From eight yards he got little more than half-way, his next went about eight inches past, and his third ran nearly all the way round the hole and stopped out. It was impossible to get up in two at the fourteenth, and another five went down against him; another stroke went at the short hole through a pulled tee shot, and at the last he had three putts again.

Alliss reached the turn in 39, or one better than Mitchell, having holed putts of about five yards for threes at the third and seventh. He had a 'birdie' at the tenth, but fell behind Mitchell by registering fives at the next two, a second shot being bunkered behind the green and a chip going astray. At the short hole he made Mitchell's putting look all the more piteous by playing from a bunker and holing a good putt for three. With the exception of the last, where he got his four, he played the remaining holes evenly with Mitchell.

Not far behind the British pair was Hagen, consolidating his position by excellent play. He did not drop a stroke until the seventh, where he was bunkered and narrowly missed a putt of three yards. He

Hagen's fourth title in eight years merits the congratulations of Henry Cotton. Hagen, says A.L.L., is the Ol'Man River of Golf.

was bunkered again at the eighth, and had to be content with a five. The ninth also was played in five, but nothing better could be expected to-day. At the turn, therefore, he was 37, and his aggregate was four better than that of Alliss.

He missed his four against the wind at the twelfth, and when he bunkered his tee shot at the thirteenth he lost for a few minutes all his jauntiness of carriage. He played poorly out, but then emphasised the differences between a champion and his challengers by holing from seven yards. The next hole was dead against the wind, and after his second wooden shot had run round the edge of a bunker he played like a long-handicap man. His pitch was very short, his approach putt was much too strong, and he nearly missed with his sixth from a few inches. A stroke gained by a single putt at the fifteenth was lost at the short hole, and another went at the last, where his second was bunkered. A 75, however, was good enough to give him a lead of four strokes over Alliss, and all seemed over except the congratulatory speeches.

Meanwhile Diegel had been performining as none of us had dreamed he could perform. He had reached the turn in 43, having taken three putts on five greens, four of them in succession, and having taken five to get on the ninth without visiting a bunker. He improved coming home, but could get no threes, and his aggregate at the finish was level with Mitchell's. Only a stroke behind these two was Farrell, whose 76 was evenly divided between the two halves. His only 'birdie' was at the second, and he had three threes and a four at the short holes.

The afternoon proceedings were merely an uninteresting procession that became a bore when Mitchell and Allis reached the turn in 40 and 41 respectively and Hagen got there in 35, which included a six at the ninth, where he pulled his second against a wall and could not get on in three. He had played the eighth brilliantly, deliberately driving into the rough on the right in order to cut off the dog-leg bend, sending a mashie niblick shot about three yards from the flag, and holing the putt. The three there put him on velvet, and coming home he slackened so much that he took three putts on each of the three greens and got into two bunkers.

He could have played even more carelessly and yet have had no anxiety. He knew that Mitchell and Alliss were giving no sign of producing the brilliant strokes that were necessary to create any excitement. Mitchell, it is true, had a single putt where he had used four in the morning, but for the rest he and his partner were just ordinary, and when they finished not a dozen hands were put together to applaud. Their better-ball score was 72, so even with that way of counting they would not have displaced Hagen.

After that the only interesting question was whether Farrell or Diegel, or both, would finish in front of the British pair. Farrell, after going out in 39 with a bad six at the eighth, played steadily, equalled Hagen's round, and took second place, whilst Diegel gave America the first three places by playing the last nine in 36.

A.L.L.

The scores

292: Walter Hagen (USA) (winner of Championship Gold Medal and £75) 75, 67, 75, 75

298: Johnny Farrell (USA) (£50) 72, 75, 76, 75

299: Leo Diegel (USA) (£25) 71, 69, 82, 77

300: Abe Mitchell (private) (£15) 72, 72, 78, 78; Percy Alliss (Berlin) (£15) 69, 76, 76, 79

301: R. Cruickshank (USA) 73, 74, 78, 76

303: Jim Barnes (USA) 71, 80, 78, 74

304: Gene Sarazen (USA) 73, 74, 81, 76; Al Watrous (USA) 73, 79, 75, 77

305: T. Armour (USA) 75, 73, 79, 78

1930

'BOBBY' JONES WINS A GOLF 'DOUBLE'

Ten strokes better than Hagen

Robert Tyre Jones, the famous American amateur, is the British Open champion for the third time in five years, but his final progress has been much more exciting than it seemed likely to be last evening, when with 36 holes to play he led by one stroke.

The great feature of the day's play occurred in the morning, when Compston gained six strokes on Jones and wrested the lead from him by creating a new record for the Royal Liverpool links by registering 68, which included two sixes. Compston, however, gave a very poor exhibition in the fourth round, and in the end they were Americans who chased Jones home.

Jones had the satisfaction of equalling John Ball's performance in 1890 of winning both our titles in one year, and as he is also the holder of the American Open Championship he is in a position which no other man is likely to attain. Jones's score of 291, made up of 70, 72, 74, and 75, beat Hagen's winning total here six years ago by ten strokes, and it is noteworthy that although 301 had never been beaten here in a championship, eight men have this week beaten 300.

As was the case last year, three Americans are at the top of the list, but instead of eight Americans figuring in the first ten, as there were then, there are only five. Robson did remarkably well for a man of 45 in finishing as the first Englishman, and Tom Barber, formerly of Buxton, had a score that would have won in Hagen's year.

The morning's play started at eight o'clock very quietly, the only interest being in Horton Smith, who began three strokes behind Jones, and who had immediately handicapped himself by taking six and five for the first two, and in the part of the links where recovery is expected he developed a hook in his second shots. Jones did not begin until after nine, and when he played the first hole in four rather luckily – his drive hit a bunker but came back on the fairway – everybody regarded that as the beginning of a triumphal march. At the second, however, he bunkered his niblick shot and lost a stroke, whilst at the third he hooked his drive out of bounds, found the rough on the other side of the course with his spoon, and chipped short, so that for the second time in succession he registered six there.

As usual, he then fell into monotonous regularity, nine holes being played in the exact figures without the slightest promise of failure. He was two under fours with five to play, but then – an astonishing thing this with Jones – four fives came in succession. At the fourteenth he was in the rushes to the right with his second; at the fifteenth he was bunkered in front of the green; at the next he took three from just off the edge of the green; and at the seventeenth he spared his second and required three to get down from twenty yards.

Compston, who went off thirty-six minutes later than Jones, said before he began that he felt wonderfully fit, and was going to do either 69 or 79. He soon showed that the lower figure was likely, as one putt of seven feet sufficed on the second green, and at the fourth a putt of eight yards made his total for the forty holes the same as Jones's. Then he killed the elation of his followers by taking six where four is often recorded; he pulled his drive into a grassy hollow two hundred yards from the tee, contented himself with a safe shot out, but was short with his third. His first putt at the seventh was poor, but he got his three, and after a magnificent shot with wood to the eighth green he nearly holed his first putt. He reached the turn two strokes worse off than Jones, and then had a marvellous run.

At the tenth and twelfth his iron shots finished five feet behind the flags and he hole the putts for threes. At the thirteenth he became seven under an average of fours by holing a six-yard putt, and the cheer which greeted the feat was even louder than earlier ones that had warned Jones that his rival was doing great deeds. His attitude as soon as he had hit his second at the fourteenth clearly showed to those who could not see the ball that it had gone awry. It finished in the rushes, as Jones's had done, and his pitch out narrowly missed a bunker. He hit the hole from the edge of the green, but had to be content with five. At the next he chipped dead from the right-hand edge of the green, but he disappointed at the long dog-leg hole. His second did not quite get home; he was very short with a chip, and after he had putted fifteen inches past the hole his ball rolled round and refused to drop. He finished with two safe fours and had to work hard to avoid being carried to the club-house, where he was received with another round of cheering. The figures of Compston's record-breaking round were:

Out: 4 3 4 2 6 4 3 4 4–34
In: 3 3 3 2 5 4 6 4 4–34

Diegel took third position by means of very accurate putting. With four threes going out he reached the turn in 33, but lost his chance by getting into trouble at the twelfth and fourteenth. Jolly made a promising start, but at the seventh he missed a very short putt and then lost his touch so completely that on four of the next five greens he took three putts. Boyer, the man from Nice, kept himself among the leaders with a score of seventy, which included seven threes, two of which came right at the finish, and Barber also had a very good round of 72. He had twos at the fourth and eleventh, but missed the one he should have had at the seventh, and found the long holes coming home very trying.

Jones's third title was part two of his historic Grand Slam in which he won the British and US match-play Amateur Championships as well as the Opens. The British double had been achieved only once before – in 1890 by John Ball, who played in the Open until 1927, when he was sixty-five.

In the afternoon there was much more wind than there had been at any time in the week, and the quality of the play suffered. The strain undoubtedly had an effect, and Jones was not impressive at the start, although he had a three at the second, where his drive was pushed out so badly that the ball hit a spectator, went across the fourteenth green, and finished in a bunker. The lie was an excellent one, and his shot was so good that it inspired him to hole a putt of about eight yards. On each of the next two greens, however, he used three putts through not getting up to the holes. At the eighth he had a remarkable lapse, as he took seven, pulling his second below the bank against the green, making a very moderate pitch, and taking four putts, the last that was missed being of the sort that could be knocked in with the back of the putter.

His 38 out seemed to leave Compston an excellent chance, but the news about Compston was depressing, and it was felt that Jones had only to return steadily to win. He missed threes at the short holes, taking three putts at the eleventh and being bunkered at the thirteenth, but little else was wrong. He saved two strokes by very good chips, but fluffed a similar shot at the fifteenth and holed a three-yard putt for an ordinary four at the seventeenth. He finished with

a very sound four and retired to the clubhouse amidst great applause.

An hour earlier it had been realised that Compston had gone to pieces. He rarely hit a shot right, and when he did make an exception he immediately threw the advantage away. His putting, too, deserted him, and he took 43 to reach the turn, and at the thirteenth he was fourteen strokes worse than he had been in the morning. A worse collapse has not been known since Mitchell squandered his long lead at Deal.

Robson and Horton Smith played very well, but without any hope of overtaking Jones, and then all the attention was given to Diegel, who needed to return in 35 to tie. He dropped a stroke at the eleventh, as Jones did, and when he missed a yard putt at the fourteenth he needed level fours for the remainder. A very good putt at the fifteenth gave him the right figure, but his next drive went into a bunker, and three putts from ten yards left him no hope of anything but second place. Macdonald Smith played steadily all day, and had the best round of the afternoon (71), which enabled him to tie with Diegel. His return in 35 was a model of perfection, a five at the fourteenth being a very small blot.

A.L.L.

The scores

291: Mr R.T. Jones (USA) 70, 72, 74, 75

293: L. Diegel (USA) 74, 73, 71, 75; Macdonald Smith (USA) 70, 77, 75, 71

296: Horton Smith (USA) 72, 73, 78, 73; F. Robson (Cooden Beach) 71, 72, 78, 75

297: L. Barnes (USA) 71, 77, 72, 77; A. Compston (Coombe Hill) 74, 73, 68, 82

299: H. Cotton (Langley Park) 70, 79, 77, 73

300: T. Barber (Derbyshire) 75, 76, 72, 77; A. Boyer (Nice) 73, 77, 70, 80; C. Whitcombe (Crews Hill) 74, 75, 72, 79

1931

Carnoustie, 6th June

OPEN TITLE AGAIN 'GOES WEST'

Armour beats Jurado by a stroke

For the eighth year in succession the Open Championship Cup is going to America, and the bitterness of the event is decreased but little by the fact that it is being taken there by a Scottish American player. Thomas D. Armour won with 396, beating Jurado, an Argentine, by one stroke, and the best Britain could do was to tie for the third and sixth places.

Armour is 36, and before 1925, when he went to America and turned professional, he was a well-known Edinburgh player, where he learned his golf on Braid Hills. He won the French amateur title in 1920, and in the following year played for Britain against America at Hoylake. Whilst in America he has won the Open and Professional Championships. A sparely built man, he has a very quick swing, and is a magnificent user of irons.

Before to-day there was some doubt about his staying power, but he dispelled that doubt with a fourth round of 71. He was fortunate, however, in that his chief challenger failed to withstand the strain over the last nine holes. Armours is not a brilliant putter, but once again it has to be written that British players have failed through moderate work on the greens. Cotton, who lost seven strokes to Armour during the day, threw the Championship away by erratic short play, and no new British player came to the front except in single rounds.

The winning score is the highest of the last six years, but that is explained by the cold and windy weather. The conditions to-day were the pleasantest of the week, although there was still a cold north-east wind, which was responsible for many of the failures over the last nine holes. The Prince of Wales arrived early in the morning, and has gone all over the links. While Jurado was struggling homewards he took his chance with the rest until the last hole was played. There he walked along the fairway, whilst from the tee to beyond the green ordinary folk were kept from encroaching by wire fencing. That was another testimony to Carnoustie's mangement. There were probably over 12,000 spectators, and although many were content to sit round the first tee and the home green as if they were at a cricket match, those who followed the play were kept so well in order that no trouble whatever was caused.

The third round is regarded as the most searching of the competition and it usually provides many surprises. The early play this morning suggested that there were going to be upheavals, but after Cotton had failed, Jurado obtained a lead of three strokes with a very good round of 73. He was playing with Davies, and the Wallasey man went out in 34 against 36 by playing seventh, eighth, and ninth in three, two, and three, all being 'birdies'.

The Prince of Wales became a spectator at the tenth and had a few words with Jurado, who was a fellow-voyager on his return from Buenos Aires. They chatted all the way along the eleventh fairway, but Jurado continued his steady play, and the Prince was much interested by what happened at the 'Spectacles' hole, so named because two great bunkers in front of the green bear some resemblance to American hornrims. Davies pitched out of one bunker to within five feet of the flag, and Jurado from the other did the same, so that both succeeded with one putt. Jurado dropped a stroke at the sixteenth through being short from the tee and at the last his second found the burn. The Prince then joined Davies and they saw Jurado's pitch leave him a two-yard putt which he holed.

Cotton's failure was almost tragic, but it did not surprise those who watched him carefully on the greens on Thursday. He made a great start with a three, but soon lost all faith in his putting. He enlisted his caddie's aid in deciding on the line to the holes and then revealed his nervousness by standing for long periods with his club motionless behind the ball. When he did make up his mind to hit he was frequently off the line, and when he did get straightness his length was defective. The trouble began because his shots to the greens were usually wide or short, but even so there was no excuse for putting failures which led to three strokes on each of four greens.

He made an amazing shot at the tenth: his ball was two yards off the green, but where many a long-handicap player could have chipped almost dead, Cotton sent the ball right over the green and only a very good putt saved him from dropping more than one stroke. He was bunkered at the seventeenth and was cheered for succeeding with an eight-yard putt, but his last drive was pushed into the burn, and after a magnificent but daring slash with wood which carried the last lot of water he fluffed a chip shot and registered six.

Compston, who began soon after eight o'clock, topped his first drive into the burn not 80 yards away, but that woke him thoroughly, and a 'birdie' at the fourth helped to give him 36 for the first nine. His short game was very good until after he had got over the burn at the home hole in two. Then he made a poor chip and his first putt was badly off the line.

Lister Hartley did best of the amateurs with 74, diverging from par figures at only two holes. Horton Smith went out in 34, his best performance in the competition, and Alliss obtained a strong position by overcoming previous unreliability with his putter. Macdonald Smith and Havers shared the lead for a time, and Havers would have started the last round with an advantage had he putted well. His long game was wonderful, and although he was always struggling on the greens he did the best homeward half of the contest with three threes and six fours. Macdonald Smith and R.A. Whitcombe played very fine golf together. Whitcombe, who reached the turn in 34 against 35 was two under fours with two holes to play, but he used two strokes in a bunker at the seventeenth and, short with his second at the last, finished with fives. Macdonald Smith, very deliberate everywhere, missed his three at the short thirteenth, but holed from five yards for a 'birdie' at the seventeenth, and a pretty third and a four-yard putt gave him one of the few fours registered at the home hole.

The last round started with the leaders in the following order:

> 220, Jurado; 228, Macdonald Smith and Havers; 224, R.A. Whitcombe and Farrell; 225, Armour, Alliss, Davies, Sarazen, and Hunter; 226, Cotton and Williamson.

The order in which they went out and the scores gave Horton Smith the lead until Genta, one of the longest of drivers, tied with him. Churio, an Argentinian, deprived them of their minor distinction by equalling the record with 71, only to be himself dispossessed in a few minutes by Alliss, who had reached the turn in 35 and seemed a probable winner when he had played the thirteenth. He finished with 5, 5, 2, 5, and 6 – the worst figure being the result of going out of bounds.

Armour, in the next couple behind Alliss, had equalled Alliss in going out in 35, his only blot being three putts at the second. Armour played a brilliant second at the eleventh, where the flag was behind a high hillock, and got down a three-yarder for a three; spoilt the effect of that success by taking three putts on the next green, and at the short hole did well to register three after missing the green from the tee. His adventurous career was continued by a sliced second at the fourteenth and a successful putt for four from the edge of the green, whilst after being

Tommy Armour, the Scottish-American professional, won by one stroke from Argentina's Jose Jurado while other rivals flagged in wet and windy weather.

bunkered at the fifteenth he missed from two yards. He had a lucky three at the short hole, for his tee shot went astray and his single putt was from fifteen yards. He had a three-yard putt for a three at the seventeenth and missed it, and when putting for four at the last he took extreme care and went a yard wide.

Cotton was little better than in the forenoon, and as Farrell was out in 38, Sarazen in 36, and Havers and Hunter in 40 each the probables were reduced to Macdonald Smith, R. Whitcombe, Davies, and Jurado. Davies had set himself an impossible task by starting with five and six, and Whitcombe delayed the smashing of his hopes until his tee shot at the short thirteenth went over the green into a bush; he tried to get out, buried the ball deeper, and then picked out under penalty, so that he took six.

Macdonald Smith played the first nine finely with eight fours and a three, but coming home he lost his accuracy, and his chance almost disappeared with a five at the sixteenth, where he was bunkered from the tee and very short with his first putt. Even worse followed, for he went over the seventeenth green, made a very poor chip, and used three more strokes in getting down.

Only Jurado was left to challenge Armour, and he had dropped a stroke at the fifth in going out in thirty-six. That meant returning in thirty-nine to win. A pulled second cost him a stroke at the tenth, and when he took four at the thirteenth through getting into a bunker his task was a heavy one. At the next he was short all the way, and, just on in three, he took three putts. At the fifteenth he holed a ten-yarder for a four, and a three at the sixteenth left him to play the last two in ten to tie.

Then the crack opened wide, for he duffed his drive into the burn, was bunkered from a very long second, and took six. At the last he declined the risk of attempting to carry the last water with his second, and placed a pitch and run within four yards of the hole. All his hopes depended on the next stroke, and with very little hesitation he made the putt. The line was, perhaps, an inch inaccurate, and the ball trickled over the side of the hole. Jurado was beaten by one stroke, and Armour was champion.

A.L.L.

The scores

296: T. Armour (USA) 73, 75, 77, 71

297: Jose Jurado (Argentine) 76, 71, 73, 77

298: P. Alliss (Berlin) 74, 78, 73, 73; Gene Sarazen (USA) 74, 78, 73, 73; Macdonald Smith (USA) 74, 77, 71, 76

299: J. Farrell (USA) 72, 77, 75, 75

300: W.H. Davies (Wallasey) 76, 78, 71, 75; M. Churio (Argentine) 76, 75, 78, 71

301: A.L. Lacey (Selsden Park) 74, 80, 74, 73

302: H. Cotton (Langley Park) 72, 75, 79, 76; A.G. Havers (Sandy Lodge) 75, 76, 72, 79

1932

Sandwich, 11th June

OPEN GOLF CHAMPIONSHIP

Sarazen wins easily with record aggregate

Gene Sarazen, born of Italian parents in New York, sets a new record aggregate of 283 in winning the 1932 Open.

The slight hope that remained on Thursday evening of a British victory in the competition for the Open Championship was dispelled to-day, and for the ninth year in succession the cup is to cross the Atlantic. Gene Sarazen, who was born of Italian parents in New York thirty-one years ago, has won it with rounds of 70, 69, 70, and 74, and his aggregate of 283 has set up a new record for the competition, the previous best having been 285 by R.T. Jones five years ago at St Andrews, which is 400 yards shorter than Prince's. That score stamps Sarazen as a marvellous player. Not once in the four rounds has he taken a six, and although numerous putts have hit the holes without dropping in he has not allowed what many deemed bad luck to perturb him. Instead of flinging his putter about and looking very angry, as some of our players have done, he has taken the hard knocks smilingly, and has earned great praise from older men who won championships because they, too, had the right temperament for a very trying game.

Although the week's test has put the best golfer at the top, the result is exceedingly exasperating from a British point of view because the young men of whom much was expected have failed, and have left what fight there has been to men who have seen their best days. Even the older men have disappointed, and early to-day Havers alone had a chance to overhaul Sarazen. Havers broke the course record in his third round and might easily have knocked two strokes off his 68, but when he went out the fourth time, needing 70 to tie, the hope he had inspired slowly died. When he realised that his task had become impossible he 'cracked' and finished with 5, 4, and 5, six strokes behind Sarazen, and had to surrender even the second place, of which he had seemed certain, to another American, Macdonald Smith. The distinction of being leading amateur fell to W.L. Hope.

Sarazen made pursuit almost hopeless when he set off in the morning, first of all the leaders, and produced figures with the accuracy of a calculating machine. True, he made a slip at the fourth which cost him a stroke, but there was some slight excuse, as he had to play a mashie niblick shot off a very hard patch. He partly socketed the shot, finished near the edge of the green, and took three more. At the seventh, nearly 400 yards long, a putt of six yards gave him a three, and at the next (438 yards) he played his second over the high sandhills with a cleek, hit the pin, and holed from three yards for another three. More threes might easily have come at the eleventh and twelfth, the holes being hit without the ball dropping. His second mistake was made at the thirteenth, where his approach went over the green and his chip back was too strong, so that he took five.

That stroke was regained at the sixteenth, a putt of three yards giving him another 'birdie' three. All the spectators hoped to see his famous spoon shot repeated at the seventeenth, but he had a hanging lie, half-topped the shot, and finished short of the green, so that he had to be content with a five. An easy four at the last made him 70, and it was realised that barring a miracle the new champion had been found.

The nearest Englishman at this stage was Lacey, who was eight strokes behind, and Macdonald Smith's 71, obtained by perfect golf except that he had two fives instead of fours, was regarded as of little importance. Mitchell began well, but soon fell into errant ways; Davies took six at the seventh and 38 to the turn; Alliss had a six at the same hole and was 40 at the turn; Charles Whitcombe went out in 37, but took six at the twelfth; and Compston, out in 36, finished poorly. These failures left Havers as the only British hope, and he shouldered the responsibility so bravely that he set up a new record of 68 for the course. A successful putt of three yards for a two at the third put him on good terms with himself, and from there onwards he obtained par figures quite comfortably, so that he reached the turn in 33. Another fine putt of six yards at the tenth improved his chance, but at the short fourteenth he dragged an uphill putt off the line and finished about four feet short. He missed with his next, and for the first and last time in the round he went above par score. At the fifteenth he hooked his drive into the rough, but a putt of twelve yards gave him another 'birdie' three. The sixteenth was played correctly, but at the seventeenth his second barely reached the green, his approach was eight feet too strong, and he missed the return. He caused some disappointment by failing to get a three at the last, where his first putt was from two and a half yards.

Sarazen began his final round quite soundly, but at the short fifth he missed the green and was short with a pitch, and a four caused him to lose some of his cheerfulness. When he took three putts at the sixth, British stock improved considerably, but it sagged again when for the second time in the day he had a three, at the eighth, holing out from about 11 yards. He began the homeward half one under fours, and immediately dropped a stroke through going into a bunker against the tenth green. At the eleventh he was lucky. The sandhills there stretch diagonally across the fairway and are farthest from the tee at the point where they cross the direct line to the hole. Sarazen went for the long carry, missed it, and found his ball lying on the only good patch that there is in that area, with the result that he got the par figure of four. Another stroke went at the twelfth when he drove into the rough, but with true American pertinacity he holed a twelve-yarder for a two at the fourteenth. His position then seemed unassailable, but three putts at the next and two shots in the rough at the sixteenth made him realise that one more inaccurate stroke might put him in peril. Instead of his spoon he used an iron at the seventeenth, making sure of a five, and at the last he got an easy four.

Havers, who was finishing his third round when Sarazen was beginning his fourth, had in his gallery for the last few holes the Prince of Wales, who afterwards followed Sarazen. When Havers went off again it soon became known that he needed a 70 to tie, and hopes sank when he took five at the first, pushing his pitch and going seven or eight feet too far with a chip over a low bank. Try as he would, the 'birdies' did not come, and when he had completed the first nine his position was hopeless. His long game was not always accurate and his putting became poor, so that when he took three putts on one green soon after passing the turn many of the spectators went home. Mitchell played the first nine holes in the afternoon in 31 with only two spectators, and several men who beat an average of fours in their last round did so without interesting anybody but their markers.

A.L.L.

The scores

283: G. Sarazen (USA) 70, 69, 70, 74

288: Macdonald Smith (USA) 71, 76, 71, 70

289: A.G. Havers (Sandy Lodge) 74, 71, 68, 76

292: C.A. Whitcombe (Crews Hill) 71, 73, 73, 75; P. Alliss (Beaconsfield) 71, 71, 78, 72; A.H. Padgham (Royal Ashdown Forest) 76, 72, 74, 70

293: A.J. Lacey (Selsdon Park) 73, 73, 71, 76; W.H. Davies (Wallasey) 71, 73, 74, 75

294: F. Robson (Addington Palace) 74, 71, 78, 71

295: A. Mitchell (private) 77, 71, 75, 72; T.H. Cotton (Langley Park) 74, 72, 77, 72

1933

St Andrews, 8th & 10th July

AMERICANS TIE IN GOLF 'OPEN'

Easterbrook fails by one stroke in most desperate finish

8th July

For the tenth year in succession the British Open Golf Championship will go to the United States. In the most exciting finish the tournament has ever provided, Densmore Shute (USA) and Craig Wood (USA) yesterday tied for first place a stroke better than two other Americans – Sarazen, the holder, and Diegel – and they will play off over 36 holes to-day for the title.

The extraordinary consistency of Shute's play – he took 73 strokes on each round – has no parallel in the history of the competition. Craig Wood won his tie with the third 68 of the competition proper, and provides another example of the success of a man who scraped through the qualifying test.

Although we find five Americans in the first six there is an Englishman only a stroke behind the leaders, and six Englishmen finished only four strokes behind. The crucial last round, a test of 'nerves' as much as of golfing skill, destroyed many hopes, especially British ones, for after three rounds five players – Mitchell, Cotton, Easterbrook, Diegel, and Kirkwood (USA) – were level with scores of 216. Cotton early lost his chance, and Mitchell, although playing gallantly, had a bad hole at the seventeenth, and the British hopes centred on Easterbrook, who went out last player but one. Diegel played bravely in the last round, and Sarazen had surmounted a bad spell. For hours these two Americans had stood at the head of affairs with 293.

A fierce wind sprang up from the sea, making the homeward half exceptionally difficult, and when Craig Wood finished with an aggregate of 292 it was though he had won the Championship. An hour later, however, there was another sensation when Shute returned an equal score, and just as the crowd gathered at the home hole had resigned themselves to an American tie hopes were raised by the knowledge that Easterbrook was making a magnificent battle.

For two hours British hopes rose and fell with the news of how Easterbrook was progressing. Fifteen thousand people surged around Easterbrook as he played the finishing holes, and the excitement rose until there were tumultuous scenes at the close. Every window that overlooked the home green was full of spectators, some stood on balconies, and the ground behind the green was one sea of faces, all looking with hope at the young Briton who had a chance of fighting again for the title.

There was a groan when Easterbrook pulled his second shot to the eighteenth and the ball finished near the steps. When his third shot was two yards from the hole the crowd realised that all was over. There were rousing cheers when Easterbrook holed his putt for a 77, but the young Ryder Cup player's great effort was unavailing.

One of the surprises of the day was the dismal failure of Walter Hagen, the leader at the half-way stage. He took 79 for his third round, and, probably dismayed by his misadventures, he required 83 for his final round for a total of 301. Never before in the competition proper had Hagen got into the eighties. The Old Course, which has been described this week as a drive and pitch links, regained all its former reputation to-day, when a strong south-easterly breeze has made play over the homeward half extremely difficult and has made many players respect Hell bunker, instead of ignoring it. Only five scores better than 72 have been made, and the best of all was Wood's 68 in the morning.

The third round started at eight o'clock with the leaders as follows: 140, Hagen; 141, Dudley; 142, Mitchell and Robertson; 143, Tolley; 144, Cotton and Boomer; 145, Spark, Kirkwood, Diegel, Sarazen, and Easterbrook. Sarazen, one of the first out, played perfect golf until he was short with his second to the seventeenth, and was so strong with his next that he had to chip back off the road and did well to get down in six. Diegel handicapped himself by taking six for the first. He drove into Swilean burn, and, having picked out, went in again; then he took off shoes and stockings and just managed to play out. He gained strokes by holing four-yard putts at the third and eighth and another by driving the tenth green. Fives at the two long holes were neutralised by good putts which gave him birdies at the fifteenth and sixteenth, but he finished with two more fives, taking three putts on the last green.

Kirkwood, Diegel's partner, also took 71. He was encouraged by holing his first putt at the first and copying Diegel's two at the eighth, but his putting deserted him at the tenth. He went on to Eden Bank at the eleventh, and he finished with only ordinary figures. Cotton dropped a stroke by sending his first drive into Swilean and another by taking three putts at the fourth, but he putted beautifully at the seventh and eighth and was two under fours with six holes to play. Then he had to face the full force of the wind and had three fives in succession, and although he had a birdie three at the sixteenth his total was 72 and his aggregate was the same as Diegel's and Kirkwood's. A little later Mitchell tied with the three, and would have gone ahead of them but for repeating Thursday's error of pulling his second at the last hole and taking five. Previously Mitchell had played almost perfect golf, and had had half a dozen putts of two inches or less. His only putting mistake was at the tenth, where he required three strokes after reaching the green from the tee. He also dropped a stroke at the short eleventh, where he went over the green. Dudley fell from the second place through taking two strokes in a bunker at the eleventh.

The only question which seemed to be left for decision was whether Hagen could retain his earlier form. He fell much below it, and played the worst round he had had in a British championship. He was lucky to escape with the loss of only one stroke when his second drive went amongst gorse, from which he was able to chip out, and additional evidence of deterioration was given when he topped on the ninth tee and took five. He was in gorse again at the tenth, holed from five yards at the eleventh after playing from the Eden Bank, missed a putt at the thirteenth, and then for the first time in a British championship took seven for a hole.

Going to the fourteenth, he topped with his brassie into the Kitchen bunker, and after he had played out his fourth finished short of the green and his chip was poorly judged. His 79 left him tieing with three others for tenth place, and play in the third round ended with Easterbrook drawing level with Cotton, Mitchell, Diegel, and Kirkwood. Easterbrook had a curious card. Magnificent golf gave him five threes in succession, beginning at the eighth, but afterwards, however, the winds affected him and he had five successive fives, three of them through getting into bunkers.

Sarazen, as last year, had an advantage in setting a standard for his rivals to beat if they could, but as his final aggregate was 293 his pedestal was more insecure than had seemed likely; for he reached the turn in 35 and played the next four in par figures. His hopes, however, had a great blow at the fourteenth, as his second went into Hell bunker; he took two to get out, and after chipping short required three putts. Cotton fell two strokes behind Sarazen going out, mainly through faulty putting, and his last chance disappeared when he took three putts at the thirteenth and fourteenth. Diegel gained two strokes on Kirkwood over the first twelve holes, and Kirkwood took 32 for the remaining holes, including a seven at the seventeenth, where he had two strokes in the bunker against the green. Diegel seemed sure to wrest the lead from Sarazen when his second at the last reached the green, but his approach putt finished about a yard from the hole and he missed with his next, a failure which caused him to throw his putter down in disgust. Boyer, a Frenchman, had a real chance when he went out in 35, but he had an even worse experience than Sarazen's at the fourteenth. He drove out of bounds, found a bunker with his brassie, took seven to reach the green and was down in nine.

By that time Mitchell had disappointed, going into Swilean and taking 39 for the first nine, and Hagen had begun moderately, so that many of the spectators turned to Craig Wood, who had reached the turn in 36. He improved his prospects with a three at the thirteenth, a great iron shot leaving him a putt of only two feet. His next drive went near the wall, and a shot with wood nearly buried his ball in the sand of Hell bunker. He exploded out sideways and luckily obtained a five, a ten-yard putt that would have been much too strong had it not been straight hitting the hole, jumping, and falling in. At the fifteenth he was lucky again, as he found a playable lie among gorse, and at the seventeeth his second finished a yard from the road. He made a long chip safely and was down in five. He went to the last tee needing a four to take the lead. This he accomplished easily and was loudly cheered as he left the green. Mitchell, wanting two fours to tie, reached the seventeenth green in three and then took three putts.

As Hagen had four sixes in his homeward journey everything depended on Shute and Easterbrook. Shute had started with two fives, but he reached the turn in 36, and on the seventeenth tee wanted two fours to win. Five at the seventeenth was not surprising, but when putting for victory from seven yards on the last green he was weak. From his final putt the ball hesitated on the lip of the hole, and then fell in.

A.L.L.

CHAMPIONSHIP PLAY-OFF

Shute beats Wood after leading from first hole

10th July

Densmore Shute, of Llanerch Country Club, Pennsylvania, aged 28, the American-born son of a Westward Ho man, is the new British Open champion. To-day he beat Craig Wood, of the Hollywood Club, New Jersey, with whom he tied on Friday at 292 for 36 holes, by 149 against 154 in a 36-hole play-off. As two Americans were the contestants it was not expected that there would be many spectators, but in the afternoon fully two thousand were present.

Shute, the smaller man in height and girth, earned the title by steady play. He had the remarkable record of playing each of the four rounds of the competition proper in 73, and this morning he registered 75, whilst in the afternoon, when the conditions were more difficult, he took only 74. He took the lead at the start, as Wood put his second into the Swilcan burn, and although he played out he took three putts, so that his score was six, against Shute's four. At the second hole Wood bunkered his second, and again required three putts, whereas Shute had the regulation score of four. Shute's lead was increased at the fourth, where Wood's putting was faulty; but he got a stroke back at the sixth in lucky fashion, an approach which might have gone almost off the green hitting his opponent's ball and stopping six yards from the hole. He holed that putt and Shute missed with his. He also had an advantage at the short hole.

Both played the eleventh badly, Shute being bunkered from the tee and Wood going into the same hazard from his chip. Both took five there. The thirteenth reduced Shute's lead to two, his drive going into gorse, but at the long fourteenth, which caused so much trouble on Friday afternoon, Shute pitched beautifully from a bunker and holed for four from over three yards, whereas Wood, who did not get on in two, required two putts. The fifteenth also helped Shute, his opponent playing a poor iron shot, and at the seventeenth Shute performed what some natives of St Andrews deemed almost a miracle. He went on to the road at the back of the green, and there was a danger of his return pitch reaching a bunker from which it would have been difficult to avoid a second experience of the road. His pitch was perfect, and he was nearly down in four. At the eighteenth Wood had a chance of a three, but a putt of ten feet went a little wide, and he finished the round three strokes behind.

In the afternoon Wood steadily fell farther behind. He had three putts on the second green, but Shute was similarly at fault at the fourth. At the seventh Wood drove into a bunker, pitched into another hazard, and from the back of the green required three putts. Wood also putted badly at the eighth, and when 27 holes had been played he was six strokes behind – a hopeless position against a player who, although often outdriven, was playing his seconds with great skill. Both beat the par score at the tenth, but at the short hole Wood dropped another stroke, and after that the play varied. Whenever Wood gained a stroke he lost it almost immediately. Shute was bunkered at the twelfth, Wood took three

Denmore Shute wins the 1933 play-off after a superb recovery from the road at the notorious seventeenth.

putts at the next, Wood was the more accurate at the fourteenth and fifteenth, both took five at the Road hole, and there was no excitement whilst the last was played in par figures.

A.L.L.

The scores

292: Densmore Shute (USA) 73, 73, 73, 73; Craig Wood (USA) 77, 72, 68, 75

Play-off: Shute 75, 74, 149
Wood 78, 76, 154

293: Gene Sarazen (USA) 72, 73, 73, 75; Leo Deigel (USA) 75, 70, 71, 77; S. Easterbrook (Knowle) 73, 72, 71, 77

294: Olin Dutra (USA) 76, 76, 70, 72

295: Reginald Whitcombe (Parkstone) 76, 75, 72, 72; A.H. Padgham (R Ashdown Forest) 74, 73, 74, 74; Ed. Dudley (USA) 70, 71, 76, 78; Henry Cotton (Belgium) 73, 71, 72, 79; Abe Mitchell (private) 74, 68, 74, 79

1934

Sandwich, 30th June

COTTON'S OPEN GOLF TITLE

Brews second, five strokes behind: Padgham third

T.H. Cotton to-day won the British Open Golf Championship and equalled E. Sarazen's record total of 283, set up at Prince's in 1932. An Englishman has thus won the Championship for the first time since 1923 after ten victories by players from the United States. The trophy does not, however, return to England, as Cotton is attached to the Waterloo club in Brussels. Not only was the victor an English player but there was not one American in the first three. Cotton led by five strokes from his nearest rival, Brews, the South African, with Padgham third on the list and two Americans tying for fourth place, nine strokes behind Cotton.

Long before Cotton made his appearance on the first tee this morning a crowd of three or four thousand people were lining the fairways up the first green. Cars clustered in the parking places like great shining blackbeetles. Cinema cameramen mounted their talkie machines on the tops of their vans, and laid long, wriggling cables across the tee. It was an uncertain morning; there were black clouds in the sky and, much more ominous, a stiff breeze, which would make play difficult, particularly at the fifth and the tenth, as it was blowing up from the north-east.

Sandwich 1934, and the long night for British golf is over. After ten victories by US golfers, T.H. Cotton – here watched by Whitcombe driving from the 4th – wins by five strokes, his second round of sixty-five never bettered until 1977 and giving a name to one of the most famous of golf balls.

The stage was set for an occasion, and had a rule repealed three years ago, according to which all those players fourteen strokes behind the leader would automatically have dropped out, been still in force only five players would have walked to the tee for the third round instead of to-day's 48. By the time Cotton came out at 10.30 the wind had plainly settled in for the day; it was tricky and swirling and gusty, the kind that was bound to deal unexpected blows to the most certain golfer in the world.

Cotton began with yesterday's assurance at his back. At the first two holes, both of them long, he played steady fours. At the third he had a three, still playing to yesterday's form, at the fifth an unexpected five, though a forgivable one, at a hole 450 yards long, and so up and down in the wind. With a three at the sixth, a five at the seventh, another three at the eighth, and a four at the ninth the game went on, Cotton still unruffled and apparently untired in the face of a rising wind. Witness of this a superb recovery out of a sand bunker at the ninth, where for his third he laid a mashie dead to within a foot of the pin. Those whose spirits were beginning to droop cried 'Bravo!' and strode on fortified to the next tee, but it was plain that Cotton was becoming disturbed by the wind and his not too delicate approaches and putts.

At the eleventh, at the end of a putt of ten yards the ball dropped into the hole at a tangent, but with such force that it leaped out again, so that another putt was needed for a poor five. Two putts at the twelfth meant another four, two more at the thirteenth another odd-looking five coming from yesterday's wizard. A five at the Canal hole, a four at the fifteenth, and it had become clear to everyone that Cotton would not to-day repeat his dazzling achievements of earlier in the week. At the sixteenth, a short 160-yard hole, the master walked again, laying a superb iron against the wind within four feet of the pin, and sank the ball for an almost miraculous two. He was now level fours again. At the seventeenth he lofted a mashie for his second shot to within three yards of the flag, and sank a superbly straight putt for a three at a hole of 423 yards. A poor five brought his first round to an end in 72.

The afternoon can be described only as disappointing by those who expected that a player of mere flesh and blood could go on playing celestial golf for a week at a stretch. Again in the afternoon there were ups and downs, peppered with miraculously long drives against the wind and one or two brilliant shots to save the hole at the moment when all seemed lost. There was a brilliant putt of four yards at the second for a four, a chip shot from the edge of the green at the third, and a short putt for a three, but there was bad luck here and there and as many as three putts on several greens, and at the turn we were confronted

Ironically, the Open trophy goes back not to Britian but to Cotton's home club of Waterloo, Brussels.

with the bulging figure of forty. Then to darken the skies came a string of three fives, though it was known that Cotton had still a good margin of strokes to spare. But at the thirteenth with a long putt came inspiration and steadiness again, and Cotton finished the last six holes in 4, 4, 3, 4, 5, marvels of consistency considering the strain, the wind, and the occasion.

Cotton's aggregate was 283 over the four rounds, and only miraculous play from Dallemagne could interfere with his chances, for Brews, the much-feared South African, who had accomplished wonderful rounds of 70 and 71, had by his previous day's play built up a total of 288. In a quarter of an hour's time all fears were at rest, for Dallemagne had collapsed badly on the homeward journey, taking 77 for the last round against a beautiful 71 in the morning.

Of the others, taking them over the four rounds, there is little to say, though one might put in a word for a fine round of 73 played in the morning by W.H. Davies, of Wallasey, who piled up an inglorious 82 in the afternoon. The Americans were virtually nowhere right from the start of the morning's play, Kirkwood and Macdonald Smith tieing with Dallemagne for fourth place with 292, and Shute, the holder, with 301, twenty below the leader. Of Padgham one can say that his score of 290 does not do justice to his approach work and his drives. It was his putts against an uncertain gusty wind which ruined his chances.

The scores

283: T.H. Cotton (Waterloo, Brussels) 67, 65, 72, 79

288: S.F. Brews (South Africa) 76, 71, 70, 71

290: A.H. Padgham (Sundridge Pk) 71, 70, 75, 74

292: Macdonald Smith (USA) 77, 71, 72, 72; J. Kirkwood (USA) 74, 69, 71, 78; M. Dallemagne (France) 71, 73, 71, 77

295: B. Hodson (Chigwell) 71, 74, 74, 76; C.A. Whitcombe (Crews Hill) 71, 72, 74, 78;

296: E.R. Whitcombe (Meyrick Pk) 72, 77, 73, 74; P. Alliss (Beaconsfield) 73, 75, 71, 77

1935

A. PERRY NEW OPEN CHAMPION

Breaks record for course and wins by four strokes

Alf Perry from Leatherhead, born on the edge of a Surrey course, is the unexpected 1935 winner at Muirfield, having qualified with only two strokes to spare.

The new British Open Golf champion is A. Perry of Leatherhead, Surrey, who took the lead in the third round this morning by setting up a new record for the Muirfield links with 67, and who played so much better than his nearest rivals in the afternoon that he finished four strokes ahead of the second man. His aggregate, 283, equalled the record for an Open championship set up by Sarazen at Prince's three years ago and equalled by Cotton at St George's twelve months ago. Perry's success was not expected, for he would not have played had he taken two strokes more in the qualifying rounds, and he failed to qualify at Southport recently, but he has earned it by avoiding the fault of many other competitors, that of not playing up to the holes. He adopts a wide stance and his swing is by no means compact, but in a slashing style he attains great length, whilst on the greens his ball rarely finishes short of the holes.

Perry was born on the edge of a Surrey course thirty years ago, and was once assistant at Walton Heath. He has won the assistants' tournament twice, has been Surrey champion three times, has been third in a Dunlop–Southport competition, and played in the Ryder Cup match two years ago in the foursomes. Hitherto his highest place in the Open Championship was nineteenth in 1932.

Little, the amateur champion, had the best score of the afternoon, 69, in which there was a two and only two fives; he finished as the leading American, tieing for fourth place six strokes behind Perry and eleven ahead of the second amateur, P.B. Lucas, the left-handed Cambridge University player.

Play began at eight o'clock with Whitcombe leading Cotton and Padgham by one stroke and Perry, Kenyon, and Branch by three strokes. Kenyon went round in 74, holing only one long putt and taking three putts three times. Branch fell out by taking 41 for the first nine, but Whitcombe was considered to have done well in reaching the turn in 37, and when he finished in 73 there were few who thought that he would be caught. Whitcombe's driving was so well controlled that the wind had little or no effect on his ball; his putting, however, was not that of a real champion, for his approaches usually were short, and although he only twice needed three putts even his friends criticised him for not hitting his first putts more boldly.

Cotton started when Whitcombe had played nine holes and soon dissipated his chance of drawing level. He fell two strokes farther behind in playing the first three holes, and although he recovered one of them before the turn he was not hitting the ball as well as usual and he lost several strokes through weak approach putting. He took 38 for the first nine holes, and his figures were repeated in exactly the same order on the homeward journey.

Perry was immediately behind Cotton. He did nothing out of the ordinary until two great shots gave him a four at the fifth. Then on successive greens he holed putts of five yards, four feet, and six yards. At the ninth, almost dead against the wind, he could not get up in two, but he pitched dead and a four meant the equalling of Gadd's feat on Wednesday of playing the outward half in 32. A sliced second at the tenth lost him a stroke, but he continued to putt grandly, seeming unable to miss anything under seven feet. He had his second two at the thirteenth, and when he nearly had another at the sixteenth a new record was well within his reach. Then came his first real mistake; he bunkered his second at the seventeenth, sent his third about eight feet from the flag, and putted two inches short. At the last hole, where few competitors hit their seconds well enough to find the green, Perry got well on, and he beat Cotton's record for the links by one stroke. His figures were:

Out:	5	4	4	3	4	3	2	3	4–32
In:	5	4	4	2	4	4	3	5	4–35
									67

Padgham kept his position with a steady 74, the inches on the greens which separate the ordinary from the excellent being all against him, and Picard moved into fourth place, six strokes behind Perry, with a 72, which hardly represented the quality of his play.

The position when the final round began was: 211 Perry, 212 Whitcombe, 216 Padgham, 217 Picard, 218 Cotton, Gadd, and Kenyon. Of those seven Kenyon dropped far back by taking 79; putting again was his weakness. Whitcombe marred his prospects by taking five at the third and by being weak from the tee at the short fourth. He had a fine three at the eighth, where his iron shot finished only a few inches from the hole, but at the ninth he cut his second and failed to pitch within holing distance. He took 38 to the turn, and lost another stroke by driving into a bunker from the next tee. He took three putts at the fourteenth and seventeenth, and finished with a poor six, being short with his second, over the green in three, and weak with his chip back.

About that time Cotton reached the turn in 35 and needed another 35 to tie with Whitcombe, whilst the news about Perry was that he was doing well enough to win. Some brief excitement was provided by Gadd, who was four under an average of fours for thirteen holes, but although Gadd has been French champion he was incapable of maintaining that form, and finished with 5, 5, 3, 6, 4. Padgham, who went out in a do-or-die mood, was soon in a moribund condition, and as Cotton found that the rolling up of his sleeves did not bring increased efficiency he too became hopeless. Cotton provided the large number of spectators round the home green with a sample of the play which had ruined his prospects; he could not be blamed for hitting his first putt too strongly, as the ball was on the edge of a bunker and his feet were in moving sand, but there was no excuse for leaving the return two inches short.

Perry was then about two holes from home, and it was clear that he had the championship within easy reach. He had begun with a six by pulling his drive into rough and taking three putts, but he gained a stroke at the third, where he sank a three-yard putt, and he showed how unlikely he was to crack by his play at the sixth. There his second went over the green, but a perfect chip made only one putt necessary. He nearly went out of bounds at the eighth and was trapped at the ninth, but fives there made him no more than 37. The remainder of the round was easy, especially after his spoon shot at the tenth had gone dead and had given him a birdie three. He refused to play pawkily, and his boldness cost him a stroke at the twelfth, where his ball went down the bank at the back of the green. He played the last six in one under fours. There was a loud cheer from about 10,000 spectators when his second at the last hole soared over all the trouble, and it was renewed when he obtained the four which made his score 72.

Padgham had an unexpected revival; after the turn he had seven fours and two threes, which gave him second place. He was the most consistent golfer of all, as his best round was 70 and his worst 74.

A.L.L.

The scores

283: A. Perry (Leatherhead) 69, 75, 67, 72

287: A. Padgham (Sundridge Pk) 70, 72, 74, 71

288: C.A. Whitcombe (Crews Hill) 71, 68, 73, 76

289: B. Gadd (Brand Hall) 72, 75, 71, 71; W.L. Little (USA) 75, 71, 74, 69

292: H. Picard (USA) 72, 73, 72, 75

293: T.H. Cotton (Brussels) 68, 74, 76, 75; S. Easterbrook (Knowle) 75, 73, 74, 71

294: W.J. Branch (Henbury) 71, 73, 76, 74

295: L. Aytonsen (South Shields) 74, 73, 77, 71

1936

PADGHAM'S OPEN CHAMPIONSHIP

Adam's gallant effort narrowly frustrated

Dallemagne and Cotton equal third

Twenty-nine-year-old A.H. Padgham, one of the most consistent scorers the world has ever seen, to-day achieved the life's ambition of every golfer by becoming the British Open champion. His winning score of 287 was four shots higher than that returned by E. Sarazen in 1932 and equalled by T.H. Cotton in 1934 and A. Perry last year, when Padgham was fourth, third, and second respectively, but he has the satisfaction of knowing that he achieved his success on the longest championship course in the world. On his own admission he won the Championship without playing his best golf and he confesses that he has never worked so hard in his life, but the fact remains that he produced four magnificent scores 73, 72, 71, and 71, and though three or four players had opportunities of tieing with him they all failed and there has never been a more popular victory.

From the time that Padgham won the Professional Match Play Championship last September he has almost continuously been in the public eye, and since the beginning of the present season he has won the Bramshot tournament, the professional tournament at Moor Park, the Dunlop–Southport tournament, and now the Open. The prize money that he took away to-night was but a drop in the ocean compared with that which he has won in the purely professional tournaments, but to him the title of Open champion is beyond price, for it establishes him, for the time being at all events, as the greatest golfer of to-day.

His victory becomes all the more remarkable when it is realised that throughout his rounds to-day he had to struggle against a hook which threatened to destroy him by its persistence. When it became only a matter of waiting for the cup to be presented he confessed that the hook was produced by the strain of the occasion, which, like a snowball, became greater all the time; he showed his abnormal courage by returning 71 in both the morning and the afternoon rounds when nothing but his putter was working well.

One cannot exaggerate the tension that electrified the atmosphere towards the end of the day; even the most conservative estimate placed the crowd at 20,000, and to the poor scribes who had to try to keep in touch with half a dozen players it seemed like 40,000. Towards the close of the play uproarious cheers greeted every good shot, whether it was played by a potential champion or not, and it was by far the most exciting finish that championship had produced for many years. The crowd, by the way, was regarded as the largest that has ever attended the last day of the Championship on any English course, though the Scots will not admit that it beat the great number of people who saw the final of the 1930 Amateur Championship at St Andrews.

The golf undoubtedly was magnificent and it was played in an ideal setting. From early morning until late this evening there was an almost continuously clear sky and glorious sunshine, and though there was a fair breeze from the sea it made the course no greater test of golf than it has been throughout the week.

Hoylake scratch score

Hole	Yards	Scr.	Hole	Yards	Scr.
1	435	5	10	455	5
2	419	4	11	193	3
3	480	5	12	464	5
4	158	3	13	179	3
5	424	4	14	511	5
6	438	4	15	443	5
7	200	3	16	532	5
8	527	5	17	419	4
9	393	4	18	408	4
	3,474	37		3,604	39

In years to come we shall still remember the great effort that J. Adams, the Romford professional and Scottish international, made to overhaul Padgham; he finished the day as runner-up in the Championship and he missed a tie almost by a hairbreadth. The morning round had finished with Adams and T.H. Cotton tieing for the lead at 215. Padgham and T. Green (Burnham Beeches) came close behind at 216, with E. Sarazen, the only American of real importance, at 218. Though there was a strong group of professionals at the 220 mark it was soon realised that they had no real chance of producing the winner, and it became obvious that the fight was to be between Adams, Cotton, Padgham, Green, and Sarazen, with the odds on a tie at the end of the day. We were spared the tie, which would have prolonged the championship to unheard of lengths, but there was not one of us who did not hope that Adam's last crucial putt on the home green would drop.

Padgham, whose morning round of 71 had represented magnificent scoring if not superb golf, was the first of the probables to finish this afternoon. He had started his final round by dropping shots at the second and third; he was so badly bunkered at the second that he could only chip sideways on to the fairway, and he was, perhaps, fortunate in obtaining a five. More bunker trouble cost him a five at the third, and eventually he reached the turn in 37; under such a humbling strain it was an excellent score, and when he played the first four holes of the homeward half in 4, 3, 4, 2, it became obvious that he would not crack. He holed a longish putt for his two at the short thirteenth, but the hook that had annoyed him all day reared its ugly head at the fifteenth and cost him a five. A second shot pushed into the rough at the sixteenth resulted in another five, and at the seventeenth he hooked his drive for the last time; fortunately he was able to hole out in four, and a four-yard putt on the home green which went down for a three, enabling him to repeat his score of the morning.

Alf Padgham from Sundridge Park took the 1936 Open. The last-day crowd numbered 22,000, a sign of golf's growing popularity.

Padgham then came into the clubhouse to sit out the interminable wait while one distinguished player after the other went out to try to catch him. The strain of waiting was almost as bad as that of playing in the Championship, but as each gratuitious report of the progress of other players was brought to him he must have felt a growing confidence, though his score was precisely the same as that which left him runner-up in the championship at Muirfield last year.

First came the failure of Adams, who had been playing at the top of his form all week. He had started his fourth round by misjudging the pace of the greens and by taking three putts far too often for his peace of mind. His 38 to the turn meant that he had to return in 33 to beat Padgham and 34 to tie. If he had been faced with such a prospect in a calmer moment he would probably have despaired, but in the heat of the moment anything seemed possible, and when he sank a fifteen-yard putt for a three at the tenth and a seven-yarder for a two at the eleventh it meant that he had only to finish in level fours to win. He took a five at the twelfth, however, and when he was bunkered at the fifteenth, took four to reach the green, and was still ten yards from the pin, it looked as though he had thrown his chances away, but he sank the putt for a five and still lived.

He was then faced with the prospect of finishing with three fours to tie, and having got his four at the difficult sixteenth we thought that he would succeed. His second shot to the seventeenth was pulled, however, and it finished in a bunker; having exploded the ball out Adams took infinite pains with his putt; perhaps he was too careful with it; at all events it refused to drop and he came to the eighteenth tee needing a birdie three to tie. Thousands of people saw his last putt look into the hole for a three and then switch out again, and the cheer that greeted his courageous effort was almost deafening, though in his disappointment he buried his face in his hands.

The excitement now became even greater, and the crowds which had been following Adams tramped out to meet the already enormous gallery which was following Cotton's fortunes. Cotton had begun the afternoon with a cut, second shot to the first green which sent the ball flying out of bounds. He made up for this with a fine three at the second, but he went out of bounds again at the seventh and reached the turn in 36. He started home with a five at the tenth and another five at the twelfth, where he played a poor approach. He was fighting against ever-increasing odds, for a bunkered second shot to the fourteenth cost him another five and on the seventeenth tee he needed a four and a three to tie.

A second shot that carried his ball right through the seventeenth green and cost him five left him in the impossible position of having to hole his second shot to the home green. W. Hagen was once in a similar predicament at St Annes in 1926; he came to the eighteenth with a two to tie with R.T. Jones; one remembers that he sent his caddie forward to take out the pin in the vain hope that the ball would go down. Cotton did no such thing to-day, and he finished with an ordinary four for third place with M. Dallemagne at 289.

When Cotton had failed it became a question of whether Sarazen or Green could catch the waiting. Padgham. Sarazen, having gone out in 35, knew that he had to come home in 34 to catch the leader; he failed, for he was up against the stone-wall defence of a man whose score was already on the board, and when he needed two three to tie he finished 5, 5. That left only Green with a chance of success, but he too 'blew up' in a minor degree, and his last round of 75 enabled him only to share fourth position at 291 with Sarazen and P. Alliss, who had a splended last round of 71.

A.D. Locke, the young South African Open and Amateur champion, finished with an aggregate of 294 in the honoured position of first amateur; his nearest rival was the Amateur champion, H. Thomson, at 299. In his morning round of 72 Locke took three putts on three occasions and holed only one putt of respectable length – a five-yarder for a three at the seventeenth. In the afternoon he finished in 74, though he went out of bounds at the third and missed short putts at the sixth and ninth. It has been made clear this week that Locke is a particularly fine young golfer, and he entirely deserved his distinguished place in the Championship.

The finest round of the afternoon was played by Dallemagne; his score of 69 represented magnificent golf. He began the round with birdie threes at the first and second and a birdie two at the short fourth. These startling figures were the result of sinking five-yard putts at the first and second and a three-yarder at the fourth, but his grand finish was of no avail for it only enabled him to tie with Cotton.

One of the first players out to-day was W.J. Branch, the Henbury assistant, who promptly showed that the conditions were ideal for good scoring; he went out in 33 and came home in 35 for a card of 68, which equalled Cotton's record for the course. His figures were 4, 3, 4, 3, 4, 4, 4, 4, 3 – 33 out; 4, 2, 4, 4, 4, 4, 5, 4, 4 – 35 in; total 68. Green's morning round of 70, which enabled him to tie with Padgham, was another masterly piece of work, his iron play being particularly good, and if he had had the slightest bit of luck it would have been a record-breaking round.

Did space allow, one could go on writing of the great adventures of the competitors for days, and certainly this Championship will live in the memory for many years to come.

The scores

*Amateur

287: A.H. Padgham (Sundridge Pk) 73, 72, 71, 71

288: J. Adams (Romford) 71, 73, 71, 73

289: T.H. Cotton (Waterloo, Brussels) 73, 72, 70, 74; M. Dallemagne (St Germain) 73, 72, 75, 69

291: P. Alliss (Templenewsam) 74, 72, 74, 71; G. Sarazen (USA) 73, 75, 70, 73; T. Green (Burnam Beeches) 74, 72, 70, 75

294: R.A. Whitcombe (Parkstone) 72, 77, 71, 74; *A.D. Locke (South Africa) 75, 73, 72, 74; A.J. Lacey (Berkshire) 76, 74, 72, 72

1937

Carnoustie, 9th July

COTTON AGAIN OPEN CHAMPION

Great exhibition of the game in mud and rain

Playing superb golf under weather conditions which had to be experienced to be fully believed, T.H. Cotton won the British Open Championship here to-night with a score of 290. Cotton began the week as the favourite for the title, and his magnificent last round of 71, which was marred only by a five at the last hole, was for the most part accomplished in almost blinding rain. He has every reason to feel proud that he is the only British golfer who has won the Championship twice since the war. His own faith in the ability of a British golfer – not necessarily himself – to resist the challenge of the greatest professional golfers of the United States was completely vindicated, and even before he had finished his last round most of the visitors had faded from our calculations. C. Lacey, an Anglo-American younger brother of A.J. Lacey, a British Ryder Cup player, threatened Cotton for a time, but in the end even his effort failed, and Cotton was left supreme.

Once more it was clear that Cotton is the greatest golfer Britain has produced since the days of the famous triumvirate. Though his score was seven shots more than the total with which he won the title at Sandwich in 1934 it probably represented a greater achievement, for the average length of the course has been more than 7,000 yards, and it has undoubtedly provided a finer test of golf than has ever been known before in the history of the Championship. When the Championship was last decided here the course did not measure more than 6,900 yards on any day; yet the winning score of T. Armour was 296. Cotton beat the Americans at their own game, for he won the Championship by superb pitching and putting. The machine-like accuracy in driving and iron play that we used to expect from him was not always seen to-day, and his mashie niblick and putter were the two most valuable clubs in his bag.

At the end of the day everyone must have been full of admiration for the way in which Cotton conducted himself. He knew full well what he had to do in his last round to beat R.A. Whitcombe, who was runner-up with 292; he had to fight not only against great golfing odds but also against the enormous gallery. If he was under any strain he showed no sign, and though there were moments when the gallery became entirely out of control Cotton went calmly on his way, refusing to be disturbed. Towards the end he had a gallery of fully 10,000 people, who stampeded like a herd of crazy buffaloes after each shot, and the only way one saw him play the last hole was from a bedroom window of a house overlooking the course. At least nine thousand of the ten thousand people could have seen little of the golf, though they persisted in blocking the view of those whose duty it was to record the happenings.

There were moments during the afternoon when we expected the championship committee to cancel play in the last round. When P. Alliss and W.J. Branch began the fourth round the first green was almost completely flooded, for the heavy rain had never stopped since morning. Wisely, they refused to putt, for there were nearly three inches of water round the hole. Messengers went hurrying back to the starter's box, and the start of the competitors who followed was delayed for nearly half an hour while groundsmen swept water from the green. But for the thrilling finish that Cotton provided it would have been an entirely miserable day's golf, for even an avowed golf enthusiast has a limit to his endurance, and the greatest passion for the game can be dampened when one has had to spend the day with rain trickling down one's neck and soaking through 'guaranteed rainproof' clothing. The position became so bad that officials of the championship committee had to walk off into the wilds to examine the greens, but in the end it was decided to allow the Championship to continue. Groundsmen tried their best to keep down the water on the greens, but almost every competitor had to move his ball for every putt so that he could get a clear line to the hole.

The day began with R.A. Whitcombe, youngest of the three golfing brothers, leading the field with an aggregate of 142 for two rounds. At least four of the American Ryder Cup players and several British golfers had chances of overhauling him, but he had an excellent third round of 74 and kept his lead. Whitcombe reached the turn this morning in 37, having bunkered his tee shot at the fifth and driven into the rough at the ninth. He started home with a great three at the long tenth hole, where he got home with two splendid wooden club shots and holed from seven yards, but the strain of setting the pace for the remainder of the field began to tell; he had three putts at the eleventh, took three to get down from the edge of the green at the twelfth, missed the green from the tee at the short thirteenth, and finally bunkered his tee shot to the fourteenth. He should have played these four holes in one under fours, but he holed them in three over. Then he pulled himself together manfully and played the last four difficult holes in 4, 3, 4, 4, for a round of 74. This gave him an aggregate of 216, and he began his fourth round as he had done in the morning with a two-stroke lead over the field.

C.A. Whitcombe came in this morning with the same score for the third round, but E. Dudley, the most consistent American challenger, who had begun the day sharing second place with C.A. Whitcombe, fell back with an unfortunate round of 78. Cotton, with 73, clipped one stroke from the lead which R.A. Whitcombe had had from him at the beginning of the day, though once again his scoring seemed to be better than his golf from the academic point of view. Cotton's theory of swinging from inside to out is well known, but occasionally he swung the ball a little too much from right to left; at the fourth hole this morning, for example, he pulled his approach and had to hole a two-yard putt for his four; he repeated the process at the next hole, but this time he missed a putt. He reached the turn in 37 and started home with two good fours, but he took three to get down from the edge of the green at the twelfth and pulled a shot into a bunker at the fifteenth. At the sixteenth his tee shot was so badly pulled that it ended on the seventeenth teeing ground, well to the left of the green. He saved himself by holing an eight-yard putt for a birdie three at the home hole, and it became obvious that Whitcombe would have to play brilliant golf if he was to beat Cotton this afternoon.

D. Shute, the champion of 1933, took 39 to come home in a round of 76. At the last hole his approach plunged into the Barry burn, and the ball remained so firmly wedged between two stones that it could not be released. Having dropped another ball, he holed out in six. A.H. Padgham, who to-day surrendered his title to Cotton, also took 39 to come home for a round of 76. One had never before seen Padgham show obvious disgust with his golf, but he did to-day when he misjudged his approach to the tenth. The hole measures little less than 500 yards from the back tee, and though the competitors who did reach the green in two required a full wooden club second, Padgham pinned his faith to an iron, and his ball fell monstrously short into the Barry burn. We could read his thoughs as his club fell from his hands to the wet turf. At the thirteenth he changed the tune by overclubbing himself, and it was by then almost certain that his title would slip from his grasp. W.J. Branch, the young Leicestershire professional, returned an excellent 73 and took fourth place behind Cotton, and a little later H. Picard and C. Lacey, who were playing together, holed out in 70 apiece, though at that stage their scores meant little in the general scheme of things.

R.A. Whitcombe began his fourth round knowing that he would have to return at least another 74 to have any chance of keeping in front, but after fours at the first three holes he pulled his second shot to the fourth and took a five. At the 560-yard sixth he was short in two and missed a two-foot putt for his four. At the seventh, where he recorded a six, the wet grip on his driver caused the club to slip almost out of his hands, and he took four shots to reach the green.

Henry Cotton beat the entire US Ryder Cup team to win his second Open at Carnoustie in 1937. Many regard it as his greatest triumph. On waterlogged greens, players had to place almost every putt.

Whitcombe had the worst of the weather conditions, for Cotton was at least able to play several holes without rain. Whitcombe required 39 shots to reach the turn, and though he played the last nine steadily in 37 for a final round of 76 he did not, unfortunately for him, put the issue beyond even reasonable doubt. It meant that Cotton could win with a fourth round of 72. C.A. Whitcombe needed 73 to win, and Branch 71; Padgham, B. Nelson, Dudley, and Shute all required 69's

Padgham, who lit a cigarette which was quickly reduced to pulp by the rain, appeared to regard his chance as an impossible one, but he reached the turn this afternoon in 36, and he at least gave himself a chance of breaking 70. But 33 home on a course like this and in such conditions would have demanded almost miraculous golf, and by the time he cut the tee shot into the burn at the last hole and took a seven his chances had faded.

Then the herds of spectators flocked to Cotton, who they felt would overhaul Whitcombe. The maestro had a curious experience at the second hole, where the approaches of both he and his partner, W. Shankland, finished almost equidistant from the pin. Between each ball and the hole was an enormous pool of casual water. Shankland, putting first, placed his ball on a piece of turf that gave him a clear run to the hole, but he was short with the putt. Cotton decided on the same method of approach to the hole, placed his ball near to the spot from which Shankland had putted, and he holed out for a birdie three.

Cotton's start was truly magnificent, for he played the first six holes in one under fours – 4, 3, 4, 4, 4, 4. He got home with a chip and a putt for a birdie four at the long sixth, and his only mistake going out was at the seventh, where he was short with his approach. But his 35 to the turn meant that he was already one shot better than R.A. Whitcombe at that stage and that he had only to come home steadily to win the Championship and to become the first British golfer to win when the field has included every member of the American Ryder Cup team. It was an enormous responsibility, but he went boldly about his task. His second shot to the tenth went over the green, but he chipped back dead for his four. He holed out with a chip and a putt at the twelfth, and at the fourteenth holed a three-yard putt for a four.

The crowd became almost hysterical when he continued to produce a superb short game, and there was a moan of disappointment at the fifteenth when he missed a four-footer after chipping beautifully from the edge of a bunker. Another chip and a putt gave him his three at the short sixteenth, but he had to hole a long putt at the seventeenth for a four. Here his second shot, which was slightly pushed out, pitched on a spectator's umbrella, but the accident did not affect Cotton's chances, for the shot would not have reached the green if it had not been impeded. As he walked to the eighteenth tee each side of the fairway was lined ten deep and it looked as though it was a royal procession that we were about to see. Unfortunately Cotton did not play the hole well, for after cutting his iron club approach he failed to sink a fairly short putt for a four, but his score of 71 made him almost certainly safe.

Little remains to be told. C.A. Whitcombe had a chance to overhaul Cotton, for he was only one over four for 13 holes, but the rain beat him, for he half-hit his drives to the fourteenth and fifteenth, and in the space of two holes he slipped back to four over fours. Then C. Lacey came to the seventeenth tee needing two birdie threes to tie, but he did not get them. If he had done so no doubt Cotton would willingly have been runner-up.

The scores

290: T.H. Cotton (Ashridge) 74, 73, 72, 71

292: R.A. Whitcombe (Parkstone) 72, 70, 74, 76

293: C. Lacey (USA) 76, 75, 70, 72

294: C.A. Whitcombe (Crews Hill) 73, 71, 74, 76

296: Byron Nelson (USA) 75, 76, 71, 74

297: Ed Dudley (USA) 70, 74, 78, 75

298: A.J. Lacey (Berkshire) 75, 73, 75, 75; W. Laidlaw (Ashridge) 77, 72, 73, 76; A.H. Padgham (Sundridge Park) 72, 74, 76, 76

299: Horton Smith (USA) 77, 71, 79, 72

R.A. WHITCOMBE CHAMPION

Tearing wind adds to competitors' troubles

Fates at last were kind to the Whitcombe family at Sandwich in 1938. R. A. Whitcombe, youngest of three golfing brothers, took four putts on two greens but made a last-round seventy-eight in a howling gale to win with an aggregate 295. The 520-yard fourteenth was almost unreachable with three full woods but with the wind Alf Padgham drove the 380-yard eleventh.

At last a Whitcombe has won the Open Championship. It must be said softly, almost reverently, for at last the fates have been kind to a family which has been in the front rank of the world's professional golfers for longer than a good many people care to remember. We have sometimes wondered whether the Whitcombes would be remembered as the family which won everything but the greatest of all golfing crowns, and now at last R.A. Whitcombe, the youngest of the three brothers, has won.

His winning total of 295 to-day on the course of the Royal St George's Club was little short of miraculous, for the day will be remembered not only because it opened a new era for the Whitcombes but because it produced the most difficult golfing conditions within living memory. A few could cast their minds back to the 'Open' of Hoylake in 1913, but as the gale grew in force to-day even those who believe that the modern age can produce nothing which is either quite so good or so bad as the products of 25 years ago began to agree that to-day's wind beat everything they could remember.

Golfers in whom one has considerable faith confessed that they were beaten and confounded by the gale. It was wellnigh impossible to stand on the exposed tees, much less to swing a club on them. The ball quivered like a live thing on the greens, and R.A. Whitcombe must be the only man in golfing history who was won a championship after taking four putts on two greens.

R. Burton, who cracked with a disastrous last round of 85, took 44 putts. Like others, he was having to allow anything from a foot to two feet for the action of the wind on the greens, and if he reached a point at which he did not care very much whether the ball went in or not no one would blame him. A number of players who were blown from their balance as they started the down swing hit the ball with the socket of their clubs, and several were eventually reduced to that state of complete desperation in which they were not quite sure whether they were hitting the ball off the 'name' or off the sole. Moreover, it did not make much difference to their scores whether they were or not.

What a riotous time the wind had! It reduced the majority of players to the level of handicap golfers, though it may be said that the average club player of handicaps would not to-day have holed the links in fewer than 100 strokes. At 441 yards the first hole was almost unreachable in two, the second at 370 could be driven downwind, the third at 238 could scarcely be reached, and the short sixteenth at 163 demanded the truest of drive strokes. The 520-yard fourteenth became a true par six late in the day, and, while the eleventh, twelfth, and thirteenth holes were made easy by the following wind, the last four holes were transformed into the most testing that one can imagine. To be short of the fourteenth with three full wooden-club shots was a common experience, and there were more eights there than could be counted.

Therefore a little enthusiasm is forgivable about the performance of R.A. Whitcombe in winning the Championship and about the achievement of J. Adams, of Royal Liverpool, in being runner-up for the second time in three seasons.

Whitcombe, having risen when the early fishing-boats were going out, started his first round soon after the exhibition marquee had undergone its unfortunate transformation. Playing with Adams he led the way for everybody, just as he did at Carnoustie last year, when he was runner-up. Instead of the expected string of sixes, he played with almost unbelievable accuracy. He had every hole in strict par until he came to the ninth, and he was playing with such grim concentration that he did not appear to know that there was a gale. At the ninth, however, he was forcibly reminded of the storm because he was blown twice from his balance as he putted, and he took four putts to hole out from the front edge of the green. Nevertheless he was out in 36, against Adams's 38, and he started home 4, 4, 3, 4 to be one under fours in spite of the gale's fury. A five at the fourteenth was expected, but his six at the fifteenth was most disappointing.

A perfectly struck driver shot for his second caught the very top of a bunker, and when he played out with a niblick the ball was blown back on the fairway by the wind when it seemed to be on the point of reaching the green. A five to the seventeenth was budgeted for, but unfortunately he dropped a stroke at the home hole, where he took three for the back of the green. Nevertheless his 75 to Adams's 78 was a stout effort and, standing at 217, he could for a while sit back to watch the others having their hopes blown to glory.

A.H. Padgham, who celebrated the occasion with a monstrous drive to the 384-yard eleventh and by holing a shortish putt for an eagle two, also came in with a 75, but at 221 he was rather too many shots behind to cause Whitcombe any real worry.

Then the first of the leaders, J.J. Busson, cracked as he played his third round with one of his co-leaders, R. Burton. His 39 out with a six at the ninth was not very distressing, but with a seven at the fourteenth and a six at the fifteenth he took 44 strokes to come home for a round of 83. Burton's story, however, was a rather different one, for, in the circumstances, he played extremely sound golf for this third round of 78. This gave him a three-round aggregate of 218, and, being only one shot behind Whitcombe, he seemed to be lying comfortably. His only reason for regret lay in the fact that in this round he missed three putts of two feet, though each failure was directly due to the wind.

Then J. McLean and V. Greenhalgh (Prestwich) came in with cards of 83 and 84 respectively, and A.D. Locke arrived home with an 81 and a conviction that he had been blown out of any sort of position in the Championship. A.J. Lacey strolled along with an 82, and Cotton, who had been playing well until he took seven to the fourteenth hole, where he cut a brassie second out of bounds, finished in 77.

A. Perry, who finished 6, 3, 6, 5, dropping four strokes in four holes, had a card of 77. J. Fallon had gone out magnificently in 36, but needed 46 to come home. M. Dallemagne took 86, and S.F. Brews holed out in 84. W.J. Cox, playing with N. Sutton, of Leigh, who had an 87, took an eight at the fourteenth, and celebrated the round with an 84.

R.A. Whitcombe and Adams started out on their last round this afternoon with two strokes separating them, and the Hoylake golfer picked them both up at the first hole, where Whitcombe took four putts for the second time in the day. Then Whitcombe settled down to steady golf, and though he missed his threes at the short sixth and eighth he had no more mishaps, and he arrived at the turn in 39. Adams took 38 to go out. The two players knew that they were against each other, and the many so-called experts who had expected Adams's full-flowing swing to lead him into serious trouble were disappointed. Fives began to creep on to his card, however, while Whitcombe, with his interlocking grip and solid, smooth swing, was recording one four after another, and with four holes to go Whitcombe had a four-stroke advantage on Adams.

After Whitcombe had chipped dead for a four at the terribly difficult fifteenth Adams calmly holed a chip for an eagle three. That picked up one stroke, and he retrieved two more at the short sixteenth, where Whitcombe, having been bunkered short of the green, exploded into another bunker and took five. The position then became most exciting, but, unfortunately for Adams, he bunkered his second shot to the seventeenth (the wind was the culprit) and took six, while Whitcombe chipped dead for a valiant four. To the home hole Whitcombe, short in two, took five to Adams's four, but both finished in 78 for Whitcombe to retain his lead.

At this stage we knew that Burton had to do 77 to tie, Cotton a 71, and Perry a 73. Burton was working valiantly, but his 42 out wrecked his chances and he finished in 85. Perry, with a seven at the fifth – among other troubles – was also out in 42, so we struck him from our list.

That left only Cotton with any real chance of overhauling Whitcombe, and he put the cat among the pigeons by starting 5, 2, 3. He drove the second green

– a matter of a mere 370 yards – and sank a putt from the edge of the green for an eagle two. Then he almost holed his putt for a two at the 'short' third, and he came to the ninth tee needing a four for a 34 out. In any circumstances this would have been good, but this afternoon it was superlative, and there is perhaps no other golfer in the world capable of such a magnificent achievement.

Unfortunately he missed a shortish putt at the ninth, but, needing 36 home to tie with Whitcombe, he started back brilliantly with a four at the tenth and birdie threes at the eleventh and twelfth. That gave him a sporting chance, but he could not take it. He took three putts at the thirteenth, took a five at the fourteenth, a five to the fifteenth, and he bunkered his tee shot at the short sixteenth and took four. He needed 43 to tie, but hooked his tee shot at the seventeenth into the rough, pitched into a bunker, went from that into another, and took six. That was the end, but he finished with a four for a round of 74, which was the best score of the day.

So the day ended with Whitcombe the winner, Adams runner-up at 297, and Cotton a brave third at 298. The winning score was the highest since T.D. Armour won at Carnoustie with 296 in 1931, but its greatness may perhaps be judged from the fact that the leading amateur, E.F. Storey, had an aggregate of 316, that C.J.H. Tolley had a total of 317, that H. Thomson had 319, and that the English amateur champion, J.J.F. Pennink, finished at 320. It was a memorable day, and Whitcombe was a worthy winner.

The scores

295: R.A. Whitcombe (Parkstone) 71, 71, 75, 78

297: James Adams (R Liverpool) 70, 71, 78, 78

298: Henry Cotton (Ashridge) 74, 73, 77, 74

303: A. Dailey (Wanstead) 73, 72, 80, 78; J.J. Busson (Pannal) 71, 69, 83, 80; A.H. Padgham (Sundridge Park) 74, 72, 75, 82; R. Burton (Sale) 71, 69, 78, 85

304: F. Bullock (Sonning) 73, 74, 77, 80; W.J. Cox (Wimbledon Park) 70, 70, 84, 80

305: A.D. Locke (South Africa) 73, 72, 81, 79; C.A. Whitcombe (Crews Hill) 71, 75, 79, 80; B. Gadd (West Cheshire) 71, 70, 84, 80

1939

R. BURTON'S OPEN CHAMPIONSHIP VICTORY

Great last effort after Fallon had taken lead in third round

When we were all but ready to see the cup being handed over once again to an American, R. Burton, the Sale Ryder Cup player, this afternoon played some of the bravest golf ever seen on the Old Course here and won the Open Championship for himself, upholding the dignity of British golf for us all.

For the Manchester people who were here the end was almost too exciting to watch, and if there was one cool man on the golf course it was Burton. He knew what he had to do just as if the figures he needed were chalked on a notice-board before his eyes. He knew that J. Bulla, the tall, powerfully built United States golfer, had this afternoon finished in 73 for an aggregate of 292, and that he was sitting in the clubhouse with his score on the board waiting as patiently as could be for anyone who was brave enough to beat it.

By the time that he reached the twelfth hole this afternoon Burton realised that he needed a 73 to tie and a 72 to beat Bulla, but in the end he holed a six-yard putt on the last green for a 71 and an aggregate of 290, which won him the Championship with a stroke to spare. What a magnificent ending it was for British golf. We had almost curled up to admit that Bulla had won, and it was not until Burton reached the turn this afternoon in 35 shots that we realised he had any chance.

Burton's morning round of 77, when the wind blew almost a full gale from the south-west, left him four shots behind the third-round leader, J. Fallon, and his hopes of winning seemed forlorn. He began his last round this afternoon in most unconvincing fashion by taking three putts from quite a short distance at the first hole, and he was two over fours with six holes played against the wind. That would have been reasonable scoring for an early round, but it did not seem good enough at this late stage. Burton, however, risked the prophecy of his partner that if he could steel two threes round the 'loop' he would win the Championship.

The gods love a brave golfer, and as luck or destiny would have it he did not get only two threes but three, for he holed from seven feet for a birdie at the seventh and from four yards for another birdie three at the ninth, and he turned in 35, with his confidence entirely restored. A four-foot putt nearly went down for a three at the tenth, but to make up for this disappointment Burton sank a six-footer for a two at the short eleventh, and he came round to the twelfth three under fours and with the wind ready to help him home. A three-foot putt that ought to have gone in missed the hole at the thirteenth, but by this time Burton was fully aware of what had to be done, and he knew that he could play the last five holes in three over fours and still win.

Even so he did not alter his style of play in any degree, but there were no mock heroics when he came to the long fourteenth that had been the graveyard of so many scores before. Rather than risk a tee shot which might have curved out of bounds to the right or fallen into the 'Beardies', he played well to the left with his drive, and his next shot was still to the left down the fifth fairway. If other players had adopted these tactics earlier in the Championship the tale might have been a different one, for they undoubtedly repaid Burton, and a five here was eminently satisfactory. Unfortunately for his peace of mind, however, he was far from being out of the wood, for at the fifteenth he hooked his second shot so badly that it finished 80 yards to the left of the hole. On the huge double green the pin must have seemed half a mile away to eyes that could not help being anxious, but Burton took out his putter and contrived to scramble the ball six feet from the hole and to sink the putt for a four.

That was another hurdle surmounted, and to the sixteenth Burton played well to the left from the tee to avoid both railway and bunkers. Unfortunately, he rather overdid it, for the drive stopped in thick rough and left him an almost impossible pitch to the green. By this time Burton was being followed by an enormous gallery, and, even if he had wanted to he could not escape the knowledge that he needed 5, 5, 4 to win and 5, 5, 5 to tie. Wherever one turned the whispered information could be heard, and there were ten thousand anxious faces when Burton's pitch from the rough stopped short and his chip came within a hair's-breadth of rolling back into a bunker. It was a weak shot but more than excusable in the circumstances, though if the ball had rolled back Burton

Dick Burton from Sale, who learned his golf with a cotton-bobbin and a walking-stick, to the joy of St Andrews won the 1939 Open by two shots from the American Johnny Bulla. Qualifiers were now 130 with a maximum of forty players on the last day.

might have let his chance slip. Luckily, however, it stayed on the edge of the green and, though he left his approach putt wide of the hole, he put the next one in for a five.

The crowd stampeded down the seventeenth fairway like a herd of buffaloes and it seemed to take hours for the stewards to marshal them into some sort of order. Burton had to drive down a fairway lined with people who were as excited as if they were waiting for a royal procession, and luckily for someone's scalp the ball hit true as a die down the middle. Before he allowed Burton to play his next shot the caddie marched solemnly down the fairway so that his man should follow him to shape his plan for the all-important approach to the Road hole, but the precaution was unnecessary, for Burton had a number two iron out of the bag long before he reached the ball from his tour of exploration. Again there was nothing ridiculously brave about his shot, for he played carefully for the opening to the green and was content with a five that might easily have been a seven if he had gone boldly for the hole with wood.

This, of course, left him with a four to win and a five to tie, and, though in the morning Burton came within six inches of slicing out of bounds from the eighteenth tee, he took out his driver and lashed an enormous shot up the very middle of the fairway. The crowd cheered as though the Championship was already won, but as he had done throughout the round, Burton sauntered along with a cigarette in his lips and an expression of complete unconcern on his face. No one would have though the Championship cup was about to be his, but he made no bones about chipping well past the hole to be morally certain of a four.

Memories of the occasion in 1933 when C. Wood and D. Shute, the Americans, tied for the Championship here must have crowded back into the minds of the thousands of spectators for when Burton, with the utmost calm, holed his six-yard putt for the three there was a burst of cheering such as has rarely been equalled even in this enthusiastic town. Bulla, with fame sitting on the fence and not knowing which way to fall, heard his fate with cheer, and as Burton was shepherded into the clubhouse the American was one of the first to give him generous-hearted congratulations.

With the Championship cup in his hands it must have seemed to Burton a far cry to the days at Darwen when as a schoolboy he tried to learn the rudiments of golf with a cotton-bobbin and a walking-stick. Golf has brought him many rewards since then; but none richer than that of to-day. There can be no doubt that his careful plan of attack at the fourteenth and seventeenth holes carried him to victory, and to those who knew his methods it was obvious that for all his apparent unconcern he was fighting like mad to win. He attacked the holes with commendable shrewdness and he undoubtedly deserved his victory.

The day that led up to his great victory began with the pouring rain to which we have grown accustomed at St Andrews. Fallon was an early starter and,

St Andrews Old Course card

Hole	Yards	Bogey	Hole	Yards	Bogey
1	374	4	10	314	4
2	411	4	11	170	3
3	387	4	12	316	4
4	424	4	13	422	4
5	576	5	14	564	5
6	377	4	15	424	4
7	354	4	16	380	4
8	163	3	17	466	5
9	339	4	18	381	4
	3,405	36		3,437	37

Total length: 6,842 yards Bogey: 73

though he had to play six holes in heavy rain, he escaped the gale until he was three holes from home. He took every advantage of this blessing from the weather and by holing snorting putts at the second and seventh holes he went out in 33. He chipped dead at the tenth, becoming four under fours, and even with mishaps at the eleventh and sixteenth holes he finished in 71 for an aggregate of 215.

Behind him came T.H. Cotton, who again took seven at the fourteenth. He finished in 76, and was somewhat out of the running. We were a little disappointed to see R.A. Whitcombe, the then reigning champion, take 39 to come home after an excellent outward half of 35. A.D. Locke, the South African, who lost the championship because he was unable to master the fourteenth hole, crashed with a 39 to the turn and a round of 76. J. Bruen took 38 to the turn and finished in 75, but Bulla, after a horrible start with a first round of 77, again returned 71, thus thrusting himself once more into the limelight. Bulla this week has changed putters almost as often as he has changed his tie, but, though he declared that he had to-day putted 'like a washerwoman', the fact is that he had seriously to be considered when the fourth round began.

In the morning one felt deeply sorry for M. Pose, the Argentine golfer, who had the misfortune not to know that the grass between the path and roadway at the seventeenth is part of the hazard. He grounded his club on it and thus suffered a two-stroke penalty, and though in the end he did not have more than a slight chance of winning the title, no one will know how much the incident affected his later golf. Pose's morning round of 76 might well have been 74, and if it had been there would have been no knowing what he might have done.

Another player who caused excitement during the morning was W. Shankland, the Templenewsam professional, who brought in a card of 72, which brought him only two strokes behind Fallon, and, as one has already said, we considered Burton virtually out of it when he required 77 shots.

This afternoon, when the wind had veered slightly to the north but was still terribly troublesome, Fallon came a cropper with a seven at the fifth hole, and he holed out in 79 for an aggregate of 294. The excitement ran high and the strain was intense when Pose missed a shortish putt on the home green and tied. Then Bulla, the eventual runner-up, came along having had a triumphal progress to the turn in 35. He blessed and admonished his putter by turns, but when a six-yard putt went in for a three at the home hole he kissed his ball in mock affection. This round of 73 meant that he had knocked two strokes from Fallon's then leading aggregate.

Shankland, out in 38, arrived on the last green needing a three to tie, but his long putt slipped so far past the hole that he eventually required two more and joined Fallon at 294. A. Perry, with two sixes in the last nine holes, also returned 294, and when R.A. Whitcombe joined them with a similar aggregate we knew that only Burton or Rees could tie or win. With a six at the fifth and a five at the sixth Rees faded out of the picture, and in the end the responsibility of beating off the American challenge rested entirely with Burton. Golfing history will record how admirably he met his responsibility.

The scores

290: R. Burton (Sale) 70, 72, 77, 71

292: J. Bulla (Chicago) 77, 71, 71, 73

294: J. Fallon (Huddersfield) 71, 73, 71, 79; W. Shankland (Temp'n'sam) 72, 73, 72, 77; A. Perry (Leatherhead) 71, 74, 73, 76; R.A. Whitcombe (Parkstone) 71, 75, 74, 74; S.L. King (Knole Park) 74, 72, 75, 73

295: M. Pose (Argentina) 71, 72, 76, 76

296: P. Alliss (Ferndown) 75, 73, 74, 74; E.W.H. Kenyon (Beac'sfi'd) 73, 75, 74, 74; A.D. Locke (South Africa) 70, 75, 76, 75

1946

SNEAD WINS THE 'OPEN'

By four strokes

S. Snead, the thirty-three-year-old American golfer, won the British Open Championship on the Old course at St Andrews yesterday with a total of 290 (71, 70, 74, 75), four strokes ahead of J. Bulla (USA) and A.D. Locke (South Africa), and five in front of the four leading British competitors. It was the same total that gave R. Burton the Championship on the course in 1939, when it was last played.

Snead was a worthy winner, if only because in an astonishing series of mishaps to others and to himself in the last round, he was the only one to recover. At the end of the third round, Snead, Bulla, and D.J. Rees (Hindhead) stood together in the lead with 215. One stroke behind came T.H. Cotton.

The afternoon began with Cotton, who had surrendered the lead with a third round of 76, finding the Swilean burn guarding the first green. The strong west wind of the morning was blowing more fiercely, and the burn is almost on the front edge of the green. Cotton limped along until a six at the fifth made him five over fours.

Rees followed with a seven at the first. His drive would have been out of bounds over the railings on the right had it not struck a spectator. He had, however, still to carry the burn from a difficult spot, and when he boldly – perhaps rashly – went for it St Andrews exacted a terrible revenge for his record 67 of the day before. The ball dropped on the far side of the burn and then rolled back into it. Rees took four to find the green and then required three putts. He sorrowfully went his way to the turn in 42.

Before Snead was fairly on his way, the first pacemaker, A.D. Locke, came in. He had reached

Sam Snead won the 1946 Open at St Andrews with Johnny Bulla second, as he had been seven years earlier. 'Slamming Sam' became Sneed's soubriquet but, in its results, the post-war Guardian *confined itself mostly to initials for British golfers and Christian names for Americans.*

the turn in 36, but on four of the five greens from the thirteenth to the seventeenth he had taken three putts, and when he committed the same sin on the home green, his last putt being one of no more than two feet, he could do no better than 294.

Cotton was next. He had been told that he needed a three at the last hole to tie with Locke, whereas a four would have done. He went for his three from seven yards, missed, went two feet past, and missed again.

Bulla, out in 39, was four over fours for sixteen holes, but the Road hole, which had stampeded him into a seven in his first round, this time cost him six, and he failed to get his 78 when, like the others, he missed from two feet with his second putt on the last green.

Rees wanted two threes to bring him level with Locke and Bulla. He got a three at the Road hole with a second shot almost up to the pin, but failed with a seven-yard putt at the last. That left the way clear for Snead. Like Rees, he was almost out of bounds at the first, played safely out to the left of the green and was down in five. What with missed short putts, a six at the fifth, after visits to Hell bunker from a pulled drive, then the whins on the other side of the fairway, and then a pot bunker out of the whins, he was far from impressive in an outward half of 40. Snead, however, put such frailties behind him and thereby showed his greatness. He chipped to within a yard of the pin at the tenth for a three, nearly holed his chip at the thirteenth, and got down from two and a half yards for a triumphant four at the fourteenth. He faltered a moment with a poor approach to the sixteenth, but it was only for a moment. Although his run up at the Road hole ran six yards past the pin, he holed the putt, and a safely played four at the last gave him the title.

A band of five fought for the position of leading amateur. It was won by R.K. Bell of Accrington and District. Bell has had a remarkable season. He won the Manchester District Amateur Championship at his first attempt, added the Lancashire title to it, and for the time being at any rate is the country's leading stroke-play amateur.

The scores

290: Sam Snead (USA) 71, 70, 74, 75

294: A.D. Locke (S Africa) 69, 74, 75, 76; J. Bulla (USA) 71, 72, 72, 79

295: C.H. Ward (Little Aston) 73, 73, 73, 76; T.H. Cotton (Ryl Mid-Surrey) 70, 70, 76, 79; D.J. Rees (Hindhead) 75, 67, 73, 80; N. von Nida (Australia) 70, 76, 74, 75

298: F. Daly (Balmoral) 77, 71, 76, 74; J. Kirkwood (USA) 71, 75, 78, 74

299: Lawson Little (USA) 78, 75, 72, 74

1947

DALY'S OPEN CHAMPIONSHIP

Fine recovery after losing all his early lead

F. Daly (Balmoral) won the British Open Golf Championship at Hoylake to-day with a score of 293, one stroke ahead of R.W. Horne (Hendon) and F.R. Stranahan (USA).

Daly is a worthy champion. As a golfer of undoubted class he has been for some time on the verge of big things. To-day he had his chance and he took it like a man. Any player leading in the final round of a championship who can hole the last nine holes at Hoylake in 34 strokes, including a six, is of the stuff of champions. That is what Daly did and two strokes at least in those last nine holes he will always remember. Both of them were putts.

The first was the 15-yard putt holed at the thirteenth for a three he needed desperately, a three which gave him the heart for those last five terrific holes. The second was on the last green where he holed from ten yards for a three, a putt that made amends for a six at the seventeenth which, when it occurred, bore all the signs of tragedy. No man can win a championship without his share of luck and Daly was doubly fortunate in his early place in the draw and in the breeze that sprang up when he had almost finished.

Once Daly was safely in with a score of 293 no one seriously challenged him until late in the piece when Stranahan came to the sixteenth requiring 4, 4, 3, to tie. He got his four most bravely from a bunker at the sixteenth, but the seventeenth cost him a five when he went for a three from 12 yards and then missed his return putt of three feet. Needing a two to tie Stranahan struck one of the finest golf shots that can ever have been played in a championship. His drive was on the fairway, leaving him a pitch to the flag 160 yards away. The ball was beautifully struck, pitching eight feet from the flag, pulled up sharply and ran on to the hole, finishing with exactly the right strength less than a foot to the left.

There never can have been a championship when so many players were in the running with one round to go. At lunch-time two shots only separated nine players. Daly, Cotton, Lees, and von Nida led with 221, Stranahan was 222, and Horne, Ayton, R.A. Whitcombe, and Perry were 223. In the morning Daly had slipped with a six and two fives late in his round, and for twelve holes Cotton was four over fours and struggling for his figures. A brave finish, however, of four fours and two threes gave Cotton a respectable score of 74. Von Nida played beautifully in a round of 71 and hardly made a mistake while Perry, Whitcombe, Horne, and Stranahan with rounds of 70, 71, 72, and 72 respectively each improved his overnight position.

Although he was not one of the leaders W. Shankland produced the first excitement after lunch. He

Daly signs an autograph after his magnificent last-nine score of thirty-four.

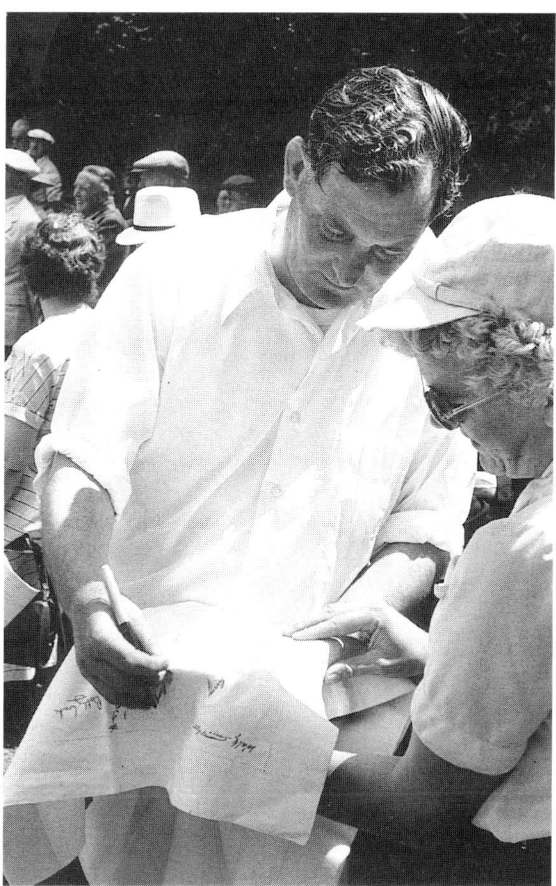

reached the fourteenth tee six under fours, after reaching the turn in 34 and starting back with four threes. A steady finish would have enabled him to set a stiff pace for the others. However, the fourteenth cost him a five and the fifteenth, where he was bunkered, a six; and the best he could do was 70 and a total of 295, good but not good enough. As expected this total was soon beaten by Daly, whose two second shots with a spoon to the fifteenth and sixteenth were sights to delight the eye. Then one after another those playing behind him met disaster.

Cotton was out in 36, but started back with a six at the tenth, where he drove into the rough and was too strong with his third. Thereafter he did not recover, and never looked like threatening Daly. Lees had slipped on the first nine holes, and von Nida began his last round by missing putts of five feet or less on four of the first five greens.

The scores

293: F. Daly (Balmoral, Belfast) 73, 70, 78, 72

294: F. Stranahan (USA) 71, 79, 72, 72

294: R.W. Horne (Hendon) 77, 74, 72, 71

295: W. Shankland (Templenewsam) 76, 74, 75, 70

296: R. Burton (Coombe Hill) 77, 71, 77, 71

297: J. Bulla (USA) 80, 72, 74, 71; T.H. Cotton (Royal Mid-Surrey) 69, 78, 74, 76; S.L. King (Wildernesse) 75, 72, 77, 73; A. Lees (Dore and Totley) 75, 74, 72, 76; N.G. von Nida (Australia) 74, 76, 71, 76; C.H. Ward (Little Aston) 76, 73, 76, 72

1948

Muirfield, 10th July

COTTON WINS GOLF 'OPEN'

His third success

Henry Cotton became the Open golf champion for the third time yesterday, when he completed the 72 holes at Muirfield with an aggregate score of 284. His figures for the four rounds were – 71, 66, 75, 72. Last year's winner, F. Daly, with a final round of 73, finished second, five strokes behind. Among the first to congratulate Cotton was the veteran James Braid, who gained the title five times between 1901 and 1910.

Cotton's previous successes were at Sandwich in 1934, with a score of 283, and at Carnoustie in 1937, when his total was 290. Those who remembered that he is now 41 years of age had some misgivings after his first round to-day, but he regained his mastery in the afternoon, and, in spite of a high wind, returned a magnificent 72. A crowd of 12,000 people joined in prolonged cheering as he sank a putt of two yards on the last green. 'I didn't think I should get away with it among so many fine young players,' he said afterwards.

His 75 in the morning was chiefly attributable to uncertainty on the greens. At the long fifth, after a colossal drive, he was short with his second, and took the first of his three fives. A simple putt went astray on the eighth, and then followed a pulled drive at the ninth, but here he saved himself with a great iron shot from the rough. Thirty-nine for the nine holes was not promising, but S. King, of Knole Park, with

Henry Cotton, aged forty-one – here playing his second shot at the 2nd – provided a major tonic for British golf, not least for the over-forties, with his third Open success.

whom Cotton was playing, seemed to act as a spur. King had made their totals level at the eleventh, but a three at the twelfth and a two at the next put Cotton three strokes ahead again and these he held to the end of the round.

When Cotton began his last round. Alfred Padgham, the winner in 1936, who had been six shots behind overnight, had got to within two of the leader, and King was bracketed with A. Lees, R. Vicenzo, the Argentinian, and van Donck, of Belgium, with 215.

Cotton started with three steady fours, and then dropped a stroke at the short fourth, where he took three from the edge of the green. Thereafter he had little cause for anxiety until he came to the fourteenth, where a tuft of thick grass 'killed' his pitch from the rough and he took another five. This slight setback was quickly overcome with a great three at the 393 yards fifteenth, where he put an iron shot five yards past the pin. Another three at the sixteenth followed, and only by the narrowest margin did he miss another after two fine shots to the long seventeenth.

Cotton struck a long drive down the left of the fairway at the last hole, and in trying to miss the bunker between himself and the pin his ball was caught by the treacherous wind and finished in the hazard on the right. There, hitting the shot off the socket of his club, he left the ball in the sand. The crowd groaned in sympathy, but immediately afterwards cheered lustily as Cotton put the ball two yards from the hole and sank his final putt.

A five at the eighteenth hole this morning put a burden on Padgham's shoulders which he was unable to shake off. After playing in his most attractive, effortless style, he arrived at the eighteenth tee needing a four to get within a stroke of Cotton or, after his approach shot, a three to tie. It appeared to be a reasonable chance, for he was less than five yards from the pin, but going for the hole, he finished two feet past, and then missed the return putt. With a rising wind in the afternoon Padgham took 39 to go out, and seemed to give up the chase. He finished with a 77. The other pursuers also slipped away. King took 76, and van Donck, Vicenzo, and Lees all failed.

J. Bulla, making his third attempt on the title, led the American challengers, with 291, and F. Stranahan, holder of the British Open Amateur title, was joint 23rd.

Cotton told me later that his victory was a tonic for British golf as well as himself: 'a tonic, too, for the over forties.'

The scores

284: T.H. Cotton (Royal Mid-Surrey) 71, 66, 75, 72

289: F. Daly (Balmoral) 72, 71, 73, 73

290: R. de Vicenzo (Argentina) 70, 73, 72, 75; N.G. von Nida (Australia) 71, 72, 76, 71; C.H. Ward (Little Aston) 69, 72, 75, 74; J. Hargreaves (Sutton Coldfield) 76, 68, 73, 73

291: B.L. King (Knole Park) 69, 72, 74, 76; J. Bulla (USA) 74, 72, 73, 72; A.H. Padgham (Sandridge Park) 73, 70, 71, 77; F. van Donck (Belgium) 69, 73, 73, 76

1949

Sandwich, 9th & 11th July

LOCKE TIES WITH BRADSHAW

Replay over 36 holes to-day

This Open Golf Championship will go down in the annals of golf as the most exciting in its long history. When the last round began H. Bradshaw (Kilcroney), A.D. Locke (South Africa), and M. Faulkner (Royal Mid-Surrey) shared the lead with an aggregate for three rounds of 213. S.L. King (Knole Park) and C.H. Ward (Little Aston) were each one stroke behind. The earlier leaders J. Adams (Wentworth) and King had faltered. King lost a two-stroke lead with a round of 74, against the 68s by Locke and Bradshaw, and a third round of 71 by Faulkner. The end of the day saw Locke and Bradshaw tieing for the lead at 283.

Everything depended on the last two holes. Bradshaw had already finished in 70 and Locke was informed that he had to get a birdie three at the seventeenth and a four at the eighteenth to be still in the Championship. He put a lovely high No. 7 iron-shot eight feet from the pin at the seventeenth and, watched by a tense and silent crowd around the green, stroked a long, gently rolling putt into the hole. He hit a 300-yard drive down the eighteenth, but his second iron-shot hit the hump of the green and kicked back, leaving him 25 yards from the pin with the hump between him and the hole. He sent a beautifully judged run-up shot to within two feet of the pin, and down it went for a tie.

The Irishman playing beautiful golf, had reached the turn in 33. Every shot was well played and he was never in the slightest trouble. He started back with four fours, and then at the difficult fourteenth hole he mis-hit a brassie shot. His ball just bounced over the ditch, and he took his first five. He scored another five at the next hole, where he was just short of the cross bunkers with his second shot, and left his pitch shot eight yards below the pin. At the short fifteenth

Sandwich 1949: a lunar landscape with a human countenance.

and the seventeenth Bradshaw had a par three and four, and at the eighteenth, all but won the Championship outright, for his 8-yard putt struck boldly and directly for the hole, hit the back of the tin, but it stayed out.

Locke accomplished the first nine holes in a grand 32. He was at that time a vastly different Locke from the morning. He sank a long 15-yard putt on the second hole for a birdie three, chipped dead at the next hole for another three, and he put down a three-yard putt at the fifth for a birdie four. He hit a lovely shot to the maiden, but just failed with a two-yard putt to get a two. He was well short with his second to the long seventh, and took an excusable five there, but again he put down a two-yard putt for a three at the eighth, and a three-yard putt for a birdie three at the ninth. The crowd was charmed by his leisurely, graceful swing, and it seemed now that nothing could go wrong for Locke. Then, without warning, he took a five at the 380-yard tenth. He was on the green for two, rather short of the pin and yet he three-putted. In a bunker at the eleventh from his second shot, Locke recovered to within four yards of the pin and stroked a good putt in for his four. The twelfth and thirteenth were played perfectly, but the fourteenth cost him a five. He had pushed out his second shot with a No. 2 iron away to the rough on the right, and was well past the pin with his recovery. He ran up nicely to the pin and then missed a short putt again. He threw away the advantage of a beautiful tee shot at the short sixteenth, where he was some six yards from the pin. He left his approach putt five feet short, and then failed to hole it.

Tomorrow's play-off over 36 holes between Bradshaw and Locke should be a most entertaining one, for two more widely contrasting players it would be hard to imagine.

LOCKE'S CRUSHING VICTORY

Faultless play in extra rounds

11th July

In this age when distance from the tee, gained as often as not by sheer smiting, seems to be the most worshipful of achievements, it is pleasant to write of the triumph of style and grace in the Open Golf Championship. The title was won at Sandwich on the Royal St George's course by A.D. Locke, the South African, at his sixth attempt and never since the days of R.T. Jones has there been so sweet a striker of the ball. It was balm to the soul of the stylists that here style was so triumphantly vindicated. Locke has a lovely wide, slow backswing; he hits the ball great distances with the utmost economy of effort and his accuracy to the green is almost inhuman. He routed poor H. Bradshaw, the Kilcroney champion of Ireland, by 12 strokes, 135 to 147, in the play-off over 36 holes here to-day. But Locke on such form might have defeated the mighty B. Hogan.

Looking back over the week's golf it astonishes one to think that Locke, the most accomplished player in the field, might never have been in the final at all, for Friday's issue hung on two putts. Bradshaw had come to the eighteenth with an eight-yard putt facing him and had struck the ball right into the hole – but it stayed out. Had he sunk it he would have been Open champion. Locke reached the seventeenth, a difficult par, four with a narrow green, knowing that he had to finish either three, four or four, three to tie. He put his second shot eight feet from the pin and ran down a beautifully struck putt for his three. He had to lay a thirty-yard chip dead over a hump at the eighteenth for his four, and it stamps the quality of the man that he did it.

When the play-off began there was much stern argument about whether the hearty unstylish Irishman could unsettle Locke, but the South African soon provided an answer. They were level to the fourth hole in the morning round but thereafter it was like an ordinary human being playing against a master and Locke seemed incapable of human emotion or human error. The slaughter of Bradshaw began at the fifth hole. Both hit lovely drives down the middle with Locke slightly ahead. Bradshaw hit a mighty wooden shot which was a trifle strong and finished in the rough over the green. Locke's ball was on the edge of the green but farther from the hole than Bradshaw's and he had to play first. His long putt ran six feet past the hole and the Irishman chipped to within five feet but Locke holed the putt, and Bradshaw missed his. Bradshaw missed a four-foot putt at the twelfth to give Locke a two-stroke lead but the Championship's destiny was practically settled at the difficult and long fourteenth, where Locke had taken seven in the second round. The South African hit a beautiful drive down wind with a No. 4 iron for fully 200 yards. The ball hit the front of the green, and running on finished less than two feet from the pin. The eagle three added three more shots to Locke's advantage, for Bradshaw had hooked his second shot into a bunker and piled misfortune on

'In this age when distance from the tee, gained as often as not by sheer smiting, seems to be the most worshipful of achievements, it is pleasant to write of the triumph of style and grace in the Open Golf Championship.' The dawning of the Locke–Thomson decade with the thirty-six-hole play-off victory of Locke over Harry Bradshaw (congratulating him above) was the start of the Guardian*'s Pat Ward-Thomas era, earning his colours as 'Our Golf Correspondent'. Locke and Thomson won eight times in ten years.*

misfortune by failing to hole a yard putt, which gave him six for the hole. Locke went on like a machine, Bradshaw dropped another stroke at the seventeenth where again he missed a normally holeable putt and Locke went into lunch seven strokes ahead. He was out in 33 and back in 34 to Bradshaw's respectable 74.

The final round began disastrously for the Irishman for he took six to the first hole against Locke's four. In the rough with his drive and short for two more, he failed to hole a four-foot putt for a five. Locke, bunkered badly in front of the green, played a grand cut-up blaster shot out which ended two feet from the pin. After that it was only a question of how big Locke's margin would be. Locke completed the first nine holes in the identical figures as in the morning, and with ten holes left to play he was 11 strokes ahead. With four holes left the South African took his only five of the day at the fifteenth, probably the most difficult hole on the course, but he holed a five-yard putt on the seventeenth to put the matter right, and concluded a wonderful performance with a par four at the last hole.

The scores

283: A.D. Locke (South Africa) 69, 76, 68, 70; H. Bradshaw (Kilcroney, Eire) 68, 77, 68, 70

Play-off: Locke 67, 68, 135
Bradshaw 74, 73, 147

285: R. de Vicenzo (Argentina) 68, 75, 73, 69

286: C.H. Ward (Little Aston) 73, 71, 70, 72; S.L. King (Knole Park) 71, 69, 74, 72

287: A. Lees (Dore & Totley) 74, 70, 72, 71; M. Faulkner (R Mid-Surrey) 71, 71, 71, 74

288: W. Smithers (Long Aston) 72, 75, 70, 71; J. Fallon (Huddersfield) 69, 75, 72, 72; J. Adams (Wentworth) 67, 77, 72, 72

1950

LOCKE RETAINS OPEN TITLE

Excellent last round decisive

Locke wins at Troon with an aggregate 279, four below the previous Open record.

A.D. Locke (South Africa) won the Open Golf Championship for the second year in succession here to-day with a remarkable total of 279 (69, 72, 70, 68), which is four strokes below the previous record for the event. Only R.T. Jones and W. Hagen have had successive wins since the days of Vardon, Taylor, and Braid. R. de Vicenzo (Argentina) was runner-up, two strokes behind Locke.

Locke's last round was a great one. It was the golf of a masterly player who was without any doubt superior to all others in the Championship. In technique and especially in temperament he again showed himself to be a worthy champion. When he went out in the afternoon, almost an hour before D.J. Rees, he must have known that he had to break 70. Most great players prefer to know what they must do. If they are in front that indeterminate feeling of whether to go out for the score or wait for it must be in their minds. Fortunately for Locke Troon was playing most easily, and he knew that he could probably score well with normal methods. This sounds simple, but with the natural strain of the event it needs a superb golfer to achieve it with the almost flawless golf that Locke showed.

From the start he never appeared likely to make a mistake. His shots to the greens after the unevitable straight drives made no demands on his putting, and at hole after hole his final putt was a matter of inches. Locke's only variation from strict par going out was to hole from eight feet for a three at the second, and after two fine shots to the gully in front of the sixth to pitch up and hole his putt for a four. His only mistake, if one can blame him for rare lapses into fallibility, came at the twelfth, where his second shot was a trifle strong, his pitch back was short and he missed the putt. At this precise moment Rees was hitting a good shot to the eighth, which he holed out for a two. He was then three under fours and one shot ahead of Locke. Whether the champion realised what the tumultuous cheer meant is not known, but he was not disturbed and played his last holes beautifully. A perfect two from six feet at the fourteenth redeemed the lost stroke. A five-foot putt was holed with utter calmness on the next hole and a safe five followed at the sixteenth. His shot to the seventeenth was short and fell between bunkers to the right of the green. It lay on a downslope but Locke pitched with superb control and got his three. The home hole was watched by a vast concourse of people, but Locke played it easily and safely for his 68.

Soon after Locke had finished Rees was leaving the twelfth tee, needing to play the remaining holes in two under fours in order to win. The chance of a dramatic victory was not to be, and Rees finished in third place. The finest total of the day was that of F. Daly, who started his first round with three threes and thereafter played with characteristic confidence, finished in 69 and then returned a 66 in the afternoon and tied with Rees. This score was equalled by F.R. Stranahan, who became leading amateur. Other outstanding achievements where those of F. Bullock, whose four consecutive rounds of 71 were the result of amazingly consistent golf, and D.A. Blair, whose style and steadiness are worthy of the Walker Cup selectors' attention.

The morning was calm and sunny when M. Faulkner and R. de Vicenzo went out. The former was playing at his best. Vicenzo was rarely out of the rough, yet at hole after hole he pitched and putted so accurately that when he holed for a two at the eighth his score was equal to Faulkner's although his golf did not compare. Vicenzo used wood – a brassy – only three times from the tee during his round: usually he drove with a 2 or 3 iron. He is not normally considered a good putter, but this morning he excelled and on each of 13 greens required but one putt.

Both he and Faulkner had extraordinary adventures coming home. Faulkner holed out from a bunker for a two at the fourteenth; each hit drives of vast soaring wildness to the sixteenth, and Vicenzo was badly bunkered from his second, but each obtained his five. Vicenzo continued to putt with extraordinary facility in the afternoon, but his erratic driving eventually took its toll. Rarely can any golfer have returned such a good score with so many wayward shots.

Meanwhile Locke moved smoothly behind them in the calm air. He also got his two at the eighth, but he missed the tenth green and failed with a shortish putt at the eleventh, dropping crucial strokes. The remainder was conventional and Locke was level with Rees and Vicenzo. Rees was the great disappointment of the morning for, after going out in 33, he had a glorious opportunity of leading the field by two or three shots, but he could only finish in 71.

At lunch-time five men were within one stroke of each other and people were talking of play-offs, but one felt that Rees's great chance had gone and that Locke would not fail to take advantage.

The scores

*Amateur

279: A.D. Locke (South Africa) 69, 72, 70, 68

281: R. de Vicenzo (Argentine) 72, 71, 68, 70

282: F. Daly (Balmoral) 75, 72, 69, 66; D.J. Rees (South Hertfordshire) 71, 68, 72, 71

283: E. Moore (South Africa) 74, 68, 73, 68; M. Faulkner (Royal Mid-Surrey) 72, 70, 70, 71

284: A. Lees (Sunningdale) 68, 76, 68, 72; F. Bullock (Royal Lytham and St Annes) 71, 71, 71, 71

286: F. van Donck (Waterloo, Belgium) 73, 71, 72, 70; *F.R. Stranahan (United States) 77, 70, 73, 66; S.L. King (Knole Park) 70, 75, 68, 73

1951 Portrush, 7th July

A GOLF TITLE COMES HOME

Faulkner's 'Open' – Brave pursuit by Cerda

M. Faulkner, 34-year-old British Ryder Cup player, won the Open Golf Championship here to-day with a total of 285 (71, 70, 70, 74) two strokes ahead of A. Cerda (Argentine). Late in the day a splendid 68 by C.H. Ward (Little Aston) brought him from obscurity to third place. F. Daly (Balmoral), after losing ground in the morning, played well for his last gallery and shared fourth place with J. Adams (Wentworth).

Faulkner deserved his victory absolutely. He had played first-class, sensible golf, and, if memory serves correctly, he had no score worse than a five in his four rounds. This unexpected consistency by Faulkner showed that for once in his mercurial career he had the head, hands, and heart of a great player. Perhaps his victory will make him into a more reliable competitor in future.

After taking advantage of his fortune with the weather yesterday, he set out on a calm morning with F.R. Stranahan, the only American competitor, as partner. Immediately his determination and control of himself were evident. Throughout the week he putted with extraordinary touch and accuracy and this more than anything else made him champion. An eight-yard putt went in at the first and it was clear that the slower greens after the night's rain were to his liking.

With a six strokes' lead from N. Sutton and Cerda at the end of the third round, Faulkner had the Championship in his grasp. No one else – though Cerda made a wonderful attempt – could win it if Faulkner played sensibly in the afternoon. And this he did, driving superbly with his wide shut-face swing and making no real mistakes. Even when a five came at the fifteenth and again at the sixteenth he remained calm. A lovely chip to the side of the hole saved a stroke at the seventeenth, and although he cut his second shot to the last green, a safe five proved to be enough.

The mercurial Max Faulkner wins Portrush's first and only Open. It was to be the last British victory for seventeen years.

A.D. Locke, of South Africa, the holder for two years, was never quite his true self. Like Sutton and others he faltered on the last morning. His judgment of the greens was below its usual exceptional standard, and a deficiency of eight strokes at lunch was too much even for him. Sutton had played finely, but a sad finish to the morning round left him too far behind. Like many others he was probably tired later, as well he might be, for Locke's slowness in the first round to-day reduced the interval between rounds for most competitors to less than half an hour. H. Weetman of Australia, who has had a fine, steady Championship, could not quite reproduce his form of yesterday.

When Faulkner had posted his excellent total, excursions to various challengers showed that only Cerda could catch him. All the way to the turn, which he reached in 34, Cerda's golf was faultless. A cut iron shot to the tenth was almost lost, but he played a great recovery, only to miss the putt from eight feet. Then came the heaven-sent break which gave him a chance of a great victory if he could play the last five difficult holes in par figures.

A glorious iron shot hit the heart of the narrow 12th green and a four-yard putt was holed for a three. From behind the 13th green, where, far beyond, the Skerries lie like low ships awaiting the tide, Cerda holed a little chip for another three. He did not get his three at the fearsome 14th, a putt lipped the next hole and he needed three fours to tie. Tragedy came for the little Argentine just as it had come to Jurado at Carnoustie long ago. Possibly the sight of the surging throng coming to meet him disturbed Cerda, for his drive to the 16th was pulled hard against the boundary bank. His third shot, played desperately for the pin on a tight line, missed the green. His chip from the rough was strong and the putt just stayed out. Poor little Cerda, dark, good-mannered, and a very fine player indeed, finished galliantly with two excellent fours on those last telling holes, the total length of which is a thousand yards.

The amateurs acquitted themselves well. C.H. Beamish, who surely must be in the next Walker cup team, and K.E. Enderby, with a high-flowing swing and calm serious approach, scored most commendably. All week Stranahan has been unable to adjust himself to the greens, but he hit the ball beautifully with a more orthodox method than previously. But he had no fortune at all with his putting, and had he putted as well as Faulkner he could have won, for the remainder of his golf was as impressive as that of anyone. Of the Italian golfers, U. Grappasonni, slim, swarthy, and strong, is a fine stroke player with a compact, crisp swing. But perhaps the most interesting of all the overseas players was the young Australian, P.W. Thomson, whose method and temperament promise a great future for him.

The scores

285: M. Faulkner (unattached) 71, 70, 70, 74

287: A. Cerda (Argentina) 74, 72, 71, 70

290: C.H. Ward (Little Aston) 75, 73, 74, 68

292: J. Adams (Wentworth) 68, 77, 75, 72; F. Daly (Balmoral) 74, 70, 75, 73

293: W. Shankland (Templenewsam) 73, 76, 72, 72; A.D. Locke (South Africa) 71, 74, 74, 74; H. Weetman (Croham Hurst) 73, 71, 75, 74; P.W. Thomson (Australia) 70, 75, 73, 75; N. Sutton (Leigh) 73, 70, 74, 76

1952

LOCKE WINS THE 'OPEN'

Two bad holes beat Daly

Locke commanded swing and nerve in a strong westerly at Lytham St Annes to ensure his third Open in four years.

A.D. Locke (South Africa) won the Open Golf Championship for the third time in four years on the Royal Lytham course to-day. His total of 287 was a splendid achievement in difficult conditions and was one stroke better than that of P.W. Thomson (Australia). The failure of F. Daly to fulfil the rich promise of victory which was his this morning was mitigated in part by the superb performance of T.H. Cotton in finishing fourth.

Cotton's total of 145 for the day was two strokes better than that of anyone else, and was a magnificent gesture by the greatest British golfer of his generation who was playing in his last Open Championship.

Locke's victory showed once again that he has no superior, if an equal, as a competitor when the game's greatest rewards are in the balance. The rain which fell during the night probably relieved his mind, for the bite had gone from the greens and they were of a pace to his liking.

A strongly westerly wind blew in gusts over the course throughout the day and it was several shots harder than at any time during the Championship. In these conditions Locke showed the greater control and consistency. His rounds were great examples of a man completely in command of his swing and himself. He must have felt that if he played steadily the others would fall by the wayside, and everyone in a position to challenge him, with the gallant exception of Thomson, did so.

Thomson fully justified the faith of those who during the past year have seen in him probably the finest young golfer in the world and one whose eminence in the game is now assured. His swing is sound and orthodox, he has a reserve of power from the tees, and is an excellent putter, but these qualities are of no avail without self-control, intelligent application, and confidence, all of which Thomson has in abundance.

After a steady round in the morning, which might have been much better with the slightest of fortune on the last five greens, he went out after lunch five shots behind Daly. He played with great steadiness and control for the finest round of the day.

Daly should have won the Championship before lunch, for, from the outset of his first round, the ball was running for him. On the first two holes his tee shots luckily eluded bunkers and he was going well until the eighth. Here, rather unwisely, he took an iron from the tee for safety, but found the bunker on the left which even a pulled drive would have carried. From a bad lie he then socketed hard towards the railway, but the ball bounced from the fence to the fairway.

This remarkable piece of fortune allowed him to escape with a six, but the worst hole of all and the one which really appeared to lose him the Championship was the eleventh. From seventy yards in front of the open green he played a wretched pitch which faded into a bunker. He needed two to get out and the hole cost seven. For the rest of the day, instead of being in command, Daly was struggling to get back some of the precious four strokes which these two holes had cost.

Locke was out an hour ahead of Daly and began his last round well. Apart from an ugly second shot to the fourth, his golf to the turn, which he reached in 34, was measured, easy, and faultless. A beautiful shot to the short twelfth brough him a two and then he had something in hand to face the fierce test of the last six holes.

Meanwhile Daly had begun shakily and his driving was suspect for a while, but from the sixth he began to play well. Every shot was straight and true, but then the fates at last deserted him. On five consecutive holes, when he so desperately needed a below-par figure, well-struck putts would not fall. A poor second shot to the fifteenth was his nemesis, for to get three consecutive threes to tie was more than any golfer could have hoped.

Locke seemed certain to finish in 71 which would have made victory beyond dispute – and, indeed, one left him after seeing a dubiously struck iron come to rest eight yards from the seventeenth hole, but he missed a putt of less than 2 ft for his four and then failed to get down in two from the edge of the home green. The outcome of this was that Thomson suddenly had a slender chance to catch him. He finished bravely in the attempt and holed a putt of five yards for a three on the last hole.

For all the victory of Locke, the sad failure of Daly, and the great finishes by Thomson and Cotton, the abiding memory of this Championship probably will be that of G. Sarazen. This lovable man, one of the tiny number of the great golfers, has further endeared himself to everyone and commanded increased respect for his immense ability.

It was wonderful to watch him enjoying his day with Daly, and at the same time incredible to think that the last time he played here was with H. Vardon in 1923. During the Championship Sarazen dropped twelve strokes from par on the last four holes, which is proof that, at 50 years of age, it is the legs and not the technique which fail. The spirit, of course, is imperishable.

The scores

287: A.D. Locke (South Africa) 69, 71, 74, 73

288: P.W. Thomson (Australia) 68, 73, 77, 70

289: F. Daly (Balmoral) 67, 69, 77, 76

294: T.H. Cotton (R Mid-Surrey) 75, 74, 74, 71

295: A. Cerda (Argentina) 73, 73, 76, 73; S.L. King (Knole Park) 71, 74, 74, 76

296: F. van Donck (Belgium) 74, 75, 71, 76

297: F. Bullock (Glasgow) 76, 72, 72, 77

298: A. Lees (Sunningdale) 76, 72, 76, 74; N.G. von Nida (Australia) 77, 70, 74, 77; E.C. Brown (Sandy Lodge) 71, 72, 78, 77; W. Goggin (USA) 71, 74, 75, 78; S.S. Scott (Carlisle City) 75, 69, 76, 78; H. Bradshaw (Portmarnock) 70, 74, 75, 79

1953

HOGAN WINS OPEN TITLE

Indelible memories of a great player

By Pat Ward-Thomas

The finest and most ruthless talent in world golf... Ben Hogan of America won the 1953 Carnoustie Open by four shots. His victories in the Masters and US Open made it a historic year.

The victory of B. Hogan (United States) by four strokes, in one of the finest Open Golf Championships ever played, was a magnificent performance and in every sense fitting, for Hogan beyond dispute is the supreme golfer of this generation, if not of all time. D.J. Rees, A. Cerda, P.W. Thomson, and F.R. Stranahan tied for second place.

Hogan was so immeasurably the greatest golfer here not only because his technique is absolutely perfect but because he has the finest and most ruthless competitive temperament in world golf. From the moment he arrived in Britain Hogan was under considerable strain. Not since R.T. Jones had one man been made such an overwhelming favourite and although Hogan's confidence, which, incidentally, was never expressed, in his ability must be immense, he was facing a tremendous test of his powers. The knowledge that the whole golfing world was expecting him to win must have been disturbing even to his cool brain. This great old links also was a true test and its nature was one to which he was not accustomed. If Hogan never wins another championship – and the possibility of his retirement is not remote – this was a triumphant ending.

The still, grey afternoon was fraught with the presence of great deeds, for after an absorbing morning Hogan and Vicenzo were a stroke ahead of Rees, Thomson, and Cerda, with Stranahan one behind them. Hogan had missed a great chance of having the Championship won by taking his only six of the week at the seventeenth, where his four wood was cut into a bunker and three putts followed. Brown, of the overnight leaders, had faltered. He does not yet appear to have the temperamental stability or consistency, of the highest level. Vicenzo had played beautiful golf all morning, but as he quaintly said, 'The hole is too small for Roberto'. Frequently he just failed to hole putts for better than par figures. His 71 nevertheless was good enough to lead with Hogan. Rees also had played finely and Cerda, who began each half with a pair of threes and who had the unenviable experience of following Hogan's vast gallery, scored superbly.

Thomson too, that splendid young athlete, with such a sensible cool approach to the game, had played strict par golf. Locke was not at his best and when he reached the turn in 37, it did not seem that he would challenge further. He plodded round in comparative loneliness after lunch and must have reflected on the ephemeral life of a champion. Thus it was all to play for and a round to go.

All the leaders, save Hogan and Cerda, were out early and their steady progress to the turn was an encouraging sign that Hogan's path was not going to be made easy. Rees looked composed and determined, for once like his old attacking self. He reached the turn in 35 and started home splendidly. He was unlucky when, after under-clubbing to the fifteenth, he played a good chip and then saw a nine-foot putt hit the hole and stay out. He missed the sixteenth green as so many have done and lost another stroke, but there was nothing faint-hearted about two brave fours which gave him the lead with Stranahan.

Stranahan just previously had completed an extraordinary exhibiton of competitive putting under pressure. On each of the last six holes he needed but one putt and his finish of 3, 4, 3, 3, was the finest of the week. Vicenzo's driving was having wayward moments and it was clear that the slightest mistakes by anyone were going to cost dear.

Hogan by now had started with four perfect fours. Then came, if it is possible to find one, a turning point. For the second time to-day Hogan missed the fifth green on the left, but chipped from the rough straight into the hole for a three. Again he struck two unforgettable wooden-club shots to within 30 yards of the sixth hole, ran up perfectly, and holed the putt. Then one sensed finally and with conviction that the iceman was coming for the others. The greatness of Hogan's golf for the remainder of the round merits detailed description, but space forbids. It suffices to state that only two strokes failed to achieve their object. Hogan played the first twelve holes in nine fours and three threes without holing one missable putt. Then for the second time he holed out at the thirteenth for a two and although he slightly underclubbed to the twelfth and fourteenth, only the latter cost him a stroke.

In many of his great championship victories Hogan's last round has been the most telling. The reason for this is that when two rounds are played on the final day it means that he has had two opportunities of locating the position of the pins. To a golfer of his class, who can call the shots almost as he pleases, this means a great deal. Another remarkable feature of his golf was the ability to produce great length whenever he required it. Frequently to-day, without any wind, his drives measured between 280 and 300 yards.

The scene as Hogan played the last two parallel holes with strokes and strokes to spare will be etched for ever in the minds of those who saw it. Some twelve thousand people lined the 500 yards on both sides of the fairways. His four to the seventeenth was perfectly played and then down came the last long drive towards victory. The crowd stood motionless and the air was filled with a resounding silence as the slight, grey figure struck his pitch to the green and holed out. Hogan stood bowing impassively and raising his hat as the crowd roared its tribute, and an unforgettable Championship was over.

No apology need be made for devoting most of this report to Hogan. It seems unlikely that he will visit Britain again and there will be many opportunities to do justice to the golfers who acquitted themselves so splendidly in this event. Among those whom one saw playing finely were H. Thomson, whose swing is still a thing of beauty and who had the privilege and pleasure of playing with Hogan. Then there was S.L. King, unnoticed and unsung, who rarely fails to do justice to the Open, and, perhaps most important of all, the performance of P. Alliss, whose total of 291 showed that he has the ability to do justice on a testing course to his strength.

The memory of watching Hogan play golf will never die and one is proud to possess it. Not even Cotton at his finest surpassed the authority, power, and accuracy of his strokes. Imagination strains at the thought of the wonderful co-ordination of mind and body expressed in the beauty of his swing; of the will-power and courage which created and then rebuilt his technique to a pitch of perfection that probably will never be equalled. Hogan made a great impression also because of his gentle bearing and quiet charm. He dresses as modestly as he talks and only the piercing deep-set eyes reveal the force of character behind them. Imagine him as he scrutinises a long difficult stroke, with arms quietly folded, an inscrutable quarter smile on his lips, for all the world like a gambler watching the wheel spin. And then the cigarette is tossed away, the club taken with abrupt decision, the glorious swing flashes and a long iron pierces the wind like an arrow. That was Hogan. We shall never see his like again.

The scores

282: Ben Hogan (USA) 73, 71, 70, 68

286: Mr F.R. Stranahan (USA) 70, 74, 73, 69; A. Cerda (Argentina) 75, 71, 69, 71; P. Thomson (Australia) 72, 72, 71, 71; D.J. Rees (South Herts) 72, 70, 73, 71

287: R. de Vicenzo (Argentina) 72, 71, 71, 73

290: S.L. King (Knole Park) 74, 73, 72, 71

291: A.D. Locke (South Africa) 72, 73, 74, 72

292: Peter Alliss (Ferndown) 75, 72, 74, 71; E.C. Brown (unattached) 71, 71, 75, 75

WIN BY ONE STROKE

Golf 'Open' for Australian

By Pat Ward-Thomas

On Birkdale's debut in 1954, Peter Thomson, twenty-four, celebrated his first Open victory, the first by an Australian, and the birth of a new child.

After a wonderful finish to a glorious day's golf at Royal Birkdale, P.W. Thomson (Victoria G.C., Australia) became Open champion with a total of 283 (72, 71, 69, 71), one stroke ahead of A.D. Locke, D.J. Rees, and S.S. Scott. This completed a remarkable year for Australian golf, for not only did her team win the Commonwealth tournament but a member of it, D.W. Bachli, won the Amateur Championship.

Thomson's victory was a magnificent performance. Aged only 24, but matured as a golfer far beyond that, he has now taken his place among the small company of world competitors for which he was destined several years ago. He was runner-up in the last two championships and since then has spent many months playing in American tournaments. This experience, without doubt, has developed his golf greatly, and Alliss should take the first opportunity of following his example.

In terms of technique, Thomson must certainly, at least, be the equal of any golfer here. His driving, always with a spoon, although a very powerful club at that, was supremely good, and his iron play was wonderfully accurate. His short approaching was most consistent, but he did not hole anything like the number of doubtful length putts which the quality of his play into the greens merited.

His temperament was quite remarkable, and perhaps his greatest asset. The self-possession, level-headedness, and unhurried rhythm of his approach to every stroke were extraordinary. In addition he is a most likeable and sensible young man. His swing, orthodox and strong, remained smooth and easy throughout. It will last him a lifetime and in that lifetime he will win many more championships.

The events of the last crowded hour, in the grey evening light of a lovely summer day, will not lightly be forgotten by the multitudes who were present – more than 10,000 had paid for admission. The morning had resolved the situation into a straight fight between Scott, Rees, and Thomson who, in that order, each returned splendid 69s for totals of 212. Locke, almost last out, was two strokes more at lunch, in his old familiar position of waiting, as only he can, for the others to make mistakes.

Spence, Cerda, and Turnesa, who kept himself in the picture with a fine 71, and repeated it later, were three strokes behind. This seemed and proved to be too great a margin in scoring conditions which could not have been easier. The wind was but the faintest of zephyrs, fairways were running, and the greens were holding.

All through the day the four leaders were never separated by more than two strokes. Scott, who had finished an hour or more before Rees, was condemned to an anxious vigil in the clubhouse before Rees came to the last hole needing a four to beat his total of 284.

Rees came down the fairway on the crest of a great throng, and it was typical of the man that he should lash his four-iron shot straight at the hole and make no attempt to steer it. It flew straight for the flag, but ran just through the green on to the little bank behind. It was not a difficult chip, but Rees hit it too strongly; the ball ran five feet beyond the hole, his putt missed, and high went his arms in despair.

Thomson by this time was on the fifteenth, and learned there that he needed level fours to beat Rees and make the task of Locke behind him almost impossible. It was then that he vindicated all one's faith in his mental control. His drive to the fifteenth was pushed a shade, but he struck a fine eight-iron shot from the rough, and almost holed from twelve yards for a three.

A glorious long drive, probably the best he hit all day, flew past the sentinel dunes of the sixteenth, and the distant green lay open for him, but his wooden club second tailed to the left, and found a bunker 25 yards from the pin. He now played a great competitive stroke, and looking at him there was no sign of the pressure he must have felt. With complete assurance he calmly examined the shot, a most difficult one to gauge because of its distance, and exploded to within two feet of the hole.

Saving some awful accident the dream of a young man's life was near fulfilment. A perfect iron shot struck and held the heart of the seventeenth and a safe three was made. His drive arrowed down the last fairway, but the mid-iron to that tiny entrance was just off line and finished on the top fringe of a bunker. He flicked it easily to within five feet, his putt lipped the hole, and then casually with the back of his putter he tapped the ball home.

Two crucial moments in Thomson's day came as early as the sixth this morning. In aiming over the formidable barrier of dunes which must be carried if the green is to be found his ball struck one of them. Remarkably it found a good lie and he pitched from 100 yards to within five feet and got his four when a six seemed probable. At the fourteenth in the afternoon he was in the rough twice on the left but pitched on to the green and then holed from 15ft, for the rest he was by no means fortunate and had to play for every figure he got.

It did not seem to be in the instinct of things that the gods would rob Thomson, but Locke never can be trusted. He came to the last with a vast throng terraced round the green and needing a three to tie. His iron shot this morning had finished dead by the hole and how he must have wished it could happen

Birkdale was at its easiest, the wind but the faintest of zephyrs.

again, but it came to rest forty feet short and his putt travelled less than 39.

In company with many one feels sympathy for Rees. The years are passing rapidly and with them the chances of winning the Open which he has deserved. No golfer tries so hard, no man at his age is so fit, and his golf throughout has been his finest, courageous and attacking. Right to the end Rees was in command of himself, holed out superbly under the awful pressure which even the most experienced must feel at the fifteenth and seventeenth after missing the greens, and he hardly deserved the remorse which must now be his.

Scott must be given the very highest praise for holding on. Although he knew the margin between him and the pack behind was so slight he never faltered. He hit the ball beautifully in his quiet pure style and best of all his short game failed only once during that last round when a championship beckoned. This was a brave performance, for Scott has yet to win an important event and posterity was within a stroke of him. Locke was Locke, the eternal machine, moving like a stately quinquireme down the fairways. Like the others he was puzzled by the greens and did not hole the proportion of putts he usually does.

Many can look back with pride on this Championship, and not least among them the Royal Birkdale Club, who organise everything so admirably on their splendid course; J. Adams, who twice to-day went round in 69, and S.L. King, who overcame a depressing start, and finished with honour; R. Halsall, who achieved the difficult task of playing extremely well on his own course; P.A. Toogood, the leading amateur, and a first-class competitor who, in his modest way, must be satisfied to have finished so far ahead of every member of a team for which he was not selected; the Italians, Grappasonni, Casera, and Angelini, who always compete most capably and attractively; van Donck for his timely return to form; and, last of all, the great little man himself, Gene Sarazen. His was a wonderful performance on this hot, sultry day, for he finished only nine strokes behind the winner. The presence of that sturdy lovable figure, with its broad grin, the charm of the man, and the immense authority that still is in his golf, brings something imperishable to any championship.

The scores

283: P.W. Thomson (Australia) 72, 71, 69, 71

284: S.S. Scott (Carlisle City) 76, 67, 69, 72; D.J. Rees (South Hertfordshire) 72, 71, 69, 72; A.D. Locke (South Africa) 74, 71, 69, 70

286: J. Adams (Royal Mid-Surrey) 73, 75, 69, 69; A. Cerda (Argentina) 71, 71, 73, 71; J. Turnesa (USA) 72, 72, 71, 71

287: P. Alliss (Ferndown) 72, 74, 71, 70; S.L. King (Knole Park) 69, 74, 74, 70

289: J. Demaret (USA) 73, 71, 74, 71; F. van Donck (Belgium) 77, 71, 70, 71

GOLF TITLE RETAINED

Thomson joins a select company

By Pat Ward-Thomas

P.W. Thomson, of Australia, this afternoon joined the small and most distinguished company of great golfers who have successfully defended the Open Championship title. In the last half-century only R.T. Jones, W. Hagen, and A.D. Locke have achieved this tremendous feat. Thomson's total of 281 (71, 68, 70, 72) was two strokes lower than that of J. Fallon (Huddersfield) and beat by four the record for the Old Course by Jones in 1927.

It has seemed throughout that victory for Thomson was in the stars and in every sense the result was right and just. There is about him an unmistakable air of success in the assurance of his bearing, the set of his head, the quick walk, the clear decisive mind, and the cool, often smiling acceptance of destiny. All these suggest the immense confidence and self-possession which one knows there is within him. In short, he has the mien of a champion as well as the ability.

The qualities of greatness in golf are abstract, once a certain standard of proficiency has been reached. Particularly is this true of Thomson, whose victories have been earned not so much by outstandingly brilliant golf but by a high order of consistency; by the resilience of spirit to accept and counter bad breaks or indifferent shots and, above all, remarkable nervous stamina and control. Within a few years he may have a record comparable with the greatest of all times.

All through the long summer day it seemed that the outcome would be closer than it eventually proved to be, for in the end Thomson, in spite of a seven at the fourteenth, was left needing two fives to win – a considerable margin which he never seemed likely to need. In conditions almost incomparably favourable for good scoring it was certain that many worthy golfers would bring themselves within reach of distinction. But it was almost equally certain that no one of them would succeed, for apart from Locke, who was just too far behind at lunch, they have not the qualities of a champion, and in the end this always decides. Gradually, inexorably the Old Course, aided by its insidious ally, the fear of winning, took its toll, a stroke here, a stroke there, and disaster for many.

Thomson chose St Andrews to join the select band to retain the Open in modern times. 'Above all,' wrote Ward-Thomas, 'he showed a remarkable nervous stamina and control.' The first £1,000 first prize; the first live coverage by the BBC.

Fallon had a great chance, for with the advance of the metal blue tide the wind freshened considerably and was at his back going out. He started finely (3–4 and 3–4) and two perfect shots left him five feet from the fifth hole, which he lipped for a three. Two lovely medium irons (how beautifully Fallon plays these shots) and two good putts brought threes at the sixth and seventh, another at the short hole, and then he rimmed the ninth from four feet to be out in 31.

The eleventh has claimed many victims and was cruel to Fallon. He played a shade too straight at the flag guarded by the Strath bunker, went in, took two to get out, and that was five. But he put it behind him manfully and continued finely until the first signs of strain came at the fifteenth, where a cut drive cost him five. An easy four followed. Then he had to decide about the Road hole whether to play short for a certain five and possible four, or go for a three or four with disaster awaiting him. He played short and that was another five. A safe four home made 70, a very fine round but he will dream a long time of what it might have been.

Jowle has been on the crest of a wonderful week, for after leading the qualifiers he went steadily on and gave everyone cause for chatter and admiration by leading at lunch until Thomson holed a putt from the back of the eighteenth green to go one ahead. Jowle, with his brisk, solid swing and dour modest manner, played extremely well, and until the last round holed out as consistently as anyone. His 69, with that of J.S. Anderson of Bruntsfield, was the only round below 70 all day.

Locke has been almost at his finest after a scrambling first round and he, too, could have caught Fallon but for the fourteenth hole, which cost him six and which later was to destroy O'Connor. Even after Thomson had finished, O'Connor arrived there six under fours, but the fourteenth swiftly put paid to any hope he might have had of a tie with an incurable eight.

Brown's morning round might have been the linch pin of the day, for he began in exquisite stillness before the dew had left the ground and whilst the sun was climbing towards perfection. He was under the whip, for the awareness of the partisan horde ready to stampede him home must have been disconcerting, and he was at his most mercurial. The Strath did to him what later it did to Fallon and though he kept going with brave putts the inspiration for the last round was gone.

Cerda, Weetman, and van Donck shared fifth place. Cerda played beautifully without the encouragement of holing many telling putts. Weetman began rather untidily after lunch and van Donck, like Bousfield, played with irreproachable steadiness without suggesting any threat to Thomson.

And so as Fallon was finishing his round, Thomson was able to take his second six of the day, at the fifth. In trying to play short and hampered by an inconsiderate camera, he was bunkered. But a long, fast putt for a two following a heavily hit tee shot to the eighth countered this and he was out in 35. He continued to play beautifully easy, composed golf until the fourteenth interfered with a vengeance. He drove into the Beardies, his third swung away into the Grave which awaits those who take the safe line past Hell, a bad lie awaited him, and most of his margin had gone. He could now play the remaining holes in one over fours to win.

And then, as only the greatest players can after a serious setback, he immediately saved a stroke with a superbly judged iron shot to within six feet of the fifteenth hole. Down went the putt, and, barring some awful accident, he was home. He played the sixteenth by the sensible left-hand route, a precaution which passed entirely unappreciated by the huge crowd. An eerie mist crept under the sun as he played for his easy five at the seventeenth, and a fine Championship ended in the old classical manner with thousands on the fences and in the windows around the last matchless sward as Thomson, casual and smiling, holed his final putt.

The scores

281: P.W. Thomson (Australia) 71, 68, 70, 72

283: J. Fallon (Huddersfield) 73, 67, 73, 70

284: F. Jowle (Edgbaston) 70, 71, 69, 74

285: A.D. Locke (South Africa) 74, 69, 70, 72

286: A. Cerda (Argentina) 73, 71, 71, 71; K. Bousfield (Coombe Hill) 71, 75, 70, 70; H. Weetman (Croham Hurst), 71, 71, 70, 74; B.J. Hunt (Hartsbourne C C), 70, 71, 74, 71; F. van Donck (Belgium), 71, 72, 71, 72

287: R. Barbieri (Argentina) 71, 71, 73, 72; C. O'Connor (Bundoran) 71, 75, 70, 71

1956

Hoylake, 7th July

THOMSON SWEEPS TO VICTORY

The finest competitor in the world

By Pat Ward-Thomas

A performance without parallel since R Ferguson in 1882 . . . Thomson wins the Open for the third successive year.

P.W. Thomson (Australia) defied history and earned lasting acclaim by winning the Open Golf Championship for the third successive year, a performance without parallel since R. Ferguson gained his third victory in 1882. Thomson's total of 286, the lowest winning score at Hoylake, was three strokes below that of F. van Donck (Belgium).

There is little more that can be written of this remarkable young man, not yet 27 years old, that has not been said in other years and will not be said again. It is beginning to seem that Thomson can win this Championship as often as he pleases and, indeed, continue to do so until some golfer, his equal in competitive ability, can be found to challenge him. His place as one of the greatest international golfers of all times is as assured, and as Hogan's career draws to a close there is probably no finer golfer in the world to-day. Without question there is no greater competitor, for winning championships is so much more a matter of character than of technique.

Not since Walter Hagen has one seen a champion about whom the aura of success has shone so brightly, nor one so relaxed, so assured, so composed, or so completely at ease with himself and the world. His swift striding figure, with the club gently swinging, and the enigmatic smile as if wondering what all the fuss is about, is becoming a permanent part of the long summer scene. There is no reason why Thomson should not win again at Muirfield next year even if Middlecoff and company dare to venture out of their dollar kingdom, which they probably will not. Because of the insularity of so many leading American golfers Thomson must be ranked above them.

The first Open is always the hardest to win, but this was not quite as straightforward as the formality of the final act would suggest. It is never easy to go on doing what is expected of one. This morning Thomson must have known that he ought to be champion again, and there seemed to be moments when uncertainty was his companion, as if perhaps he doubted for the first time the power of his destiny. His manner did not suggest it but he had to work very hard for his 72 this morning and the early holes this afternoon were not played with his usual abundant confidence. But gradually, as victory became even more inevitable than it had been on Wednesday, the tension lightened and he cruised to victory as easily and comfortably as he had done at St Andrews.

The outcome of the whole day depended upon whether van Donck and Vicenzo, who were out almost two hours ahead of Thomson, could set a difficult or even unreachable target. Vicenzo put himself out of court immediately by starting 6, 4, 6, this morning. Three putts on the first and a bunkered tee shot to the third are easy enough mistakes to make, but they set Vicenzo off on the wrong foot and deprived him of the inspiration Latin golfers need more than most. His 79 was unworthy of him, and attention turned to van Donck, whose beginning was nothing less than inspired. He actually reached the turn in 33, figures which speak for themselves; they were achieved by beautifully accurate, elegant golf supported by fine putting.

The first of the setbacks against which van Donck was to fight so bravely, and which even the finest players rarely can avoid at Hoylake, came immediately. Twice van Donck held his shots too much into the left-hand wind from the sea and his second to the tenth finished in an awkward spot. He could not get his third near the hole and took three putts. But he thrust this six behind him, continued as if nothing had happened, and made only one further mistake when he cut his long second shot to the fifteenth. This probably did not matter for the hole was out of range in two.

Meanwhile Thomson also had begun perfectly. The first five holes were passed in eighteen strokes, and then the Briars claimed him as it had so many others. His drive was pulled out of bounds and the fine start had been counterbalanced. But Thomson had the priceless attritube of a champion in that he never falters twice in succession; he either redeems or at worst checks any suggestion of collapse. But there were slight signs of doubt about his choice of clubs for the rest of the round, and possibly because of this he was not hitting his shots into the greens as accurately as usual. At the seventeenth he saved his four with a superb shot from a bunker with the road immediately beyond the green. The crucial third round then was safety behind him, and he had three strokes in hand on van Donck and five on Bertolino, whose nine fives had condemned him to a moderate score.

The beginning of van Donck's final round was the crux of the whole Championship and examined his character to the full. If he could return another 70 then a great finish was in prospect. But immediately any idea of this vanished. His drive to the first lay on one of the grassy mounds to the left of the fairway. Unwisely he took wood and paid the penalty. The ball drifted out of bounds and ultimately he was faced with a putt of seven feet for his six. Gallantly he holed it. The second shot to the Road hole was a short pitch downwind. Van Donck overhit, and wide at that, and the ball almost reached the wall by the third tee.

He then chipped from 25 yards almost into the hole. This escape steadied him and so beautifully was he putting that there seemed no question of any disaster now. But leaving the pin unattended has become almost a fetish and cost van Donck two strokes to-day which might have made a difference. At the sixth a long approach putt gently struck the pin and would have fallen just as another would on the eighteenth this morning. Although he again played the ninth indifferently he was out in 38. Handsome, cool, and assured, he came home in 36, failing to get his par figure only at the twelfth, where his second slipped with the wind below the green on the right. With three holes to play he and Vicenzo, who had thrust himself back into the picture with some splendid golf, were level. Van Donck played these holes in faultless fours and just edged Vicenzo out of second place.

The setting, as Thomson moved out in pursuit of van Donck for the last time, did the heart good. The overcast had gone, the breeze stood firm from the sea, and the sun shone hot from the deep blue sky. Everywhere about the links the large crowds clustered after their favourites. He began a little unsteadily by chipping weakly from beside the first green, missing from four feet for his four on the third, and underclubbing to the fifth. Two strokes had gone, but he played the sixth perfectly in four and then, on the seventh, chipped short from behind the green.

It was most important that he should get his three here. He holed from six feet and all was well. By the time he had reached the turn in 37 van Donck and Vicenzo were done and the Championship was his if he could come back in 39. Failure never for a moment seemed likely. A superb long iron shot finished within four feet of the twelfth hole and he missed the putt, but, after a three at the short hole, he came to the last long holes with several insurance strokes in hand. His second shot to the fourteenth was a little fortunate to escape a bunker; he showed his appreciation by chipping dead from well short of the green. He played the last four holes safely.

Another beautiful pitch and run from fifty yards made his four at the sixteenth, he drew his iron shot away from the road to the seventeenth, and in spite of its presence played another bold bunker shot. Now he could take six strokes on the last hole and win. Four were enough.

There were many who contributed with their golf, personality, and presence, to this day but only the barest justice can be shown them. Precedence must be given to Cotton who, by his golf throughout the week and especially this morning, once again emphasised that he still, in his fiftieth year, has no equal as a stroke maker among British golfers. He loves the challenge of a great links in the wind, and, after dropping two strokes owing to a plugged ball in a bunker at the fourth hole, played superbly. His inward half was magnificent. He started back 4, 3, holed a long putt for a three at the twelfth, got his three at the Rushes, and with a glorious spoon down the tiny alley of the fourteenth to within six feet had yet another three. The fifteenth he could not reach in two and this brought his only five. He completed a memorable round wth a perfect pitch to the eighteenth and had come back in 32, the finest nine holes of the Championship.

Young Player won himself fourth place with two splendid rounds. His golf increases in stature with every widening step in experience. Panton, who seems to be casting off the defensive shackles which have hampered him in recent years, returned to his old solid best. He was faithfully followed throughout the day by a gallery whose Scottish fervour far outdid that of the larger crowds.

The scores

286: P.W. Thomson (Australia), holder 70, 70, 72 74

289: F. van Donck (Belgium) 71, 74, 70, 74

290: R. de Vicenzo (Mexico) 71, 70, 79, 70

291: G. Player (South Africa) 71, 76, 73, 71

292: J. Panton (Glenbervie) 74, 76, 72, 70

293: T.H. Cotton (Temple) 72, 76, 71, 74; E. Bertolino (Argentina) 69, 72, 76, 76

294: A. Cerda (Argentina) 72, 81, 68, 73; M. Souchak (USA) 74, 74, 74, 72

295: C. O'Connor (Bundoran) 73, 78, 74, 70;
H. Weetman (Croham Hurst) 72, 76, 75, 72

LOCKE WINS HIS FOURTH OPEN

Thomson defeated by three strokes

By Pat Ward-Thomas

St Andrews took over from Muirfield because of the Suez crisis and petrol shortages. For the first time leaders went out last in the final two rounds but it made little difference to the leading names involved. Locke won his fourth Open by three shots from Thomson.

A.D. Locke (South Africa) achieved probably the greatest performance of his wonderful career in winning the Open Golf Championship at St Andrews with the remarkable total of 279 (69, 72, 68, 70). This equals his own record for the event made at Troon seven years ago, and was three strokes ahead of P.W. Thomson, the holder these past three years.

This is Locke's fourth victory in the Open, a number equalled only by Hagen since the far-off days of Vardon. Braid, and Taylor. This victory was all the more remarkable because Locke, who first won the title in 1949, had given signs in the last season or so that he had passed his best. But this summer, since he came to Britain, he has been playing admirably and throughout this week always seemed likely to threaten Thomson, although it must be confessed that one did not think he would maintain such a wonderful level of scoring throughout six rounds. For he led the qualifiers as well.

The weather certainly was in Locke's favour, for he loves the sun on his back. The course was not playing long and the greens were holding in every round. Thus, his superb judgment of length in pitching was fully rewarded and he putted as unfallibly as of old, with the same faithful hickory putter. No man even had a truer friend. Also the shape of the old course suited his preference for hitting from right to left. But none of this would have been of much avail without highly consistent striking. His swing has been shortened slightly, probably because of advancing years and girth and is, perhaps, a shade quicker than it used to be, but the rhythm was as implacably smooth as ever, and he hardly played a false stroke all week.

And so the great Thomson lost the title which he had held since the evening at Birkdale three summers ago when he took it from Locke. It was fitting that if he lost it it should be to Locke. Not until the sixteenth hole in the last round was one convinced that he would lose it, for at that point he needed 3–4–4 to finish in 68 and a total of 280, which was the one he had anticipated before the Championship began would be good enough. If he could have achieved this Locke would have had to play the last four holes in level fours to win, against the fresh easterly wind. Thomson hit a superb long pitch, one of a countless number, to within five feet of the sixteenth but he misread the lines and missed. His drive to the seventeenth was cut a shade and finished on the path by the railway sheds, just as it had in the morning. Again he played a remarkable recovery, but this time failed to get down in a chip and a putt for his four.

This meant that Locke, two couples behind, was able to play the Road hole in a safe five, and then the noblest setting in all golf awaited him. On either side of the long, lonely sward up to the clubhouse and

Tom Morris's green, thousands upon thousands massed on either hand. The sun blazed from the pure cool skies and the most precious moment in a golfer's life was Locke's. Thinking, wrongly as it proved, that he needed a four to win, he hit his drive hard across the road, and then in the manner of a great champion pitched to within a foot of the hole.

St Andrews Old Course

Out			In		
Hole	Name	Yards	Hole	Name	Yards
1	The Burn	374	10	Tenth	338
2	Dyke	412	10	High	173
3	Cartgate	400	12	Heathery	360
4	Ginger Beer	439	16	Hole O'Cross	427
5	Hole O'Cross	567	14	Long	560
6	Heathery	377	15	Cartgate	413
7	High	364	16	Corner of the Dyke	382
8	Short	163			
9	End	357	17	Road	453
			18	Tom Morris	383
		3,453			3,489

Total length: 6,942 yards

If the Championship be reduced to one essential fact it was that putting was decisive. When conditions are favourable for low scoring and remain standard throughout the event this is inevitable. This week it was not a question of avoiding three putts but of holing out fairly frequently in one. Thomson's accuracy into the green with medium and short irons was magnificent, and unsurpassed in one's experience for its trueness of striking and judgment. Apart from his drives to the seventeenth every other one was in the right place, but sadly he did not hole sufficient putts, although he appeared to be striking the ball well and always attacked the hole.

At the day's outset there was the prospect of many players being bunched together and even a tie seemed horribly real, but before the third round was over it was obvious that the destiny of the title lay between the two supreme golfers of the Commonwealth and two of the greatest competitors of all time. Middlecoff continued to play impressively except on the greens, where again he took 38 putts and was gone; Cerda squandered a brilliant start with a sad succession of fives coming home; Brown, the leader, who usually hits from right to left, betrayed anxiety by pushing a couple of early drives at some cost. But once the prospect of victory had gone he played steadily and well and eventually missed from eight feet to tie with Thomson. Crampton collapsed and stayed more or less collapsed after taking eight at the fifth in the morning; the strokes slipped away from van Donck, and ultimately Locke, with a superb 68, led Thomson, who was round in 70, by three strokes at lunch.

Thomson should have reduced the lead immediately after perfect pitches to within five feet of the first and third. But a superb four iron to the fourth brought a three which a few minutes later Locke equalled with an even more accurate second shot. Then Thomson, after a long wait on the fifth fairway, mishit his wooden club second, was bunkered, and took six. But his unshakable poise did not falter and five beautifully played threes in succession from the seventh hole made him four under fours. Meanwhile Locke had also reached the turn steadily and uneventfully in 34 and thus had maintained his lead.

It became desperately necessary for Thomson to hole a good putt, but on the fourteenth and fifteenth possible ones slipped by the hole and then came the last error on the sixteenth. Locke's only anxious moment was at the fourteenth, which long years ago cost him a chance of a Championship. He played too far left with his third shot, but produced a masterly stroke from one of the little bunkers and got his five. Two perfectly safe fours followed, and then the Championship was his.

For several others this was a memorable day, particularly for an amateur, W.D. Smith, whose consistency was beyond all praise. He finished joint fifth and played with a steadiness and accuracy that must have been the envy of almost everyone in the field. Perhaps the Scottish selectors will now consider him worthy of a place in his country's side. In finishing fourth A. Miguel, the French Open champion, accomplished his finest performance in Britain; Thomas, with two admirable seventies on this last day, took another step towards the great fulfilment which should be his; Haliburton played beautifully all day in what was, if memory serves, his most distinguished performance in the Open; and Alliss, who began with a three in his last round and then holed his next second shot, once again proved, as in every tournament this season, that he has mastered the art of consistent scoring.

The scores

279: A.D. Locke (South Africa) 69, 72, 68, 70

282: P.W. Thomson (Australia) 73, 69, 70, 70

283: E.C. Brown (Buchanan Castle) 67, 72, 73, 71

285: A. Miguel (Spain) 72, 72, 69, 72

286: D.C. Thomas (Sudbury) 72, 74, 70, 70; Mr W.D. Smith (Prestwick) 71, 72, 72, 71; F. van Donck (Belgium) 72, 68, 74, 72; T.B. Haliburton (Wentworth) 72, 73, 68, 73

287: T.H. Cotton (Temple) 74, 72, 69, 72; M. Faulkner (St George's Hill) 74, 70, 71, 72; A. Cerda (Argentina) 71, 71, 72, 73

1958

Lytham St Annes, 5th & 7th July

THOMAS AND THOMSON IN STIRRING FINISH

Play-off to-day over 36 holes

By Pat Ward-Thomas

5th July

One of the most extraordinary finishes to any Open Golf Championship of modern times resulted in a tie between P.W. Thomson (Australia) and D.C. Thomas (Sudbury) at Royal Lytham yesterday. They will meet to-day over 36 holes in the first play-off since A.D. Locke and H. Bradshaw tied at Sandwich nine years ago. Their total of 278, the lowest ever recorded in the Open, was one stroke below that of E.C. Brown and C. O'Connor.

In a lifetime of watching golf one might never again experience a last hour like this one, because the event came perilously close to being a quintuple tie. Briefly the situation was that Brown, an hour ahead of Thomas and Thomson who, fortunately for the thousands watching, were paired together, had finished in 279. He had taken six at the last hole, and while he was suffering the agonies of the damned, Thomas and Thomson had five holes to play and eventually came to the last needing fours to beat him. Meanwhile O'Connor and Ruiz, who in the minds of the spectators and probably their own, were out of the reckoning, suddenly came with a brilliant rush and there they were also, incredibly, needing fours to tie. After Thomas and Thomson had finished they both drove into bunkers. Ruiz thereupon made a sorry mess of the hole, but O'Connor made a brave attempt to get down in two from 80 yards. He just failed to hole a long putt for his four. These were the bare facts. Their fashioning makes a brave wonderful story because of the superb golf of Thomas.

There has been no greater performance by a young British golfer in modern times and whether Thomas becomes champion or not nothing can ever tarnish the memory of a glorious day. Fortune blessedly had paired them together and, although Thomas was apprehensive of the prospect he soon realised that playing with Thomson was an immense advantage. The way in which he stayed with him shot for shot all through the long day was quite magnificent. Not only for the supremely high quality and power of his golf under the severest pressure but for the character and courage behind it. This was exciting and heartening to those of us who have had faith in Thomas as the finest British golfer of the next generation.

At Lytham, Thomson beat Dave Thomas by four shots in a thirty-six-hole play-off for his fourth victory in five years.

The story begins in the morning, long before the sun had melted the greyness into soft summer skies. It will be remembered that O'Connor and Ruiz were the leaders and straightaway it seemed that the Open, such a searching test of a man's vulnerable points, was finding them out just as, hours later, it was to find Brown wanting. On the way home O'Connor putted ill, even on these perfect greens, and Ruiz learned that rough would not always forgive. Gradually they slipped from the picture.

Thomas and Thomson, immediately ahead, were away to a tremendous start. Detail does not matter now. The simple fact was that Thomson went out in 32, Thomas in 33, and although the Australian gained another stroke with a colossal putt on the fifteenth Thomas was round in 69 and only two behind. Meanwhile Brown and van Donck had moved in as the challengers and pacemakers. At the turn Brown was nowhere, but suddenly a wonderful inspiration charged his puttting. He holed five ranging from five to twenty feet for threes and was home in 30 – surely the only man in history to do this twice in an Open. His 65 put him only three behind Thomson at lunch, with a glorious chance of getting his blow in first afterwards. The same was true of van Donck, whose 67, beautifully played in his own calm, courtly, stylish manner had put him a shot ahead of Brown. And so the scene was set for a wonderful afternoon.

Brown, still on the crest of confidence, went to the turn in 34, in spite of a six, but poor van Donck, after starting with two threes, let his drive fade with the wind out of bounds at the third and thereafter slipped quietly out of mind. Now came the heroes on to a crowded, sunlit stage, and immediately Thomas stirred hopes with a two at the first. Thomson drove into the rough at the third and they were level, but, like a great player, restored his lead with a superb three at the sixth. Thus, it went almost stroke for stroke until Thomas took three putts on three consecutive greens after the turn, twice from inside Thomson. When he missed the fourteenth fairway, his first wide drive of the day and was well short of the hole in three, all seemed over. But gallantly he holed from eight yards and still was only two behind.

By now the news of Brown's appalling failure had filtered back. As one had watched him miss the fourteenth and fifteenth fairways the truth came to mind yet again that an uncertain driver cannot win an Open. The fresh wind from the north-west had come just in time to make the finish brave and challenging. It settled Brown's fate. Two fives at these holes were partly redeemed by a fine three at the sixteenth, but the hole was utterly destroyed when he drove into a bunker at the eighteenth, ultimately putted just too strong for his four, and missed the one back. A four there and he would probably have been champion. He may never get so near again.

The fifteenth, more than any other hole, compelled the tie. Thomson pulled slightly from the tee into rough, put his third into a bunker, came out short, and took six. Thomas hit a beautiful two-iron shot boring into the wind, one of the finest strokes imaginable, got his four easily, and was level again. He then hit an enormous drive to the sixteenth and pitched perfectly to within seven feet. Thomson missed from six yards for his three, and then smiled as Thomas holed to a shattering acclaim.

The excitement now was almost unbearable. Thomas was actually, unbelievably, one ahead of his formidable companion. Vast and composed, he towered between his guardian police up the seventeenth after two perfect drives down the right. Thomson found the green with a fine shot then Thomas, as he said later, felt all tight on the shot, and who could blame him. He struck it heavy, was bunkered well short, but bravely made his five with a great approach putt. Each drove safely down the eighteenth, now a menacing tee shot into the wind. Thomas pitched rather wide on the green. Thomson beautifully, typically, fifteen feet past the hole. Thomas putted two feet past and then Thomson's putt for the title was always a little wide and Thomas had his to tie. He confessed that only then did he fully realise the awesome fact. Most sensibly he had banished scores from his head all day and played every hole as it came. But his putt went straight in, and two golfers, who had made a page of memorable history, beamed at one another.

A last tribute on this wonderful day must go to two supreme champions of other times, would that one could write more than the remarkable facts. T.H. Cotton, in his fifty-first year with a 69, 72, actually finished eighth. And the great Sarazen celebrated his American Independence Day with the distinction of finishing fifteenth with a total of level fours. He will remember his visits as long as we shall remember him.

THOMSON MAINTAINS SPELL OVER OPEN TITLE

But Thomas again calm and courageous

By Pat Ward-Thomas

7th July

P.W. Thomson (Australia), with a total of 139 (68, 71) won the Open Golf Championship for the fourth time in five years when he beat D.C. Thomas (Sudbury), 143 (69, 74), by four strokes in the 36 holes play-off at Lytham on Saturday.

Thus the Commonwealth, represented by Locke and Thomson, continue to dominate the Open Championship to a remarkable degree. Between them they have now won eight times since 1948, a sequence broken only by Faulkner and Hogan, and surpassing even the spell that Walter Hagen and R.T. Jones passed over the Championship in the twenties.

Although in one's heart of hearts it never seemed likely that the wonderful dream of a young British champion could be realised the possibility was there for 27 holes on this warm, airless day. There has been nothing finer in many a long year than the calmness, poise, and courage of Thomas in standing up to a really formidable competitor. Infinitely more experienced in the ways and strains of winning. Only once, at the sixteenth on Friday afternoon, did Thomas lead and then only for a moment. Yet never did his resolution or his superbly powerful striking falter until the strain of constantly playing the second shot first and of sustaining concentration in round after round began to tell. Then only was Thomson able to take the destiny of the Championship within his cool, strong hands.

Marathons such as this are rare and the full scores of the players, including the qualifying rounds, are revealing. Thomson: 63, 70, 66, 72, 67, 73, 68, 71. Thomas: 70, 70, 70, 68, 69, 71, 69, 74. These figures of Thomas are a striking tribute to the exceptional consistency of his golf. His driving and iron play were exciting, stimulating in their power and straightness. This huge young man, over sixteen stone and well over six feet, is not yet 24. But he is enormously strong, his swing is simple, and he hits great distances without any effort. The soft, holding greens suited him admirably and prevented too great a strain from being placed on his short game. This is not yet absolutely first-class but his putting generally was splendid and his method excellent. And, in addition, he has presence, modesty, and good manners.

It was strange how the morning round followed the pattern of the previous evening. In the still, warm air Thomson began with ruthless perfection. He holed long putts on the second, sixth, and seventh, produced a masterly chip at the eighth and was out in 31. But the massive, easy calm of Thomas was undisturbed even when his second rather unluckily went through the eleventh and he was four strokes behind. When Thomson cut his drive to the fourteenth and his second, badly, to the fifteenth, Thomas was ready with impressively easy fours. Yet again Thomas pitched close to the sixteenth hole, got his three, and again lost the stroke immediately by pulling from the seventeenth tee. When he holed a putt of six yards on the eighteenth, Thomson missed from inside that distance and went into lunch looking serious – as indeed he might. He was only one ahead.

Strokes were exchanged at the first three holes afterwards, Thomas drawing level with a majestic four-iron shot to within two feet of the third hole. Four perfect pars followed and it began to seem as if the break would never come. But when it did it happened suddenly. From the front of the eighth green Thomson putted very short. Thomas chipped well inside him but he missed, and Thomson holed. This made Thomson one ahead and then the tenth settled it – a perfect pitch by Thomson, a weakish one from Thomas followed by three putts. Thomson holed his and was three ahead. He gained another stroke with a superb chip almost into the eleventh hole, and although Thomas got one back at the fourteenth Thomson was yielding no more. The fact that Thomas took three putts on the seventeenth and the champion as many on the eighteenth mattered not at all. A memorable week, admirably planned and organised by the club and containing so much that will not lightly be forgotten, had come to a fitting conclusion in the still, evening sunshine.

The scores

278: P.W. Thomson (Australia) 66, 72, 67, 73; D.C. Thomas (Sudbury) 70, 68, 69, 71

Play-off: Thomson 68, 71 139
Thomas 69, 74 143

279: E.C. Brown (Buchanan Castle) 73, 70, 65, 71; C. O'Connor (Killarney) 67, 68, 73, 71

281: L. Ruiz (Argentina) 71, 65, 72, 73; F. van Donck (Belgium) 70, 70, 67, 74

283: G.J. Player (South Africa) 68, 74, 70, 71

284: H. Weetman (Selsdon Park) 73, 67, 73, 71; T.H. Cotton (Temple) 68, 75, 69, 72; E.G. Lester (Hazel Grove) 73, 66, 71, 74

G. PLAYER STRIDES RUTHLESSLY TO OPEN VICTORY

Van Donck once more near the top

By Pat Ward-Thomas

Gary Player's 1959 victory at Muirfield was achieved in spite of a first-round seventy-five and a six at the 72nd.

G. Player (South Africa) continued the Commonwealth domination of the Open Golf Championship at Muirfield yesterday. His total of 284 (75, 71, 70, 68) reads like a sequence of Hogan's at his greatest – a ruthless improvement. Two strokes behind were F. van Donck and F. Bullock; S.S. Scott was fourth; and R.R. Jack, the leading amateur, finished joint fifth with 288, a magnificent performance.

Player's final round would have been one of the greatest in the history of the Championship but for the anti-climax on the last hole. A four would have given him a 66 and an unapproachable total. He was a little quick with the tee shot, pulled into one of the bunkers, pitched his third weakly short, and took three putts. This was sad in that it spoiled a wonderfully impressive exhibition of striking, and prolonged the outcome of the Championship by well over an hour.

Scott, Cerda, and van Donck now could tie if they came home in 34, and Bullock in 33. This was a tremendous order against the strict par of 35 in a firm wind, and one by one they failed. At the very end van Donck and Bullock came to the last great hole needing threes to tie, but Bullock was bunkered from the tee, and van Donck, after going for his putt from the front edge of the green, missed the one back.

The shape of victory became clear as Player reached the afternoon turn in 34. He had gained a stroke with a fine shot to the fifth and a good putt, and he played the ninth, still menacing as ever, in a safe five. In fact, he missed a holeable putt for his four. This hole more than any other had played a decisive part in the Championship. It had destroyed Thomson. Van Donck also had a seven there in the first round, and two hours after Player he took a tired, laboured six. This was his undoing in spite of a most unyielding finish. He had played most accomplished beautiful golf yet again in the Open.

Jack also had a six at the ninth just as Player in the couple ahead was getting a memorable three at the tenth. A long second held the wind beautifully and a ten-foot putt with a borrow of several inches went straight in. After a safe four Player had his one uneasy moment. An iron, pushed under the wind, drifted off the twelfth green and he recovered over strongly. But he holed from six yards for his four. One felt certain then that he would win.

Player set about confirming expectation by pitching eight feet from the thirteenth and holing for a two. The fourteenth was still out of range, and he just failed to make his four, but a two iron rifled to within twelve feet of the fifteenth hole, and another pitch ended four feet from the sixteenth. He missed the first putt, holed the second for another two, and the championship was over if he could finish with two fours. He got the first of these, and then came the last hole and, for him at least, an agony of suspense.

Player, at 23, is one of the best tournament golfers in the world. His record in the United States and this victory are overwhelming proof, and he deserves the fruits of success. Few young men have ever worked so hard or applied themselves with such determination as Player. In technique he was with Thomson the most accomplished golfer in this field. The evidence of watching him as long ago as Tuesday confirmed that, and victory was no surprise

After a melancholy night of pitiless rain the course was playing its full length and the greens were rich and easy, and a brave, challenging wind stood hard from the west, keeping the rain at bay. Mercifully it was constant all day, so that no one got away with it as several had been doing. It was precisely the wind a connoisseur would have chosen for the last day of a championship.

The first setting of the pace fell to Jack, whose 68 was a masterly example of control. He turned in 35, made one error of judgment at the fifteenth, but finished with a long putt on the sixteenth, two superb strokes, a drive and four iron, to the eighteenth, and a putt of twelve feet for his three. At lunch S.L. King and Bullock led with 212 and Ruiz, Rees, Hitchcock, and van Donck were 213, a stroke ahead of Jack and Bonallack.

Not since R.H. Wethered at St Andrews had a British amateur stood in a strong position to win the Championship. Jack, fully aware of this, hit the ball well nigh perfectly going out and never defensively. The thought that he might set a severe target, even win, persisted until the ninth, where his drive drifted into heavy rough, his second was again in rough, and the six which resulted made him out in 36. This was just too many and, although one or two strokes slipped coming home, he had completed a proud total.

Bonallack, playing all day in the penultimate couple, did splendidly in keeping going throughout. Wolstenholme finished his Championship in the majestic manner by holing a two-iron shot to the last green. Carr had rather a disappointing day, but the golf of the four amateurs throughout the week, three within seven shots of the winner, is a shining beacon for the future. It has done much to banish the memory of the Walker Cup and to render foolish the outpourings of little minds who were wise after the event.

There are golfers who almost invariably give of their best in the Open, and Scott and King are of these. Scott was never quite in the hunt for victory, but 144 for the final day was splendid golf spoiled only by a sad seventeenth hole. His drive finished in a horrible hanging lie or he might have joined van Donck and Bullock in the pursuit of threes to tie on the last hole. It is not hard to imagine Bullock's thoughts during the term of his leadership. Ambition and apprehension, hope and courage must all have passed through his mind, and perhaps resignation, but he went on playing his game until the very end and can be proud of his performance.

It was good that S.L. King had such a fine Championship. He has played little tournament golf recently and has had more important anxieties. His 67 in the morning was the lowest round of all, fashioned as always with marvellously straight hitting. He has been one of the most natural of golfers whose game has remained as unaffected and simple, as much an expression of himself, as it was years ago when he learned to play while making clubs from switches of hazel. To King the stirring of the seasons and the peace of nature mean more than the missing of putts. This was one of the happiest things of a beautifully organised Championship in a links which was the admiration of all.

The scores

*Amateur

284: G.J. Player (South Africa) 75, 71, 70, 68

286: F. van Donck (Belgium) 70, 70, 73, 73; F. Bullock (Prestwick St Nicholas) 68, 70, 74, 74

287: S.S. Scott (Roehampton) 73, 70, 73, 71

288: C. O'Connor (R Dublin) 73, 74, 72, 69; J. Panton (Glenbervie) 72, 72,. 71, 73; *Mr R.R. Jack (Dullatur) 71, 75, 68, 74; S.L. King (Knole Park) 70, 74, 68, 76

289: D.J. Rees (South Herts) 73, 73, 69, 74; L. Ruiz (Argentina) 72, 74, 69, 74

1960

NAGLE WINS CENTENARY OPEN CHAMPIONSHIP

A memorable contest with Palmer

By Pat Ward-Thomas

K.D.G. Nagle, a solid, likeable citizen of Australia, won a great and famous victory in the centenary Open Golf Championship at St Andrews on Saturday, after a memorable contest with A. Palmer, the most formidable competitor in the world today. Nagle's total, which equalled the lowest ever in the Open, was 278 (69, 67, 71, 71), one stroke less than Palmer's (70, 71, 70, 68).

This was, of course, the supreme achievement of Nagle's lifetime. His only other outstanding successes, apart from those in the Canada Cup as Thomson's partner, have been in Australia, where he is the open champion. He had won many tournaments there in much the same fashion as this one by making a lead and then holding it. He is known as a front runner. This needs no little strength of character, and if ever a triumph was one of character this one was. At the outset he led Palmer by four strokes and no doubt was more afraid of him than of Vicenzo, his partner, who as the pressure mounted began to miss crucial putts. Nagle knew that Palmer, immediately ahead of him, would set a severe pace, and he did by pitching almost dead at the first two holes for threes. Nagle withstood this knowledge with great heart to the very end.

With two holes to play he led Palmer by two strokes, and as he drove safely from the seventeenth tee Palmer was playing a shot of marvellous control from the bank down to the road. The American had driven too far to the left for a straight second shot but hit a fine, bold iron to the narrow green. The ball slipped over the side, but Palmer putted it up the bank to within a yard of the hole and had his four.

Prize money was up to £7,000 for 1960's Centenary Open at St Andrews, won by the Australian Kel Nagle by one shot from a young American, Arnold Palmer – a rising Ben Hogan in his own country but challenging for the first time with the small ball and bump-and-run approaches of the United Kingdom.

Nagle wisely played just in front of the green and then putted six feet short. By then Palmer had hit a prodigious drive up the eighteenth, the longest one had seen there, and pitched with a wedge four feet short of the hole.

Nagle heard the great cheers as Palmer's putt inevitably fell, and must have known that he had to hole his for victory. Like the brave man he is he struck it firmly home and now needed a four to win. The mob stampeded up the last fairway as Nagle walked towards his great moment, his rugged, handsome face tense and set. With admirable promptness he hit a superb pitch to within a yard of the hole, and now, for him, the dream of every golfer had come true, two putts for the Open from nowhere. He missed the first, but rapped a tiny one into the back and a remarkable Championship was over.

This victory preserved the Commonwealth domination of the Championship – ten victories in the last twelve years. It is easily explained, for its fashioning depended almost entirely on putting. Beyond any question Nagle is one of the great putters of the world. More than anything this put him in a winning position and helped him to maintain it, but there was more besides. He drove very safely and solidly throughout the tournament. A driver recently acquired in the United States had given him renewed confidence. He never played a rash, ill considered, or over-ambitious shot. His golf through the green was a perfect expression of the man himself in its unwavering steadiness. It was a wonderful basis for the medium of his attack, similar in effect, if certainly not in appearance, to that of Locke. At a conservative estimate he must have had ten fewer putts than Palmer over the four rounds.

It was not that Palmer putted poorly but he simply did not hole enough of the eight to fifteen feet range. A perfect example of this came before the turn. He missed from between six and eight feet on the tenth and eleventh, while Nagle holed from eight feet from the seventh and eighth. This enabled him to preserve his lead of four strokes well past the turn. The cause of Palmer's comparative putting failure is hard to determine and even his self-critical, observant mind was unable to explain it. Perhaps the answer lay in the fact that he paid overmuch attention to the slight falls and borrows about the hole, instead of putting straight at it, as those wise in the ways of the Old Course usually do. The greens were beautiful and easy in pace throughout the week and Palmer may well wonder how it was that he did not score in the sixties in every round.

Palmer admirably contained his disappointment at not equalling Hogan's feat of 1953. No doubt he was suspicious of the Old Course when he arrived and probably did not like it, but by Friday evening he was talking of its challenge and one felt that he was enjoying the strategic exercise that it set. As at Portmarnock he made a happy impression on everyone, as indeed did Nagle. No more agreeable men ever contested the last hour of a great championship.

The early play on this last day resolved itself into a question of whether a strict target could be set for the leaders. Carr, with a disastrous six at the second, and a dive at the ninth was out in 39. He rallied with great spirit and skill and in spite of a six at the seventeenth finished in 73. This was just too high. Scott was going splendidly until he became the one notable victim of out-of-bounds at the fourteenth. Then it fell to Henning and Hunt to make the pace. In every round Henning reached the turn in 33. This time he finished in a splendid 69. Hunt played perfectly for his 66, which equalled the record. Wolstenholme then had a great chance, having gone out in 31, playing and putting magnificently, but a four at the eleventh and a six at the fourteenth contained him to 68 and a total of 283, one stroke behind third place.

Hunt alone of the British professionals finished ahead of Wolstenholme, Carr, and Blair, who hit the ball beautifully throughout. Jack, in his last first-class event, played with splendid steadiness in every round. He shared fifteenth place. If ever a British Isles player wins the Open again – the last was Faulkner in 1951 – it is as likely to be an amateur as a professional, judging by the present standard.

The scores

*Amateur

278: K.D.G. Nagle (Australia) 69, 67, 71, 71

279: A. Palmer (USA) 70, 71, 70, 68

282: B.J. Hunt (Hartsbourne CC) 72, 73, 71, 66; H.R. Henning (South Africa) 72, 72, 69, 69; R. de Vicenzo (Mexico) 67, 67, 75, 73

283: *G.B. Wolstenholme (Sunningdale) 74, 70, 71, 68

284: G. Player (South Africa), holder, 72, 71, 72, 69

285: *J.B. Carr (Sutton) 72, 73, 67, 73

286: H. Weetman (Selsdon Park) 74, 70, 71, 71; S.S. Scott (Roehampton) 73, 71, 67, 75; D.J. Rees (South Herts) 73, 71, 73, 69; *D.A. Blair (Royal and Ancient) 70, 73, 71, 72; E.C. Brown (Buchanan Castle) 75, 68, 72, 71; P.W. Thomson (Australia) 72, 69, 75, 70

OPEN TRIUMPH PUTS PALMER AMONG THE GREAT PLAYERS

Courageous performance by Rees

By Pat Ward-Thomas

Another great golfer, in the powerful and personable figure of A. Palmer (Laurel Valley, Pennsylvania) has joined the illustrious list of those who have won the American and British Open Championships. Their names make a noble procession, Vardon, Ray, Hagen, Barnes, Armour, Jones, Sarazen and Hogan. Palmer is truly worthy of their company.

His right to victory was beyond dispute. Although the total of 284 (70, 73, 69, 72) was only one stroke less than that of the gallant Rees (68, 74, 71, 72) the margin in effect was greater. Palmer had holed his final putt before Rees approached the last green needing a two to tie, but this in no way diminishes a performance of sustained courage and endurance by Rees, who maintained his pursuit to the last putt of all with a wonderful finish of 3, 4, 3, 3.

It was always probable that Palmer would win, because he was immeasurably the strongest golfer in the field. At this time he is without doubt supreme to the world. Victory in Britain may not mean a great deal to some American golfers who, understandably perhaps, prefer to remain at home and gather dollars in the sunshine than make what must appear to be a hazardous pilgrimage, but it is more than that. For an American golfer to succeed in conditions that are entirely foreign to those of his own land requires an ability, not only to adapt his technique but to revise his strategy and thinking. The change of ball in itself must be trying, particularly in becoming used to its greater liveliness in the short shots. Obviously, in the winds that afflicted Birkdale, a small ball has an advantage, but it still requires altered judgment of length and flight, as well as the fact that it lies tighter on the turf. Palmer, like Hogan eight years ago, mastered these things as only a great golfter could have done.

Arnold Palmer's first victory at Birkdale in 1961 led to the restoration of the Open as the world's premier championship. He mastered wind and small ball as only a great golfer could, Ward-Thomas wrote.

Finally, there is the fact of a desire to compete in the Championship which, with Palmer, goes beyond the acquisition of a title. Financially victory means comparatively little to the man whose income must be in the region of £70,000 a year or more. But his presence last summer and this, and probably next year at Troon, where he has already reserved accommodation, revealed one of the true qualities of greatness. There is in him a will to learn all there is to know about the playing of this game, to make his technique as complete as possible, and to overcome the personal challenge that varying conditions can offer.

Palmer had the courage and the ambition to accept this challenge and, at the second time of asking, has conquered. He will have returned to the United States yesterday a proud and deserving golfer, and one of the most likeable champions of all. In the great event of the modern world Hogan alone has a greater tally of success, and when he won the two Opens and the Masters in the one summer of 1953 he was ten years older than Palmer. The same achievement has taken Palmer 15 months, and imagination boggles at the thought of what the future may bring if his ambition so desires it.

There was an awful suspense about the early hours of this last day. Would the weather hold and avoid the ghastly anticlimax of abandonment, and also spare the wrath that would have descended upon the championship committee? By the grace of some benevolent fate it did, and although the skies frequently menaced, and there was an hour or so of rain astride noon time, the course played remarkably well, and was a great compliment to the greenkeepers.

The pattern of the day was set on the very first hole, still exceedingly difficult into a fresh wind. Palmer played it in four, Nagle, his companion, in five, and a moment later Rees and Henning, the last pair, took seven and six respectively. This meant that Palmer was in front, and for the rest of the long day no one ever drew level with him. As on Thursday it seemed that command was to be his from the outset. He went to the turn in 32, having made no semblance of serious error that was not immediately redeemed by superb chipping and holing out. There was an inevitability about the sight of his strong, hard figure bent low over the ball, with knees locked together, arms close to the body and firm low stroke. This putting, and his formidably powerful, controlled striking, suggested a ruthless progress to victory, but it was far from being so.

There came a moment, again on the sixteenth, when it appeared that the Championship might not be his after all. His drive failed to clear the left-hand hill; his third shot flew high on to the scrub-covered dune above the right-hand side of the green, and was within inches of being unplayable, and a few feet from the out-of-bounds fence. Thence he played a marvellous stroke, cut up deeply, which fell within two feet of the hole. He deserved this fortune after his cruel experience in the second round.

Meanwhile, Rees, playing with the determination so typical of him, had redeemed his seven by the turn, came storming home in 71 and had maintained his position, only a stroke behind. But O'Connor, it was, who had the round of the morning, a beautifully played 67. Watching the effortless rhythm and confidence of his iron-play to the soft greens it seemed that he could well make Palmer's final task severe, for he was six holes ahead, but inspiration left him after lunch and 73 was not quite good enough.

Nagle, as was feared, could not quite withstand the pressure of playing with Palmer, and although he came back strongly when hope of keeping his title had almost gone, he was six behind at lunch. The retirement of Player owing to food poisoning was most unfortunate for him, and also for White, but he did win the distinction of being leading amateur, finishing three strokes ahead of Christmas.

The task of pacemaking fell, therefore, first on O'Connor, and then on Coles and Thomson. Coles played beautifully throughout the day, with a quiet poise and confidence that emphatically confirmed his recent swift progress. He is clearly in the highest company as a striker, and should now be certain of a place in the Ryder Cup team. Even at the end his swing never lost its rhythm and to tie third with O'Connor was an exceptional performance. The afternoon made splendid watching, and there was even sunshine for a while. Palmer's putting had lost its morning deadliness, save at the sixth, where an unwise overclub from the tee into a bunker might have cost him a stroke. He missed several holeable putts around the turn for threes, but his golf through the green now was implacably solid. It was clear that if he could come home in the par of 36 no one could catch him. He did miss the thirteenth green, not for the first time, but immediately redeemed a stroke with two immensely powerful hits up the fourteenth, and what proved to be a crucial putt of eight feet for his four.

Palmer's drive to the fifteenth was pushed, and lay a foot from the fairway inches deep in scrub. Then we saw the last, and perhaps the most vivid, example of the frightful strength in his hands. He used a six iron, where most people would have been hoping with a blaster, and, hitting with all his might, he crashed the ball on to the green, a carry of some 140 yards. A phenomenal stroke. There were no more crises; he nearly had a four at the sixteenth, hit a perfect shot to the seventeenth, a huge drive straight down the last fairway, a firm controlled approach to the back of the green for an unshakeable four, and the task of Rees was hopeless. It was fitting that the last, and most moving moment of all these days should belong to Rees, for his unyielding courage, wonderful fitness, and enduring skill.

The scores

284: Arnold Palmer (USA) 70, 73, 69, 72

285: D.J. Rees (South Herts) 68, 74, 71, 72

288: N.C. Coles (Coombe Hill) 70, 77, 69, 72; C. O'Connor (R Dublin) 71, 77, 67, 73

289: E.C. Brown (unattached) 73, 76, 70, 70; K.D.G. Nagle (Australia) 68, 75, 75, 71

290: P.W. Thomson (Australia) 75, 72, 70, 73

291: K. Bousfield (Coombe Hill) 71, 77, 75, 68; P. Alliss (Parkstone) 73, 75, 72, 71

293: S.S. Scott (Roehampton) 76, 75, 71, 71; H. Henning (South Africa) 68, 74, 75, 76

1962

Troon, 14th July

PALMER'S ATTACK AND CONTROL MAKE HIM A GREAT CHAMPION

Nagle's gallant struggle proves in vain

By Pat Ward-Thomas

Palmer won again at Troon in 1962 with 'the greatest exhibition of golfing supremacy Britain has seen in modern times'. His aggregate of 276 was a record and his six-stroke margin over Nagle the greatest since Hagen in 1929. Yet, to Ward-Thomas, 'for all the sum of his mighty achievement in title and money, Palmer remains a delightful, friendly human being who commands respect and affection.' A chubby young American named Jack Nicklaus had a first-round eighty including a ten at the eleventh hole.

The victory of Arnold Palmer in the Open Championship at Troon was the greatest exhibiton of golfing supremacy that Britain has seen in modern times. It was a rout without parallel. Palmer's total of 276 (71, 69, 67, 69), was two strokes lower than the previous record, and his winning margin, six ahead of the gallant Nagle, was the largest since Hagen won at Muirfield in 1929. Palmer was 13 strokes ahead of B.H.G. Huggett and P. Rodgers.

Nagle so richly deserved to be second, for he had withstood the pressure of playing with Palmer in most courageous fashion throughout the day and, at its end, had endured the acute discomfort and discourtesy inflicted upon members by the disgusting exhibition of a huge stampeding crowd. Never has one seen such a revolting disregard for stewards and police; the players and caddies might well have been injured on the last hole, and heaven knows what would have happened had Palmer or Nagle had a corpuscle of Scottish blood in his veins. Fortunately they are men of abundant good nature. The whole conception of stewarding must be revived. It was pathetically inadequate for crowds which behave in this manner.

This day was so overwhelmingly Palmer's triumph that little space need be given to the rest, save for the splended performances of Huggett and Rodgers. The young American played with remarkable resource and composure in his first tournament with the small ball. It was for him a technical triumph of no small order. No praise is too high for Huggett who finsihed with a 69. Surely this young man will go far as a tournament player. His scoring was a great tribute to the soundness of his method and rapidly developing competitive temperament. And now for Palmer.

Palmer took absolute command of the Championship with his magnificent morning round which scattered the field like feathers in a gale. At lunch only Nagle, five behind, and Charles, eight, were within 10 strokes, and yet at the beginning there was no sign of the cold murder that was about to be done.

Card of Old Troon

No.	Name	Yd	No.	Name	Yd
1	Seal	360	10	Sandhills	445
2	Black Rock	390	11	The Railway	485
3	Gyaws	385	12	The Fox	480
4	Dunur	545	13	Burmah	400
5	Greenan	210	14	Alton	175
6	Turnberry	580	15	Crosbie	460
7	Tel-el-Kebir	385	16	Well	565
8	Allsa	125	17	Rabbitt	225
9	The Monk	420	18	Craigend	410
		3,400			3,645

Total: 7,045 Yards

Long before Nagle and Palmer began their duel in the sunshine the sweet breath of summer was in the air. Across the limpid seas Arran rose from the mists like a dream fragment, and a tiny cool breeze stirred from the West. Legions and legions poured into the old links, and the cars shimmered in their thousands nearby. Straightaway the contest was alive, for Nagle holed good putts on the first two greens for threes, and the two men were even on the tournament. Then once again the fourth was the hole of destiny for Palmer.

This time his drive was pulled into the left-hand bunker; his third missed the green, and he took six. Nagle, after a fine pitch, had a putt of five feet to become two ahead, but missed. This six, as on Thursday, was the spur for Palmer. His temperament, which thrives so strongly on challenge, seems to need the sting of adversity, and invariably it reacts in formidable fashion. He struck a perfect 3-iron shot six yards from the next flag and holed the putt; Nagle took four and was behind. Never again did he draw level.

Palmer played the remaining holes in seven under fours, an exhibition of golf that will have etched itself deeply on the minds of all who were blessed in seeing it. He was hole high in two at the sixth and played a perfect bunker shot so that Nagle's conventional five cost him another stroke. Nagle did hole from eight feet for a two at the Postage Stamp, but this was his last thrust of the morning.

The eleventh hole once again saw two strokes of unforgettable power and control from Palmer. A spoon shot drew to the fairway's centre, and a 2-iron rifled straight at the flag but slipped just through the green. From a tight lie Palmer underhit the chip and missed a shortish putt, as did Nagle for a four after a wonderful recovery shot from the rough by the railway wall.

Thenceforth Palmer was merciless. He holed from 10 feet after being bunkered at the twelfth, from six at the next, and from about the same distance at the fifteenth for threes. He pitched dead by the sixteenth hole and holed all across the seventeenth for a two. He played the last six holes in four under par, and for the three rounds his total for the homeward half was 99. Nagle missed holeable putts on the sixteenth and seventeenth; otherwise his game never for an instant had wavered. He played with great character and it availed him nothing.

The early afternoon was simply a marvellous exhibition of Palmer's immense power and control, crushing power and technique. He holed a good putt on the third, and another on the fifth for a two; two huge blows reached the sixth green, and when Nagle took five at the seventh Palmer was 10 strokes ahead of him and Rodgers. His absolute mastery of the eleventh hole was confirmed for the last time with a 1-iron which streaked through the now greying afternoon, on and on to the heart of the green. Surely no one has ever hit long irons such enormous distances; this must have been 230 yards or more.

It was perhaps inevitable, particularly with the crowds pressing behind him almost before he had completed the stroke, that Palmer would drop one or two strokes coming home, but he and Nagle contrived a magnificent finish. Again Palmer got his four at the sixteenth; Nagle holed a huge putt across the seventeenth, and did so again on the eighteenth after he and Palmer had been permitted to reach the green. Finally Palmer holed for a three, and his fantastic conquest was over.

Palmer beyond question could rank with Hogan as the supreme golfer of this generation and is quite alone in the world today. As a driver and long iron player he has no peers; his pitching is wonderfully firm and always bold, save when strategy dictates otherwise, and his putting under pressure is superb. It has been fascinating to watch him improve day after day, ever learning a little more and working a little harder until at the precise time he begins to hole one after another.

If one adds to this, technical ability, an active, inquiring mind, that rare blend of immense self-confidence and true modesty, the ability to acquire concentration through a relaxed approach, and a truly formidable desire to win that is never outwardly aggressive, there is a remarkable man. For all the sum of his mighty achievement in titles and money Palmer remains a delightful, friendly human being who commands respect and affection.

Palmer has mastered the small ball and British conditions as only Hogan did and could have continued to do so. The essence of Palmer's game is attack, and thus it is more suited to the uniform watered conditions of American courses, and yet, though he would prefer these fairways and rich, holding greens, he does not complain but responds to the challenge. In technique, attitude and manner he makes some of his famous rivals seem puny and such outbursts as that of Player, after he had failed to qualify, even more ridiculous.

Palmer's presence these past three years has brought greatness once more to the old Championship. It has inspired others to compete and has set a new standard which can only benefit all who follow. Now the organisation of the championship must match the quality of a great champion.

The scores

276: Arnold Palmer (USA) 71, 69, 67, 69

282: K.D.G. Nagle (Australia) 71, 71, 70, 70

289: B. Huggett (Romford) 75, 71, 74, 69; P. Rodgers (USA) 75, 70, 72, 72

290: R.J. Charles (New Zealand) 75, 70, 70, 75

292: P.W. Thomson (Australia) 70, 77, 75, 70; S. Snead (USA) 76, 73, 72, 71

293: P. Alliss (Parkstone) 77, 69, 74, 73; D.C. Thomas (Sunningdale) 77, 70, 71, 75

294: S.S. Scott (Roehampton) 77, 74, 75, 68

1963

CHARLES PUTTS HIS WAY IMPECCABLY TO TITLE

First left-handed Open champion

By Pat Ward-Thomas

Bob Charles of New Zealand becomes the first left-hander to win a major championship in a play-off with Phil Rodgers of America.

The great company of those who play games left-handed has acquired a member of rare distinction in the person of R.J. Charles of New Zealand. He beat P. Rodgers (United States) by the overwhelming margin of eight strokes in the play-off for the Open Championship at Lytham St Annes on Saturday.

No left-handed golfer in the history of the game has achieved eminence in any way comparable to that of Charles, whose position now is quite unique. All over the world when children grasp the club 'the wrong way round' parents henceforth may think again, before insisting on the change. Left-handers are common in other games but in golf they are rare birds who, with notable exceptions like P.B. Lucas, look strange and often ungainly.

The golf of Charles, in its simplicity of style and ease and constancy of rhythm, should have banished this conception for evermore. At the same time it does not suggest the absolute authority and strength of a great champion, but in conditions where straightness and putting were the transcendent virtues, he was supreme.

Charles, without question, is one of the world's finest putters, and this alone is proof of his competitive quality. Under the acute and mounting pressure of the last round his wonderfully true, firm and deliberate strokes never faltered. He gave an exhibition of putting which has rarely been surpassed; it tortured and destroyed Rodgers with a merciless finality, which was almost inhuman.

It brought visions of other distant ages when cold, dark, slender young men moved silently through the secret places of the night, and one could feel only sympathy for Rodgers, who is probably superior in technique to Charles. It availed him nothing. In the peaceful morning sunshine, while the tents and the trappings of a strange championship were being dismantled elsewhere, Charles was round in 69.

Card of the course

No.	Yds	SSS	No.	Yds	SSS
1	208	3	10	336	4
2	439	4	11	483	5
3	456	4	12	200	3
4	393	4	13	339	4
5	212	3	14	445	4
6	466	4	15	462	4
7	553	5	16	356	4
8	394	4	17	462	4
9	164	3	18	389	4
	3,285	34		3,472	36

Total length 6,757 yds: SSS 70

Rodgers was unfortunate to be three strokes behind at lunch for Charles was down in a single putt no less than eleven times. This revealed, with some truth, that his golf through the green was less accurate than that of Rodgers. Palmer had said the previous evening that if Rodgers started putting well he would win. As it happened he did not, and when erring shots cost two more faults in the early afternoon all seemed over.

Then Charles quietly pulled his drive to the third on to the railway; Rodgers made his first good putt on the fourth, but Charles also holed implacably for a three. Rodgers holed out well on the next two greens, and was only one behind. The tide was turning but it was dammed ruthlessly on the next two holes.

Charles was fortunate to find a fair line in the rough at the seventh, but Rodgers bunkered his second shot, seemed to half-shank his recovery and took six. Instead of being even he was two behind again, but his spirit was not broken. Bravely he holed a huge putt on the eighth, and how hope must have stirred anew in his hunched little frame, but Charles cruelly holed from eight yards, and that in effect was that.

The feeling of hopelessness which must have overwhelmed Rodgers at that moment could be sensed, and he is far from lacking in courage, but the dies were cast. Charles gained strokes on each of the next six holes and the rest simply was a formal walk in the sunshine.

The day had a pleasant epilogue but a sense of anticlimax was inescapable. No matter how close the contest may be the urgency, compulsion, the mounting excitement and the tension are gone and 36 holes seem unnecessarily long. Eighteen as in the United States would be quite sufficient.

The organisation of the Championship was incomparably better than ever before. The control of the crowds, who co-operated splendidly, was excellent; the wooden palings protecting many fairways suggested a stockade, and would have looked less aggressive if painted green, but they were most effective, and, in so far as could be gathered, prompted no complaints.

The services for scores, refreshments, rest tents and the admirable closed circuit television were splendid; there did not seem to be undue congestion and, all in all, the hospitable club and the Royal and Ancient Committee have made vast improvements. Continuing efforts must be made to preserve high standards, and ensure that the dignity and quality of the old Championship is maintained.

The scores

277: R.J. Charles (New Zealand) 68, 72, 66, 71; P. Rodgers (USA) 67, 68, 73, 69

Play-off:	Charles	69, 71	140
	Rodgers	72, 76	148

278: J. Nicklaus (USA) 71, 67, 70, 70

283: K.D.G. Nagle (Australia) 69, 70, 73, 71

285: P.W. Thomson (Australia) 67, 69, 71, 78

286: C. O'Connor (R Dublin) 74, 68, 76, 68

287: G.J. Player (South Africa) 75, 70, 72, 70; R. Sota (Spain) 69, 73, 73, 72

288: S. Miguel (Spain) 73, 69, 73, 73; J. Garaialde (France) 72, 69, 72, 75

LEMA'S MAGNIFICENT VICTORY

Two fine challenges withstood

By Pat Ward-Thomas

Tony Lema's first Open brought victory at St Andrews after only two practice rounds. The American's career was to end tragically with a fatal air crash in 1966.

Tony Lema, a great, handsome golfer from California, resisted in a magnificent fashion a wonderful challenge from Nicklaus and a very gallant one from Vicenzo in the Open at St Andrews and won by five strokes. He became the third American to win on the Old Course at his first attempt, and this was by far the finest victory of all.

Throughout a lovely, fresh golfing day everything was in a minor key, apart from these two superb American golfers and two glorious rounds of 69 and 67 by Vicenzo. Lema's total was 279. Nicklaus took 284 and Vicenzo was a stroke behind. As usual the British challenge, apart from two fine steady rounds of 70 by B.H. Hunt, was negligible; but Hunt never threatened the pace. Devlin's chances evaporated in the morning when he topped his drive to the seventh, plugged the next into the face of a bunker and took six. For a while he was shaken but he collected himself and finished bravely in fifth place.

Lema's victory was one of the greatest performances in the history of the ancient Championship. That an American, on his first trip to Britain, could master the Old Course, with only two practice rounds, in such manner defied all expectation. He proved, as did Nicklaus, that if a golfer has the technique, the intelligence to observe and learn swiftly, an excellent caddie (as he had in Anderson), the courage to ignore turns of fortune to which he is unaccustomed, and difficult weather . . . then nothing is beyond his power.

Furthermore, Lema putted quite superbly in the middle two rounds, and needed only 65 in all. This, together with his magnificent striking from the tees, and the fact that he did escape the worst of the weather on Wednesday, laid the foundation of his triumph. It is of interest that over four rounds for the six holes of the Loop he was 16 under fours, and after this in the last three rounds he had only two fives – wonderful consistency.

It is a pleasure in these days of efficiency and power to see a golfer who combines both with rare grace and elegance of style. Lema is a handsome man, mature in looks for 30, with flecks of grey in his dark hair. He is lean but has the blessing of a long, strong back and beautiful hands. Like his two great predecessors in the ranks of tall men, Nelson and Middlecoff, he has a dip in the swing, but much slighter than theirs; and the whole swing is a beautifully free, firm, and flowing movement with a superb high finish.

A glorious morning greeted this memorable last day. The wind had moved a pointer to the north, bringing a sharpness to the air and the lovely spreading scene. Most of the pins had been placed in their sternest middle position, and the outward holes were testing save to the few.

After the early starters had gone through the motions, the event came to life as Nicklaus pitched dead to the first, and began his tremendous challenge. A long iron to the fourth was followed by a substantial putt, and then he drove overmuch to the right at the fifth, was bunkered and only a brave putt saved his five. He holed again from 10 ft at the seventh. At last now confidence in his putter had returned, perhaps because the greens were faster.

Lema drove the ninth green and was out in 32, Charles again making the fine, cool, determined attempt that was inevitable from him. Nicklaus played with superb control coming home, using his one-iron from the thirteenth, fifteenth and seventeenth tees. The approaches into the greens were desperately tricky downwind on the ever-swiftening turf. The run of the ball was not with him but on the last four greens long putts were marvellously judged and 66 was a wonderful challenge, the lowest round ever in the Open on the Old Course.

As Nicklaus moved up the thirteenth Lema passed him after an uncertain start. He had underclubbed to the second, taken three putts from the edge of the fourth, and the pressure was mounting, for the sight of Nicklaus's burly confident figure, five under fours, must have been anything but reassuring. His reaction was magnificent and worthy of a great champion. The fires were lit and how they burned thenceforth!

Old Course

	Yds	Par		Yds	Par
Burn	374	4	Tenth	338	4
Dyke	411	4	High	170	3
Cartgate	370	4	Heathery	312	4
Ginger Beer	470	4	Hole-o-Cross	427	4
Hole-o-Cross	567	5	Long	560	5
Heathery	414	4	Cartgate	413	4
High	364	4	Corner of the Dyke	380	4
Short	163	3	The Road	453	4
End	359	4	Tom Morris	381	4
Out	3,492	36	In	3,434	36

Lema played the next five holes in three apiece and his holing-out consistencies inside 10 feet showed that his putting had lost none of the assurance and touch of the previous day. Lema's striking for the rest of the round was flawless and his choice of club for the downwind shots showed a shrewd head and wise counsel.

Never was he under the slightest strain for his figures and as Nicklaus, about to start his last round, watched from the first tee Lema holed from eight yards down the slope for his 68 and a lead of seven strokes. Even Nicklaus must have felt that this was too much but it did not deter him. Only Palmer at Troon has had a greater lead after three rounds.

The afternoon was strangely peaceful as Lema began his last task; the wind had almost died and there was no tension, especially when it was known that Nicklaus had, for the third time, driven into the right-hand bunker at the fifth and taken six. Lema continued skilfully with a dark, stately calm. He did take three putts on the fourth, but a magnificent four-wood shot, from a downhill lie, after pulling to the fifth, reached the green and gave him a four.

Now, unless Nicklaus went mad, his task was as straightforward as he could hope it to be – but Nicklaus, the mighty Nicklaus, with astonishing cheerful resilience went burning on 3, 2, 4, 4, 3, 3 round the Loop. If he could have picked up a couple more threes, Lema would really have been under the whip, but it was not to be. At last the perfect exhibition of putting was broken and he took three on the 17th; but he drove the last green for the fourth successive time and Lema needed to come back in 40 to win. Steadily, beautifully, par followed par and soon he came up the last long sward, with the teeming thousands on either hand, towards the supreme moment of his life.

The scores

279: A. Lema (USA) 73, 68, 68, 70

284: J. Nicklaus (USA) 76, 74, 66, 68

285: R. de Vicenzo (Argentina) 76, 72, 70, 67

287: B.J. Hunt (Hartsbourne) 73, 74, 70, 70

290: B. Devlin (Australia) 72, 72, 73, 73

291: C. O'Connor (R Dublin) 71, 73, 74, 73; H. Weetman (Selsdon Park) 72, 71, 75, 73

292: H.R. Henning (South Africa) 78, 73, 71, 70; G. Player (South Africa) 78, 71, 73, 70; A. Miguel (Spain) 73, 76, 72, 71

1965

Birkdale, 10th July

THOMSON IS MASTER AMONG THE GAME'S MIGHTY

By Pat Ward-Thomas

Peter Thomson of Australia achieved the supreme performance of his golfing lifetime yesterday at Birkdale when he became Open champion for the fifth time. It was at Birkdale that he won his first title 11 years ago. His total of 285 (74, 68, 72, 71) was two strokes ahead of Huggett and O'Connor who sustained a magnificent challenge to the very end, while all the great Americans, save Lema, were nowhere.

Only Harry Vardon, in the century and more of the old Championship, has won the title more often (six times); Braid and Taylor each won five. This was incomparably the greatest of Thomson's victories because the field was infinitely the strongest. All day long Thomson played composed, magnificent golf through the green, hitting the ball with authority and wonderful greatness that even he has never surpassed. The measure of this can be appreciated from the fact that, starting from the eleventh in the last round, he missed putts of six, two, nine, and four feet in succession. And the measure of his temperament was the fact that these never disturbed the superb balance and rhythm of his swing.

Frankly I did not believe that Thomson would win another Open in such company. But at the age of almost 36, after seven years in which he was rarely under pressure of contention in the final stages of an Open, he has returned, refreshed as it were, to the heights and, for the first time in his career, proved himself a masterful competitor in the presence of at least four of the greatest golfers of the generation.

It was a surpassing triumph for one of the purest swings that golf has ever known, a technique that has few peers in British conditions, a remarkable golfing intelligence, an assurance and composure of manner that have become such a familiar part of the golfing scene in this land for a decade and more.

It was an extraordinary Championship for the failure of Palmer and Nicklaus, neither of whom really commanded his game from the outset. Both, by their standards, putted ill, and certainly this was the origin of a terrible untidy last round by Palmer. Lack of confidence on the greens is a deadly saboteur. At lunch Palmer was only two strokes behind Thomson but when, for the second time in the day, he took fives at the second and third one could sense that all hope had gone. The waning of these two must have been a great source of encouragement to Thomson, and to everyone else.

Card of the course

Hole	Yds	Par	Hole	Yds	Par
1	493	5	10	393	4
2	427	4	11	412	4
3	416	4	12	190	3
4	212	3	13	517	5
5	320	4	14	202	3
6	468	4	15	536	5
7	158	3	16	401	4
8	459	4	17	510	5
9	410	4	18	513	5
Out	3,363	35	In	3,674	38

Total 7,037 yds: Par 73

The golf of O'Connor and Huggett in setting the final pace is beyond praise. O'Connor has by far the finest record of any home golfer in the last 10 years, and he scored throughout with a consistency that hitherto has escaped him this year. Bernard Hunt too had a memorable day; rounds of 70 and 71 gained him innumerable places and made the first real target. From the time that he finished, events gathered in tension and excitement to a remarkable degree. Not the least among the day's heroes was M.J. Burgess who had the proud distinction of being the leading amateur, a performance of considerable courage.

In a sense Huggett showed the greatest character of all. He had endured a wretched season without complaint, and the sight of his sturdy, tough little figure, every line of it determination, putting superbly under great pressure was moving indeed. And how he putted! He holed no fewer than four putts of medium length going out in 35; then, with victory distinctly possible, he holed at the fifteenth and sixteenth for birdies from 15 and 9 feet; his putt for a four at the seventeenth ran across the hole, and eventually he needed a four to tie with O'Connor. He got it with yet another putt of eight feet. The present from an Australian of a wooden putter with a brass face screwed on worked marvels for him. His putting was probably the finest by a British golfer in the last round for years and years.

After a strange morning when it seemed that no one save Thomson and Hunt could make a thrust for the lead, the issue suddenly began to resolve itself. It was a contest between Thomson and Lema, playing silently together and pursuing in that order Hunt, O'Connor, the mighty Vicenzo playing with Palmer and Huggett. The afternoon unfolded in sunshine the same old westerly wind eased, and a vast crowd of some 14,000 became absorbed in a compelling struggle.

At first it seemed that Thomson would take complete command. Except for missing the fourth green he played with beautiful control to the turn in 34. He might well have been more than three strokes ahead of Lema who several times saved his pars with brave putting. Then, as they turned away once more towards the sea, came the missing of short putts by Thomson. With five holes to play, he was only one ahead of Lema.

Eventually Vicenzo, needing a four to tie with O'Connor, drove into a bunker at the eighteenth, and once again this great golfer and lovable man had to be content with a fractional failure. No one has ever been so near so often without succeeding. Then, as Huggett caught O'Connor, Thomson was left to play the last two holes in nine strokes to win, and Lema the same in eight.

Thomson finished in the grand manner. A superb drive and three-iron shot flew flawlessly straight to the seventeenth, his putt for a three hit the hole and stayed out and, showing rare emotion, Thomson threw his cap to the ground. Lema had sliced and pulled his way to a five. Again Thomson repeated his superb strokes with the same clubs, Lema was bunkered by the green, and so at the great day's end the setting belonged alone to its master.

The scores

285: P.W. Thomson (Australia) 74, 68, 72, 71

287: B.G.C. Huggett (Romford) 73, 68, 76, 70; C. O'Connor (R Dublin) 69, 73, 74, 71

288: R. de Vicenzo (Argentina) 74, 69, 73, 72

289: B.J. Hunt (Hartsbourne) 74, 74, 70, 71; K.D.G. Nagle (Australia) 74, 70, 73, 72; A. Lema (USA) 68, 72, 75, 74

290: S. Miguel (Spain) 72, 73, 72, 73; B.J. Devlin (Australia) 71, 69, 75, 75

293: J. Panton (Glenbervie) 74, 74, 75, 70; M. Faulkner (Selsey) 74, 72, 74, 73

Birkdale in 1965 saw Peter Thomson join James Braid and J.H. Taylor as five-times Open champions. Birkdale eleven years earlier was the scene of his first success.

1966

Muirfield, 11th July

NICKLAUS'S MAJESTIC FINISH FRUSTRATES HIS CHALLENGERS

By Pat Ward-Thomas

In more than a century the Open Championship has known many great days but few have surpassed the last act at Muirfield where Jack Nicklaus joined the Olympians of golf. His victory by one stroke from most gallant challengers in Sanders and Thomas completed for him the modern quadrilateral of supremacy. In all history Hogan, Player, and Sarazen alone have won the American and British Opens, the Masters and The United States PGA Championships, and Nicklaus was only 26 in January of this year.

The feeling that he would win had strengthened since his intelligent play in the first round but few dreamed that at last a British golfer would make a magnificent bid, in the full awareness of what he was doing. Thomas's performance in finishing with a 69, following the same score on Friday, was the finest by a British golfer in the field of this quality since the war. Others have gained high positions by attacking strongly when victory was well-nigh impossible but Thomas knew that he could set a severe target. He did so by driving of a length and accuracy that has rarely been approached, sensible cool golf at all times

Jack Nicklaus joins golf's Olympians with his first Open victory, achieved on the narrow fairways of Muirfield, with David Thomas runner-up a second time, jointly with Doug Sanders.

Golf was entering the modern era, play over four days ending on a Saturday, the attendances more than 40,000, TV gantries all around the course and a tented village mushrooming.

and splendid putting. After all the talk of Muirfield being a defensive course, two of the world's most powerful strikers finished at the top. Thomas used his driver ten times and missed only one fairway.

Sanders showed once again that he is a great competitor and an accomplished maker of strokes. He stayed in contention until the very end by brave putting, the holing of an approach from sixty yards for an eagle on the ninth, and by fine controlled driving. He seems to have taken to British courses, and British followers should take to him for he is one of the world's finest players.

The world has grown accustomed to prodigies but since the imperishable era of Jones, almost 40 years ago, golf has had no parallel to Nicklaus. Not alone have his achievements been phenomenal for one so young but he is a man of rare sincerity and integrity, a man to respect as well as admire and one who preserves the finest image of a great champion in all that he does.

These qualities were examined at Muirfield and his courage, self-possession and technique were severely tried. For the second time he allowed a commanding position to escape but when the final ordeal faced him he met and overcame it superbly. This fashioned the climax of a great championship.

On the green of the ninth, a hole which Nicklaus always played with the greatest of good sense, never pressing for a four, he faced a putt of three feet to be out in 32. This would have given him a substantial lead over Rodgers, Sanders, Thomas and Palmer, his only dangerous pursuers. It did not seem to matter when he missed the putt. He played the tenth masterfully while Rodgers was toiling in rough where a moment before Palmer's hopes, faint though they may have been, vanished beyond recall with a hideous seven.

Palmer remains at the crossroads. This is no time to ponder his destiny but the last month has shown that he must adjust his approach to the game if the great championships are to come his way again. The swordsman must control the swashbuckler.

When Nicklaus pitched eight feet from the eleventh hole, he felt that he was playing one of the finest rounds of his life but golf is a humbling game.

He took three putts, almost unbelievably; an indifferent shot to the thirteenth and a slightly misdirected drive to the fourteenth and he was face to face with awful reality. Ahead Thomas, and then Sanders were making the pace.

The awesome prospect of a British victory became ever more real when Thomas holed a prodigious putt for a two at the thirteenth, and saved his four at the next with a racer downhill. His sixteenth tee shot hit the pin but he missed a difficult crosshill putt of seven feet. His drive to the seventeenth was so long that it left him awkwardly angled for a medium-iron shot to the green. He hit it too straight, into rough above the bunker on the right, and could only scramble the next one on to the green's edge. The last hole was flawlessly played but his putt for a three just missed. Then Sanders, twice in the rough, also failed to make a four at the seventeenth but there were no two ways about the splendid four that tied him with Thomas.

Nicklaus had to work on the fifteenth and sixteenth greens and then knew that two fours would win. As he strode purposefully up the seventeenth fairway he said with a smile: 'Interesting position, isn't it?' It was one of the most dramatic I have known. He had used a three iron from the tee and then hit a deathless stroke with a five iron twenty feet from the hole. A one iron from the last tee, a three iron, wonderfully judged to use the wind from the right, left him 25 feet from the hole. He walked into the great gathering of people and a noble victory was his.

As for the others Rodgers slipped a little but Player had a splended last round and Nagle came within a fraction of a great one. What an admirable golfer he is, always the same, solid and true in his golf. Devlin also finished his championship in great style as did the delightful Marr.

The scores

282: J. Nicklaus (USA) 70, 67, 75, 70

283: D.C. Thomas (Dunham Forest) 72, 73, 69, 69; D. Sanders (USA) 71, 70, 72, 70

286: G.A. Player (South Africa) 72, 74, 71, 69; B. Devlin (Australia) 73, 69, 74, 70; K.D.G. Nagle (Australia) 72, 68, 76, 70; P. Rodgers (USA) 74, 66, 70, 76

288: D. Marr (USA) 73, 76, 69, 70; P.W. Thomson (Australia) 73, 75, 69, 71; S. Miguel (Spain) 74, 72, 70, 72; A. Palmer (USA) 73, 72, 69, 74

VICENZO'S GREATNESS IS REWARDED IN BRAVE VICTORY

By Pat Ward-Thomas

Roberto de Vicenzo of Argentina, in his forty-fifth year, became the oldest Open champion since Vardon in 1914, when he beat Nicklaus by two shots. It was a sentimental victory for a man four times third and once second since 1948.

17th July

At last Roberto de Vicenzo has achieved his heart's desire, and all the years of striving and disappointment are as nothing now. The greatness of his golf has been fulfilled in the 45th year of a good lifetime with as commanding and brave a victory as the Open has known in a long while. Only Vardon, when he won in 1914, was as old a champion. Vicenzo's total of 278 (70, 71, 67, 70) was two strokes lower than that of Nicklaus, whose 69 completed an honourable defence of his title.

Clark's performance in sharing third place with Player was the finest by a young British golfer in modern times. When his second shot to the first fell out of bounds, and he over hit the next green, he stood in the realms of nightmare. His subsequent play vindicated all the faith in his sterling character, and what is now an absolutely solid professional swing.

Obviously he enjoyed the presence of his formidable, yet kindly, companion, Nicklaus, and played the remaining holes in three under par. Jacklin's 70 was comparable in quality and character, so, too, was that of Horton, and Boyle's 68 completed a splendid confirmation that British golf really is on a rising tide. Vicenzo said: 'I hope next year to give the trophy to a young British professional.' This charming sentiment could prove to be right.

Adversity in golf takes many forms. For almost 20 years Vicenzo has tried for victory. Ten times he had competed, and only once was he not in sight of winning at some late stage in the Championship. However accomplished a golfer may be, and Vicenzo has had few peers, repeated failure can become an insuperable burden. Apart from the sabotaging effect on his confidence, there is the growing awareness that people regard him as always vulnerable.

Vicenzo bore disappointment with grace and dignity. Never was there an excuse or complaint. Like many strong men, Roberto is a gentle soul, kind and charming to everyone. The Latin in him never explodes; rather the sad little shrug of resignation than the outburst of emotion when things go amiss. The measure of his triumph was that he never became lastingly resigned to failure, but retained faith in his magnificent gifts.

He spoke humorously of coming to see his friends this year, and of not trying so hard; this may have been partly true, and may have helped him to approach the Open in a more relaxed state of mind. With effortless ease he was among the leaders after 36 holes, and then his 67 brought him face to face with the greatest ordeal he will ever know. His whole destiny as a golfer rested on this last single round. Apart from the huge financial rewards that will come his way, there was the fulfilment of his talent and life's work at stake, and also a desire to crown the many gallant, but unsuccessful attempts by Argentine golfers since Jose Gurado let victory slip in 1931 at Carnoustie. These last mean as much to Vicenzo as the money; that, too, is a measure of the man.

All this being so, there never was a more compelling situation on the last day of an Open, nor one as sentimental in its undertones. By their voice alone one knew, as did Vicenzo, that the people wanted him to win; they would have loved a British victory, but this was not the time. Their appreciation for Nicklaus, Player, Clark, and the rest was warmly given, but their hearts were with Vicenzo.

At first he was apprehensive that play might be too slow, with Nicklaus immediately ahead, and Player, his tense partner, often deliberate in his mechanical approach. But Nicklaus moves faster these days, and Player's obvious anxiety, which led to several indifferent shots on the early holes, heartened Vicenzo. Masterly chips saved his fours at the third and fifth, and one felt that he was at peace with himself.

Then Nicklaus began what seemed likely to be a deadly thrust. He holed for a two at the Dowie, and the mightiest 4-iron shot I have ever seen, which pitched on the back of the eighth green, made another birdie. He was now only two behind, level with Player, and the golden afternoon was filled with suspense.

Card for Open

Hole	Yds	Par	Hole	Yds	Par
1	421	4	10	404	4
2	426	4	11	201	3
3	491	5	12	460	4
4	196	3	13	158	3
5	450	4	14	515	5
6	389	4	15	459	4
7	193	3	16	529	5
8	492	5	17	418	4
9	393	4	18	400	4
	Out 3451	36		In 3544	36

Total 6,995 yds: Par 72

When Player tood three putts from 12 feet on the tenth, and Vicenzo holed from six for a three, and made his par with a marvellous chip from a treacherous sandy lie at the Alps, where Player hit a terrible stroke, the issue lay betwen Nicklaus and Vicenzo. Crucially, Nicklaus could not approach close enough to have birdie putts on the first four homeward holes. He drove into thick rough at the fourteenth, and Vicenzo, after a majestic drive, watched him miss for his birdie. He said: 'He make his par like a good boy – I feel better now.'

A moment later Vicenzo was four ahead, almost holing a little pitch from beside the green, and Nicklaus had missed another holeable putt, for a three on the fifteenth. So did Vicenzo for his par, and a stroke had gone, but the decisive hole was at hand. Nicklaus, fighting now with all his tremendous competitive power, made his birdie at the sixteenth, but before he had holed out Vicenzo had driven just short of the out-of-bounds Cop. For a ghastly second, as the ball was in the air, I thought he was too strong. Happily, it came to rest five yards short, and he then hit one of the greatest strokes imaginable. A spoon thundered away to the heart of the green, and Vicenzo knew that all the dreams were about to come true.

It was typical of Nicklaus to hole for a three at the last, but Vicenzo's superb driving, which since the turn, was as fine as any I have seen late in an Open, left him only a 9-iron shot to the last two greens. Suddenly, unbelievably, he was there in the amphitheatre filled with sunshine and thousands. A great golfer and a fine human being had come into his own, a supreme climax to one of the happiest Open Championships in living memory.

The scores

278: R. de Vicenzo (Argentina) 70, 71, 67, 70

280: J. Nicklaus (US) 71, 69, 71, 69

284: C.A. Clark (Sunningdale) 70, 73, 69, 72; G. Player (South Africa) 72, 71, 67, 74

285: A. Jacklin (Potters Bar) 73, 69, 73, 70

286: H. Henning (South Africa) 74, 70, 71, 71; S. Miguel (Spain) 72, 74, 68, 72

287: H.F. Boyle (Jacobs GC) 74, 74, 71, 68; T. Horton (Ham Manor) 74, 74, 69, 70; P.W. Thomson (Australia) 71, 74, 70, 72; B. Devlin (Australia) 70, 70, 72, 75; A. Baldwin (Canada) 74, 71, 69, 73

1968

Carnoustie, 15th July

PLAYER OVERCOMES A BURDEN

By Pat Ward-Thomas

Character is the essence of greatness in any game, and this is particularly true of golf: All the champions have had to master human frailties, some to an uncommon degree, and the victory of Gary Player in the Open Championship at Carnoustie was a remarkable instance of a courageous heart and mind.

He resisted a tremendous challenge from his friend and companion Nicklaus, and the constant threat of Casper and Charles behind. His total of 289 (74, 71, 71, 73), one over par for the event, was a triumph of one of the most exacting tests of golf the Open has ever known.

Player joined the exalted company of those who have won a major championship more than once, and spoke of an ambition to repeat his victory in the Masters, American Open, and PGA Championships. Provided the call of home and seminary in South Africa do not become too intense there is little reason why he should not do so. He has overcome a great burden, similar to the one which still rests heavily upon Palmer – that of continuing supremacy. As the years go by, this becomes ever harder, especially when so much wealth in terms of contracts is involved.

Earlier I wrote of a more relaxed atmosphere around Player; he was less intense and more philosophical than at times in the past, and even when the pressure was mounting to its peak his composure never failed. Neither did the courage that enabled him to play great saving strokes when Nicklaus was thundering at his heels.

The champion's supreme moment came at the fourteenth. Charles and Casper were level with him at this point and Nicklaus, two strokes behind, was fortunate to find a wooden club lie dangerously near a spinney. He smashed his shot over the Spectacles

Gary Player's total of 289 at Carnoustie was the highest for twenty-one years, but he resisted a tremendous challenge from his friend and companion Jack Nicklaus.

then Player, wonderfully concentrated before the excited noise after Nicklaus's shot had died, hit a magnificent spoon straight down the line of the distant flag. The explosion of sound from the stand beside the green must have been music to Player's ears and, after Nicklaus had made a birdie four with a superb chip, Player tapped in his putt of no more than two feet for an eagle. He was three ahead, and then Nicklaus really unleashed the powers within him.

No golfer in history could have surpassed, and very few remotely approached, the awesome power and beauty of the drives Nicklaus hit to the last four holes. Had his long putt at the fifteenth, or one of 15 feet at the sixteenth, fallen, Player would have been desperately pressed. As it was, he saved his fours at the fifteenth with a fine pitch and a putt of eight feet, and at the seventeenth with a great approach putt. Player missed from six feet at the sixteenth.

Nicklaus's drive at the seventeenth was all of 350 yards, but he could not get the three he sorely needed, so Player still was able to play the eighteenth for a five the safe way, in the hope that Nicklaus did not make an eagle.

From an awkward down lie, Player's two-iron second shot finished in deep rough. When Nicklaus, after another enormous hit into wind, pushed a one-iron into a greenside bunker, Player was left with the long pitch to the green. He forced it there with a nine iron, putted dead from eight yards, ran to the hole, tapped it in, and turned to receive beaming congratulations from Nicklaus. The stands again massed in a great arena, roared their acclaim as well they might: the golfers had given them the substance of a lifetime's memory.

Player had completed 72 holes without a six, and only twice did he take three putts. All the other close challengers, except gallant little Bembridge, had their disasters on an unforgiving day with the east wind fresher than it had been. Charles and Brewer each took six at the little third hole, and Casper swiftly dropped two strokes. Nicklaus, unaware of this strove to use the wind from the sixth tee, aimed too straight and pulled out of bounds. His father, watching, said: 'There goes the championship,' and was proved right.

Casper, unexpectedly vulnerable, again missed several holeable putts and the fourteenth finally destroyed him. Poor Jacklin, who had started in great spirits, was moving well until, going for the bold shot, he pulled out of bounds at the seventh and hit his next tee shot into a bunker. This led to a ghastly eight.

A moment later Palmer, disaster prone nowadays, had a five at the short eight and his challenge was spent. After going out in 34 – great golf – Bonallack had three dreadful holes. Charles, inevitably it seems, did not yield further after the third, but neither could he gain.

At some point or another, the links mastered everyone, but Bembridge deserved the highest praise for his abiding steadiness. Nicklaus spoke warmly of his golf and said that he might do well with the large ball in the United States if he gave himself time there. Barnes redeemed his previous day in some measure with the afternoon's lowest round, and Coles played an admirably consistent Championship.

But the lasting memories will be of Player and Nicklaus, not least for the manner in which they fought their great contest. This was golf at its finest.

The scores

289: G. Player (South Africa) 74, 71, 71, 73

291: J. Nicklaus (USA) 76, 69, 73, 73; R.J. Charles (New Zealand) 72, 72, 71, 76

292: W. Casper (USA) 72, 68, 74, 78

293: M. Bembridge (Little Aston) 71, 75, 73, 74

295: B. Barnes (Burnham & Berrow) 70, 74, 80, 71; N.C. Coles (Coombe Hill) 75, 76, 71, 73; G. Brewer (USA) 74, 73, 72, 76

296: A. Balding (Canada) 74, 76, 74, 72

297: R. de Vicenzo (Argentina) 77, 72, 74, 74; B. Devlin (Australia) 77, 73, 72, 75; A. Palmer (USA) 77, 71, 72, 77

1969 Lytham St Annes, 14th July

INSPIRATION IN YEARS TO COME

Pat Ward-Thomas on the significance of Tony Jacklin's triumph in the Open

One year it was bound to happen that a British golfer would win the Open Championship again, but Tony Jacklin himself said that he did not think his greatest ambition could be fulfilled so soon. His triumph at Royal Lytham was magnificent indication of the mounting hope that has pursued him these past two years, of a great strength and talent for the game, and above all of sterling character.

The significance of his victory is incalculable. It will remain a source of pride and inspiration to British golf for years to come; the long dark night is over, the longest in the history of the Championship. It will command for Jacklin, the golfers that follow him, and the land that bred him a new respect whenever he plays in the US. He was the first British golfer to beat a powerful field from overseas since Cotton won at Carnoustie in 1937, and he won because he played golf of more lasting control than anyone else.

For Jacklin himself magic doors will open all over the world. It has been estimated that victory might be worth a million dollars; he is exempt from qualifying for the US Open and the Masters for five years, and in all probability from the day-to-day American events as well, not to mention life exemption from this championship. The offers, the contests, television matches, and all the ancillaries of success will come his way in abundance and it is well that he has a level, realistic approach to life and a cool, hard head.

Every young professional golfer, or amateur intending to be so, should be grateful to Jacklin for pointing the way. He has proved that given the heart, the ambition, and the patience to persevere in the United States by his own efforts anything is possible. Not long ago Jacklin, having failed to make the cut in five out of six tournaments, was almost despairing of his game, but he did not succumb to the temptatations to return home and was rewarded.

There is no conceivable doubt, as he was quick to emphasise, that without the experience and the intense competition he has faced in America he would never have withstood the pressure of the final round. Had Jacklin been content to potter along in the parish pump affairs at home his greatness might never have emerged, and greatness surely was his on the last memorable afternoon.

Jacklin said that he had never been so nervous in his life as on the previous evening, but every great golfer is nervous, the insensitive never reach the heights. The proof of Jacklin's character was that

Tony Jacklin ended the longest losing British run in the Open's history with victory by two strokes over Bob Charles. It brought him £4,250 in prize money. Max Faulkner had last won for Britain in 1951, but not in an equivalent international field.

under the severest tension he was able to play his finest and preserve the rhythm of his swing. This last was absolutely crucial because his greatest weakness has been a tendency to swing too fast, but in the last hour of his ordeal his swing had a rare beauty of rhythm and poise. It was a movement proud in its strength and consequence.

The tee shots to the last few holes that had almost destroyed him the previous evening were superbly struck. He dismissed the peril of the last hole in masterful fashion with a flawless long drive and, after Charles had given himself a fine chance of a three, which meant that a tie was possible if Jacklin missed the green, he hit the true stroke of a champion. His beautifully controlled 7-iron shot finished inside that of Charles, and a few moments later he had two putts for the Open from a range of one inch. The sun came forth for the first time in the day, as if to herald the dawn of a shining new world for British golf, and the great mass of the people rose and gave him the thunder of their acclaim.

After so many years it was strange that these momentous hours should be lacking in the desperate tension and suspense one might have expected. There was, of course, excitement and stirring expectation but no agony. This was a tribute to Jacklin, who made his thrust early with birdies at the third and fourth and never allowed anyone to catch him; it was also a comment on the failure of those about to make a challenge. It was as if destiny had decreed this day and would brook no interference. There was no mighty surge from Nicklaus, betrayed overall by his driver; Thomson and Vicenzo played many lovely shots but could not hole these telling putts.

O'Connor limped quietly out of the reckoning, as always seems inevitable, and only the courageous, implaccable Charles kept going until the very end as if, in the fitness of things, there should be a foil for Jacklin's commanding finish. No point of crisis ever came through all the long afternoon. Once Jacklin had followed a marvellous pitch by Charles to the seventh – one of the finest strokes I have ever seen – with a great bunker shot, the conviction grew that he would not fail. Thereafter an overhit pitch to the thirteenth and three from the front edges of the fifteenth and seventeenth, after surmounting the worse perils, were the only flaws in a great round.

The championship will take its place in history because of Jacklin, but will also be remembered for the perfection of its organisation, and the fulfilment of long devoted planning by the club and the Royal and Ancient. The Open must return to Lytham. The scoring services were superior to anything I have seen in the US for their speed and accuracy; the facilities for everyone seemed admirable, and the crowds behaved beautifully. Everything was worthy of the occasion, its young hero, and the greatness of the golf he played.

The scores

280: A. Jacklin (Potters Bar) 68, 70, 70, 72 (£4,250)

282: R.J. Charles (New Zealand) 66, 69, 75, 72 (£3,000)

283: P.W. Thomson (Australia) 71, 70, 70, 72; R. de Vicenzo (Argentina) 72, 73, 66, 72 (£2,125 each)

284: C. O'Connor (Royal Dublin) 71, 65, 74, 74 (£1,750)

285: J. Nicklaus (US) 75, 70, 68, 72; D.M. Love Jnr (US) 70, 73, 71, 71 (£1,375 each)

286: P. Alliss (Parkstone) 73, 74, 73, 66 (£1,100)

287: K. Nagle (Australia) 74, 71, 72, 70 (£1,000)

288: M. Barber (US) 69, 75, 75, 69 (£900)

1970

St Andrews, 13th July

JONES, HOGAN ... NICKLAUS

Pat Ward-Thomas on an historic Open

Rarely in all its long history has the Old Course at St Andrews seen a finish to a golf match that could compare to the one which Jack Nicklaus and Doug Sanders played last evening. The thousands gathered about Tom Morris's green will never forget the moment when Nicklaus's putt from six feet for victory gently fell into the hole for a play-off victory 72–73.

Nicklaus is not an expressive person on the course, but such was his longing to win at St Andrews, and such was the tension there and had been over the last four holes of the contest, that he flung his putter high in the air and turned away, obviously overcome. For Sanders this must have been one of the harshest moments in a long career; many times he has been close to a championship without winning, but never as near as on this occasion. He stepped aside to let Nicklaus's putter fall and then holed his putt of four feet, made possible by a beautiful run-shot from short of the green.

			OUT							
Nicklaus	4	4	4	4	5	4	4	3	4	– (36)
Sanders	4	4	5	5	5	4	4	3	4	– (38)
			IN							
Nicklaus	4	3	4	4	5	4	5	4	3	– (36)
Sanders	4	4	4	5	4	3	4	4	3	– (35)

Nicklaus had hit a prodigious blow from the tee, saying later that he struck the ball perfectly and was charged up as well. He had hesitated before choosing a driver instead of his spoon. The ball lay in that nasty rough fringe at the back of the green; he might have had a bad line, chipping against the grain, but fortunately the grass was leaning his way. He had to dig for the ball and chipped it to six feet. Nicklaus said later that he almost hit the putt before he was ready but admonished himself saying, 'Stop you idiot, make sure the stroke is a good one.'

When the slender old vase, symbol of so much, was presented, Nicklaus clearly had trouble in paying the handsome tribute that he never neglects. Many felt with him when he said that it should have all ended yesterday with two champions. He went on to say:

'I said at the beginning of the week, and it is more than true now, there is no other place in the world I would rather win an Open Championship than here. It was only Doug's misfortune, of course, on the last green on Saturday, that gave me a second chance. If he had holed that putt it could have stopped right there. It's some while since I won a championship, and I can't tell you what it means or what it is like, standing on the eighteenth green. I have never been so excited in my life. I shall be coming back next year.'

Nicklaus has now reached a pinnacle of achievement comparable only to those of Bobby Jones and Ben Hogan. In the past nine years he has won the United States and British Opens twice each and the Masters three times. Even Hogan did not do this, although doubtless could have done had he so wished. In every sense of the term Nicklaus is the world's greatest golfer.

There cannot have been a more gallant loser than Sanders, nor one more gracious, humorous, and generous at a moment of overwhelming disappointment for him. To come back at Nicklaus, who was playing commanding golf, after five exhausting days, when the strain and tension upon him must have been enormous, was a performance of great character, particularly because we knew that he should have won the previous evening. At Muirfield in 1966 he was runner-up with David Thomas to Nicklaus, one stroke behind. He is deserving of a championship, in every sense of technical accomplishment and competitive quality, and one hopes that his career in the United States will take a more prosperous turn in future, and that he will be true to his promise and return again to these shores.

The same grey, westerly wind, gusting to force seven, blustered over the links yesterday, straining the flags and sending the dark rain clouds hurtling across the bay. First blood fell to Nicklaus when Sanders, having saved his four at the second with a putt from nine feet, took three from only twice the distance at the third. His long second to the fourth was held too much into the wind and Nicklaus's perfect four gained him another stroke.

The fifth, where Nicklaus let his drive fade into one of the little bunkers on the right, brought his first minor crisis. His long third finished in heavy ruts and a beautiful pitch and a putt from five feet, enabled him to match a sound par-five by Sanders.

Steady pars followed and then at the eleventh, a testing shot into the angering wind, Sanders was bunkered and Nicklaus was three ahead. He gained a fourth stroke at the thirteenth where he reached the greens from rough and Sanders did not. And then out of the seemingly peaceful progression to triumph for Nicklaus excitement stirred again. Two huge hits took Nicklaus through the fourteenth green; Sanders from away on the left played a masterful chip to five feet and holed for the day's first birdie, whereas Nicklaus missed from two feet when trying for his.

In the cool light of afterthought the sweep of events leading to the play-off contrived an anticlimax, unforgettable though it was in the ancient, classic setting. To golfers who have suffered the game's agonies, and few in huge record crowds have not, there is nothing more sad than failure at the last gasp.

Jack Nicklaus (right) won the play-off 72–73 from fellow American Doug Sanders after Sanders, who had pre-qualified, missed a yard putt for the Championship the previous evening. Willie Whitelaw, captain of the R and A, is between them.

That one of the finest players of the generation, and Sanders is that for all his bizarre garb, unusual style, and recent inability to distinguish himself, should not be able to play a hole of 358 yards in four to win an Open is not exciting; it is pitiful

This was a perfect instance of cruel subtlety of the Old Course that has deceived golfers for centuries. The hole has no bunker, no hazards of any kind, and no rough, but the Valley of Sin and its attendant hollows guarding the green, wrought their havoc. The pin was 15 yards beyond them; Nicklaus drove within 25 yards of it, but putted much too hard up the steep shelf. Sanders was far back and, anxious at all costs to be up, overhit his pitch, and under-hit his first putt which looked more down hill than it was: He was then beaten by the invisible left to right borrow on the next one of a yard. Sanders is a gay, good-humoured person, but failure will haunt him a long time, and everyone was sad on his behalf.

The westerly wind, violent to gale force in gusts, swifly narrowed the conflict. No hint of a threat came from ahead although Oosterhuis, especially Henning, who played a wonderfully consistent championship in his cool, slender, unobtrusive fashion,

Coles, and Jackson kept going splendidly. And Panton's 71 at the height of the wind's fury, was the lowest score by two strokes, a wonderful tribute to the enduring simplicity and soundness of his swing.

Towards the turn Trevino began to slip shots as, not surprisingly, did Jacklin but he remained in contention until the seventeenth hole. No one with knowledge of the pressure of these affairs could have expected Jacklin to continue striking the ball superbly and to remain within two strokes of the lead for so long. His was a magnificent defence.

And so it came to a straight fight between the two men best prepared for the Championship. Sanders had qualified at Panmure; Nicklaus had allowed nothing to divert his purpose, and they played golf through the green of a very high order indeed.

At the sixteenth, Nicklaus was astonished to see his 4-iron shot fly through the green, and yet again he took three to get down. Now he was only one ahead. Never can the Old Road hole have seen two braver strokes than they played to the green. That of Sanders with a 5-iron just skirted the bunker and finished six yards beyond the hole. Then Nicklaus played the kind of stroke that the great ones muster at such moments. His 7-iron shot was perfectly judged across the wind: it pitched short of the bank and rolled 12 feet short of the hole. Both just missed the putts and they turned away towards a moment that they, all the thousands, and I will never forget.

The total attendance for the week, including the practice days and the play-off was 81,593. The attendance to Saturday was a record by 24,000.

Card of the course

Hole		Yards	Par	Hole		Yards	Par
1	Burn	374	4	10	Tenth	338	4
2	Dyke	411	4	11	High	170	3
3	Cartgate	405	4	12	Heathery	312	4
4	Ginger Beer	470	4	13	Hole O'Cross	427	4
5	Hole O'Cross	567	5	14	Long	560	5
6	Heathery	414	4	15	Cartgate	413	4
7	High	364	4	16	Corner of the Dyke	380	4
8	Short	163	3				
9	End	359	4	17	The Road	466	4
				18	Tom Morris	358	4
Out		3,527	36	In		3,424	36
	Total yds: 6,951:			Par 72			

The scores

283: J.W. Nicklaus (US) 68, 69, 73, 73; D. Sanders (US) 68, 71, 71, 73

285: L. Trevino (US) 68, 68, 72, 77; H. Henning (SA) 67, 72, 73, 73

286: A. Jacklin (Potters Bar) 67, 70, 73, 76

287: N.C. Coles (Coombe Hill) 65, 74, 72, 76:
P.A. Oosterhuis (Dulwich and Sydenham) 73, 69, 69, 76

288: H. Jackson (Knockbracken) 69, 72, 73, 74

289: J. Panton (Glenbervie) 72, 73, 73, 71;
P.W. Thomson (Australia) 68, 74, 73, 74; T. Horton (Ham Manor) 66, 73, 75, 75

1971

TREVINO HAS TRUE PLACE AMONG THE SELECT

Pat Ward-Thomas sums up the 100th Open

Lee Travino celebrates his triumph in the British Open at Birkdale to follow victory in the US and Canadian Open events in the space of a month. Mr Lu, Lu Liang Huan of Formosa, was only a stroke behind.

12th July

The genius and inexhaustible zest for golf of Lee Trevino found supreme expression in the hundredth Open Championship at Birkdale. Bobby Jones, Gene Sarazen and Ben Hogan, the only others to win the United States and British titles in the same summer, surely would agree that he deserved the right to join their company.

It was also entirely fitting that Liang Huan Lu should be second, Jacklin third, and Craig De Foy, whose 69 was the round of his life, fourth. Thus ended a Championship that will ever be memorable for the colour, flair and charm of its heroes, the vastness of its crowds, easily a record for England, and the suspense which came from nowhere at its end.

Trevino's gift of £2,000 to a Formby orphanage was characteristic of a generosity of spirit bred from a not remote experience of life's harsher realities, that most of his contemporaries never knew.

Within 23 days Trevino had played in four events, and had also won the Canadian Open, a feat of sustained golfing endurance that may never be equalled. Trevino was not able to explain the reason for such an extraordinary run of success, except that golf is his life and he exists for it, and when talking of his swing he said: 'I keep the club on line longer than any other player.' Clearly though, a wonderfully sound, constantly repeating swing was only part of the answer. He has enjoyed a formidable spell of confidence scarcely broken since he won his first American Open three years ago.

At Birkdale this was mostly reflected on the greens. He did not like their cushioned slowness and variable surfaces any more than most of his rivals did, but so true was his putting stroke, so positive his attitude, that he achieved exceptional results. In the last round he used his putter only 11 times in the first nine holes. The precision and attack of his shot making was glorious to watch; only twice did it fail when he attempted his shots easily rather than hard to the short twelfth and fourteenth.

The golf of Lu, who learned it from H.S. Chen, the famous teacher in Taiwan, was beyond praise. Admittedly the running fairways compensated for his comparative shortness, and the slow greens suited him, but no one hit the ball more consistently straight, nor with greater ease or constancy or rhythm. His one turn of fortune came at the very last, when from a hanging stance near a bunker he hooked valiantly. Had an unfortunate woman's head not intervened he might have been in serious trouble instead of on the fairway. A beautiful long pitch and one putt revealed a composure that never once had failed him: it had forced Trevino to play to the desperate end. Lamps for the little man should glow all over the golfing Orient.

Trevino's finish was that of a really great golfer. He had aimed his drive to the seventeenth hard at the huge left dune, expecting the inevitable fade. It flew straight; his next shot from sand hit undergrowth, the next flew into rough, the next two were short and disaster, such as that I saw at Portland in America two years ago when he lost seven strokes to Casper on the last three holes of the Alcan, seemed near. But his last drive was perfect: his six iron, played as swiftly as possible after Lu's mishap, equally so, and he putted with implacable certainty. He said later that he never really felt any pressure. A truly remarkable man.

The seventeenth brought a dramatic element to the finish which had never seemed likely.

Birkdale card

Hole	Yards	Par	Hole	Yards	Par
1	493	5	10	393	4
2	427	4	11	412	4
3	416	4	12	190	3
4	212	3	13	517	5
5	358	4	14	202	3
6	473	4	15	536	5
7	158	3	16	401	4
8	459	4	17	510	5
9	410	4	18	513	5
Out:	3,406	35	In:	3,674	38

Total: 7,080 yds: Par 73

When Trevino left the sixth green, where he made a rare three, he was four under par for the round and eight strokes clear of the field, except for Lu, his gentle companion who long since was endeared to the hearts of the crowd.

The Championship seemed over; those in high places, notably Player and De Vicenzo, gradually receded. Jacklin, advised by John Jacobs the previous evening to alter his right-hand grip found it hard to put into practice immediately under pressure. He was still prone to hook, and one at the second led to a six. His cause was seriously weakened but he continued with unfailing courage. His putting was his sword and his shield throughout the Championship, and when there was just a remote chance of victory remaining he mastered the last three holes in three, four, four. He could not have played a braver championship.

After watching Trevino take two putts for the first time, on the seventh green, I crossed to the eleventh fairway to see if Nicklaus could mount the massive rearguard action of which he, more than anyone, is capable at the end of championships. His drive plunged into the heavy rough. An explosive cheer for a Jacklin putt on the eighth had caught him at the top of his backswing. The five he took checked his impetus towards an almost impossible task but he made a great golfer's gesture for the huge theatre of the eighteenth with an eagle.

Craig De Foy played with splendid style and composure, quietly and most easily making his pars, and later birdies with some admirable iron shots while attention mainly was upon others. This may be the beginning of greater things for him, and how many golfers can say, as he now can, that in an Open he finished ahead of Nicklaus, Casper, Player, Coody, Sanders, Thomson, Yancey, De Vicenzo, and Nagle. Their presence at the head confirmed the greatness of the Championship.

The scores

*Amateur

278: L. Trevino (US) 69, 70, 69, 70 (£5,500)

279: Lu Liang Huan (Formosa) 70, 70, 69, 70, (£4,000)

280: A. Jacklin (Potters Bar) 69, 70, 70, 71 (£3,250)

281: C. De Foy (Coombe Hill) 72, 72, 68, 69 (£2,750)

283: J.W. Nicklaus (US) 71, 71, 72, 69; C. Coody (US) 74, 71, 70, 68 (£2,300 each)

284: W. Casper (US) 70, 72, 75, 67; G. Player (S Africa) 71, 70, 71, 72 (£1,775 each)

285: D. Saunders (US) 73, 71, 74, 67; P. Thomson (Australia) 70, 73, 73, 69 (£1,550 each)

1972

Muirfield, 17th July

TREVINO SHATTERS THE GREAT NICKLAUS DREAM

Pat Ward-Thomas on the Open

In 1972 at Muirfield, Trevino won again, holing two chips and a bunker shot, the chip at the 35th reducing Jacklin to a baffled three putts.

Long before a shot was played in the Open Championship at Muirfield the gods must have decided that Lee Trevino would retain his title, the first man to do so since Arnold Palmer 10 years ago.

No golfer could have been more greatly blessed with fortune than he was at the very moment he was yielding-hope. His victory meant cruel disappointment for Nicklaus, who finished only a stroke behind Trevino's total of 278 after a magnificent rearguard action, and for Jacklin, who for two days had withstood the wizardry of Trevino's short game until at the last gasp he could take no more.

Every great champion, and Trevino certainly is that, having won the American and British Open twice each within five years, needs a little luck because golf is a game of tiny fractions but Trevino had more than his share. The freakish finish on Friday evening, coupled with his play of the seventeenth hole on Saturday, must make him one of the most fortunate champions in a long while.

When Trevino's fourth shot had raced over the green he should have lost the Championship and his manner suggested that he had given up. Even before Jacklin had marked his ball after three shots, Trevino had hurriedly played his difficult chip from a bank against the grain to a fast sloping green, as if heedless of the results. A second later he was saying to his caddy: 'That may be the straw that breaks the camel's back.' The shock to Jacklin must have been dreadful; as everyone knows he took three putts and was one behind when he seemed certain to be one or two ahead.

Trevino's moods can switch from humour to dead earnest, from nonsense to good sense, from despair to elation within a twinkling. He took his time going to the last tee, so as not to have to wait and think about the Open, wasted no time over his drive, perfectly placed, and then hit a beautiful eight-iron shot. Poor Jacklin's second was bunkered and as he walked into the thunder of the last arena he looked a sad, forlorn figure. Once again he has played superbly, with great resource and courage, and has given the vast crowds cause for abundant pride.

Muirfield card

Hole	Yard	Par	Hole	Yard	Par
1	449	4	10	473	4
2	349	4	11	386	4
3	379	4	12	381	4
4	181	3	13	153	3
5	558	5	14	447	4
6	439	4	15	396	4
7	185	3	16	188	3
8	444	4	17	542	5
9	495	5	18	447	4
Out:	3,479	36	In:	3,413	35

Total yds: 6,892: Par 71

For Nicklaus, the great dream is over for another year just as it was in 1960 for Palmer who was warmly sympathetic to him afterwards. No other golfer could have summoned the challenge that Nicklaus made in the full knowledge, as he had said the previous evening, that he would probably need a 65. He was within a fraction of the greatest last round in history. Five times he missed putts between five and 12 feet and was round in 66.

History did not repeat itself for in 1948 Henry Cotton was round in the same score on the last occasion that royalty, King George VI, had watched the Open at Muirfield. Princess Margaret, on a private visit, watched some of the play, but could not quite work the spell for Nicklaus.

Majesty had returned to Nicklaus's game; he had discovered the previous day that hooding the club slightly gave his iron shots greater authority. He struck one after another with masterful truth and judgment; and has given his excellent caddy, Jimmy Dickinson, an instruction for Troon next year. 'Keep the club face square.' After five holes Nicklaus had the pressure on Jacklin and Trevino with a vengeance but they came back with eagles at the ninth and the Championship was poised on a knife edge.

It was lost for Nicklaus when his putt for a birdie at the fifteenth caught the hole and stayed out, and his 4-iron to the sixteenth just missed the green, as did his putt from five feet. Had he holed he would probably not have pulled from the next tee. The five he took gave Trevino and Jacklin new life but both had to get down in two from off the sixteenth green, Jacklin holing from six feet. How heroically he was playing.

As always, Nicklaus accepted defeat with great good grace and his tributes to Trevino were not simply courtesy of the hour. The respect and admiration these two supreme golfers hold for one another is sincere indeed. Yet again one marvels at the balance of Nicklaus; as I write at the lovely summer's day's end, looking out over a links at peace once more, he is playing joyful tennis in the garden below, only an hour or so after his great ambition had been thwarted. If the great men provided wonderful entertainment for the largest crowds ever to watch an Open many others contributed too. Sanders, who finished fourth, has become an increasingly welcome and popular visitor from America, for himself as well as for his artistic golf. Barnes can never have played better or with greater control in such company, and tiny Guy Hunt hit the ball extremely well alongside Nicklaus who must have been grateful for such a quiet, efficient partner.

Weiskopf's beautiful striking had its reward, Vaughan played admirably to join such illustrious company and the great old champion, Palmer himself, finished in the grand manner and had enjoyed his Championship. The course was a flawless example of the finest concept of traditional links golf and the organisation, conspicuously efficient, deserved its great success and the perfect summer days.

The scores

278: L. Trevino (US) 71, 70, 66, 71 (£5,500)

279: J. Nicklaus (US) 70, 72, 71, 66 (£4,000)

280: A. Jacklin (Potters Bar) 69, 72, 67, 72 (£3,250)

281: D. Sanders (US) 71, 71, 69, 70 (£2,750)

283: B.W. Barnes (Fairway) 71, 72, 69, 71 (£2,450)

285: G. Player (S Africa) 71, 71, 76, 67

286: D.I. Vaughan (North Wales) 74, 73, 70, 69; T. Weiskopf (US) 73, 74, 70, 69; A.D. Palmer (US) 73, 73, 69, 71; G.L. Hunt (Wentworth) 75, 72, 67, 72

1973

Troon, 16th July

WEISKOPF SURMOUNTS PERSONAL BARRIER

Pat Ward-Thomas sums up the Open Golf

Tom Weiskopf brought vast power and a delicate putting touch to Troon to win the 1973 Championship by three shots.

Now that Tom Weiskopf has won his first important championship there is no telling what fulfilment may await one of the greatest talents in the modern game. His victory in the Open at Troon, masterfully and serenely achieved, was as if he had passed through a psychological barrier. His failures, narrow though they often were, on previous occasions were of temperament rather than technique.

That he should win was entirely fitting. He had led after every round, and his last one of 70 never gave his pursuers an opening. Coles and Nicklaus, with great rounds of 66 and 65, could have made life very difficult for him had he been at all vulnerable. But, as Yancey remarked, he always kept the pressure on. His total of 276 (68, 67, 71, 70) which equalled Arnold Palmer's record set in 1962 on the same links, was three strokes lower than those of Miller and Coles, with Nicklaus one further behind. Otherwise only Yancey was in the hunt; after him came an unusual gap of five strokes.

Weiskopf and Miller have dominated the American and British Open this summer on courses which played similarly with holding greens and little wind. In figure one would hope to see them examined under more demanding conditions. Neither Oakmont nor Troon played true to character, but they were the same for everyone and these two golfers emerged as entirely deserving champions.

Weiskopf has had a rare sequence of success recently. In succession he has finished first, first, second, first, third in the US Open, fifth, and now first again. This is the outcome, as he said, of having 'really worked at my game as hard as I can,' possibly for the first time in some years. It was said of Weiskopf that apart from an impatient nature, he lacked the ultimate ambition for greatness. His performance at Troon would seem to be a splendid contradiction.

After his anxious passage in the third round, the overcoming of which was the root of victory, he practised until satisfied with his alignment. That night he did not sleep well, but perfect opening strokes revealed that his nerves were in good order. Earlier, Nicklaus cautioned him 'don't play Johnny, play the game,' invaluable advice because Weiskopf and Miller were so far ahead.

Weiskopf said that Jacklin had helped him greatly in mastering the small ball, and showing him some of the shots Troon demanded, because in practice he had felt confused. And yet he claimed that his golf in the Championship was the best, shot for shot, that he had ever played. It could hardly have been better.

The fitness of things also was admirably served by the golf of Coles, at present Britain's most accomplished player. It was his finest Open; his inward half of 32, if my researches are right, was the lowest of the week. He may never have been in a winning position, but he played supremely well, always giving the hole a chance. In the whole Championship he never took three putts, neither, for that matter, did Weiskopf, and only once did Coles fail to get down in two when he missed a green.

These facts are not quite as remarkable as they may seem because the greens are small and in the rain were always of a gentle pace. In his modest fashion Coles said that the rain made his performance possible; he has never been enamoured of fast courses. Be that as it may, he sustained a challenge to the very end which no other British player came in sight of doing.

Card of Old Troon

Hole	Yards	Par	Hole	Yards	Par
1	362	4	10	437	4
2	391	4	11	481	5
3	381	4	12	432	4
4	556	5	13	468	4
5	210	3	14	180	3
6	577	5	15	457	4
7	389	4	16	542	5
8	126	3	17	223	3
9	427	4	18	425	4
Out	3,419	36	In	3,645	36

Total 7,064 yds: Par 72

The great enigma once again was Nicklaus, who every year brings an incomparable quality of excitement to the Championship. Although starting the day nine behind he had not lost heart. Time and again in last rounds he has almost made the impossible come true. When he chipped into the thirteenth hole, after an eagle at the eleventh, and a short putt missed at the twelfth, he was seven under par for the round. Weiskopf, then around the turn, was only four ahead. Three times putts of no great length by Nicklaus lipped the hole, as did a bunker shot, and he was round in 65, 11 strokes lower than the previous day, but it was too late. Weiskopf's stately progress remained undisturbed.

Miller, playing with Weiskopf, never quite threatened to overtake him. When the issue finally rested between them alone he missed a short putt on the fifteenth, possibly because of the cheer that greeted Coles's score on the leader board as he was about to make the stroke. Again on the sixteenth he dragged a little putt wide, and when he missed the seventeenth green Weiskopf at last permitted himself to believe the Championship was his. He completed it with a one iron from the tee, and a seven iron to the green, yet another instance of his great power.

The Championship was finely presented, the marshalling was good although Troon is not comfortable for large crowds, and the scoring services, as always, were superior in speed and accuracy to any other in the world.

The scores

276: T. Weiskopf (US) 68, 67, 71, 70 (£5,500)

279: J. Miller (US) 70, 68, 69, 72; N.C. Coles (Holiday Inns) 71, 72, 70, 66 (£3,625 each)

280: J. Nicklaus (US) 69, 70, 76, 65 (£2,750)

281: B. Yancey (US) 69, 69, 73, 70 (£2,450)

286: P.J. Butler (Butler DR) 71, 72, 74, 69 (£2,150)

288: C. O'Connor (Ryl Dublin) 73, 68, 74, 73; L. Wadkins (US) 71, 73, 70, 74; R. Charles (NZ) 73, 71, 73, 71 (£1,717 each)

289: L. Trevino (US) 75, 73, 73, 68; G. Brewer (US) 76, 71, 72, 70; H. Henning (SA) 73, 73, 73, 70; B. Barnes (Fairway DR) 76, 67, 70, 76 (£1,350 each)

PLAYER'S TRANSCENDING FORM IS UNCHALLENGED

Oosterhuis a source of pride to British golf at Open

By Pat Ward-Thomas

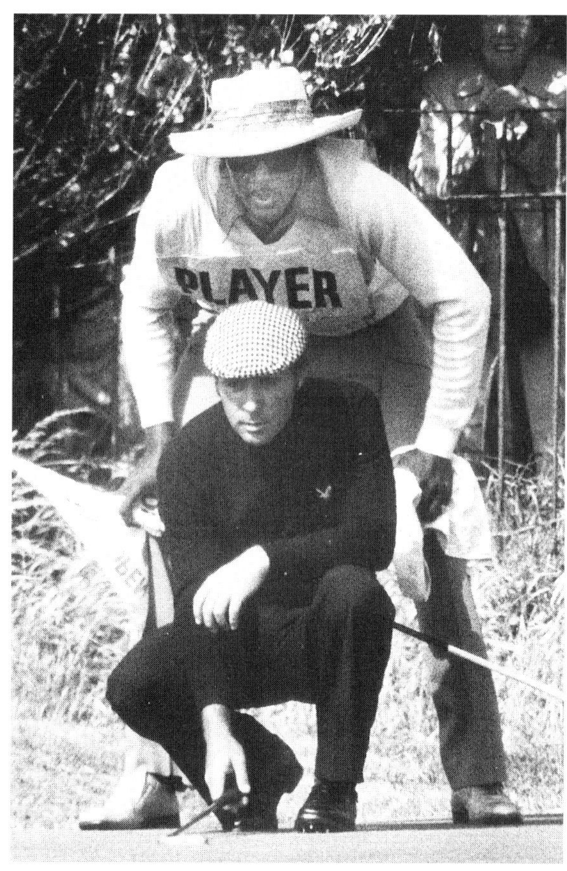

Gary Player and caddie line up at Lytham. The South African led throughout, like Weiskopf the previous year. Britain's Peter Oosterhuis was a game runner-up. The large ball was used by everyone with no complaints.

Rarely in modern times has an Open been won with greater certainty, conviction and command than that at Royal Lytham in which Gary Player's supremacy was unchallenged. He led throughout, as did Weiskopf last year, and his total of 282 (69, 68, 75, 70), two under par, was a masterful performance that even he has never surpassed. For Peter Oosterhuis four strokes behind and one ahead of Jack Nicklaus, the days were a triumph of control and composure and a source of pride to British golfers everywhere. He was beaten only by a most exceptional golfer in transcending form.

The indomitable spirit and urge for greatness that continue to drive Player to heights that few golfers have ever reached seem inexhaustible. No champion since Vardon has covered a span of 15 years and Player's eternal fitness and youthful zest make it scarcely credible that his first Open victory was at Muirfield in 1959. This was his third in Britain, and together with two Masters, two United States PGA Championships and one US Open gives him a professional tally surpassed only by Nicklaus with twelve, Hagen eleven, and Hogan nine. There is no indication that he is not capable of adding to it, as of now not even Nicklaus is his superior; as an international competitor he has had no peer in the game's history.

Anxious Player may have been the previous evening, with a lead of three strokes over Oosterhuis, but no sign of it appeared and straight away he seized, with an almost fearful tenacity, command of the situation. To begin as he did with two birdies must have been a tremendous relief. He spoke of the agony of leading, of how the four days had felt like ten, and of how on the last morning he tried to sleep again after breakfast, but that his stomach was tight with tension and he could not. Player is not famous for understatement, but one could believe him because 'no one wants to lead a major championship by so much and then lose.' Player talked also of golf being a game of chances and 'you have to find the one that fits the pattern.' He would not say what his was, apart from marvellous concentration which he described as self-hypnosis, as being in a reverie, a kind of shell, but, I believe, patience had much to do with it. He never attempted to force his game. Time and again he used an iron from the tees to ensure a safe position, confident that his subsequent iron play, which must be consistently the finest in the game, would compensate for any loss of distance.

The crux of the day depended upon Nicklaus, playing immediately ahead. He was the one man capable of the great round which would impose severe strain upon Player who, one felt, would always be able to take care of his companion, Oosterhuis. Twice previously in lesser affairs Oosterhuis had beaten him at match play, but this was different. After the second day, when Player achieved the key round of the Championship, destiny had decreed that it was to be his year.

As it proved, Nicklaus failed to take advantage of the easiest of the four days. The breeze beneath summer skies caressed from the north straight down the course; given judgment of length birdies were there for the grasping on the outward half. Player holed on the first for his third two there, hit a perfect iron to the second and thereafter was never threatened. Nicklaus could not get his putting stroke to work and although he made easy birdies on the long holes, 34 out, with two putts on every green, was not quite good enough.

Player's only anxiety came at the fourth, where he was awkwardly bunkered, and again at the fifth, but a five iron to six feet at the sixth for an eagle set these to rights. A beautiful little chip almost went into the seventh hole, and he was still five ahead. All this time Oosterhuis played bravely and looked absolutely in control of his swing; his driving was excellent and he too almost holed for an eagle at the seventh.

When Nicklaus made a four at the eleventh, and saved his worst shot of the round, a mishit one iron to the twelfth, there was still hope of a target for Player, but he missed from six feet at the thirteenth and 'this deflated me.' His drive swung across the wind into the thick rough at the fourteenth and his challenge was over.

One sensed his ebbing concentration but he summoned it, as always, in time for the final gesture to the enormous amphitheatre at the eighteenth. But he had opened the door for Oosterhuis to be second alone, and splendidly he took the chance with four successive pars. He had played wonderfully well, without recent tournament practice. It is ridiculous that he still has to prove himself in the United States school. Surely a third in the Masters and a second in the Open is sufficient indication that he can play.

Apart from the engaging Hubert Green, who seemed to enjoy himself thoroughly and finished only one behind Nicklaus, a fine effort in his first British event, as was that of Danny Edwards, all else was in a minor key. Garner, Graham Swaelens and Townsend gained many places with 69s. In every sense, save the lack of a memorable climax, it was a superb championship, as near flawless in its organisation as could be expected, and fully deserving of the record crowd for the week of over 90,000. The Royal and Ancient and Royal Lytham can indeed be proud of their labours. Lastly, any fears as to the wisdom of using the big ball proved to have no foundation.

The scores

282: G. Player (S. Africa) 69, 68, 75, 70 (£5,500)

286: P. Oosterhuis (Fiji) 71, 71, 73, 71 (£4,000)

287: J. Nicklaus (USA) 74, 72, 70, 71 (£3,250)

288: H.M. Green (USA) 71, 74, 72, 71 (£2,750)

292: D. Edwards (USA) 70, 73, 76, 73; Lu Liang Huan (Taiwan) 72, 72, 75, 73 (£2,300 each)

293: D. Swaelens (Belgium) 77, 73, 74, 69; R. Cole (S Africa) 70, 72, 76, 75; T. Weiskopf (USA) 72, 72, 74, 75 (£1,713 each)

294: J. Miller (USA) 72, 75, 73, 74 (£1,500)

1975

Carnoustie, 14th July

WATSON ON THE FAIRWAY TO GREAT FUTURE

Open Golf by Pat Ward-Thomas

A splendid young champion in Tom Watson, of the United States, arose from the damp gloom of Carnoustie yesterday when he beat Jack Newton, of Australia, by one stroke in the play-off. Watson was round in 71, one under par, after a thoroughly absorbing and finely played contest. Very few golfers have ever won the Open at their first attempt. The last instances were Tony Lema at St Andrews and Ben Hogan here, and then possibly Densmore Shute in 1933.

This remarkable achievement revealed the uncommon strength of his character. Many would have been set back by his failures after leading two successive US Opens, and by the seventh at the short sixteenth in the Masters' this spring, but he learned from the anguish of disappointment and gained in strength and adversity. Watson succeeds Armour, Cotton, Hogan, and Player, and of all the young golfers in the world at present none could be more deserving of this great honour. Watson is intelligent, extremely clear minded, and attractive in appearance, quietly and simply dressed and lacking in affectation. In short he is the type that American golf needs to perpetuate the example set by Nicklaus and Palmer of how to behave at all times. An instance of his good manners was when, receiving the trophy by the last green, he publicly apologised to a cameraman with whom he had remonstrated for moving as he was about to strike from the third tee.

Although small and lightly built, his swing develops unusual power; the movement is crisp and beautifully balanced. Speaking cheerfully but calmly afterwards he said: 'I feel confident now that my swing has held up, and that I can rely on it no matter what happens.'

He paid a warm tribute to Byron Nelson, a great champion of other years who was here to provide encouragement after Watson's failure at Winged Foot last summer, and also to give advice before Watson faced the difficult conditions on Saturday.

Of the future, Watson said: 'I would like to be known as a great golfer by my peers, and be a good human being.' I think he will achieve both ambitions.

In the play-off Watson went ahead when a four-iron shot bounced kindly for him at the second; Newton, disturbed by a child mishit his next tee shot and was two behind. The crucial point for Watson, he claimed, was at the fifth where he was twice bunkered but got down in two and avoided losing his lead. He did so, however, when Newton played a fine bunker shot and won the sixth. Watson also had to hole from 15 feet to salvage a three at the eighth, where Newton had a good chance of a two.

Newton was lucky when his stance at the eleventh was on a rabbit scrape when he had no shot for the green. Relief without penalty almost enabled him to make a birdie and then, for the first time, he drove on the fairway, made a good four at the twelfth, and was ahead... but only for one hole. If the fifth was important to Watson, the thirteenth was for Newton. From an unlucky lie in a bunker he skimmed the ball over the green but made a brave putt for a four. Even again, but then came Watson's break. Both chipped well from the fringe of the fourteenth but Watson went in for an eagle. Again Newton drew level with a beautifully judged putt up the slope of the sixteenth, where Watson, for the fifth time in the Championship, failed to make a three.

Watson's nerve and beautiful putting stroke were sorely examined on the seventeenth, where he had to hole from five feet to stay level. The ball went straight into the middle of the hole.

In the dripping rain that had beset the last few holes they came into the great amphitheatre. Many of the four or five thousand who had followed climbed into the stands and watched Watson play his winning stroke. His drive was dead down the centre and after Newton's two iron from the rough had found a bunker his shot with the same club, struck a shade heavily though it was, found the heart of the green. Newton hit a splendid bunker shot from some 25 yards but on the damp grass it skidded a little and, after Watson had very nearly holed for a three, and holed out, Newton had to hole a putt of 15ft for salvation. Sadly for him it slipped just by or we would have watched the first sudden death for an Open on either side of the Atlantic. Newton had made a very fine contest of the afternoon which, rare in such instances, did not produce an anticlimax.

Saturday's events at Carnoustie were similar to those at the United States Open. No one made a conspicuous challenge for victory but the racking-off process left unexpected survivors.

In this sense it was not a great championship, and the elements were mainly responsible. The absence for three days of a demanding test of stroke play and the over-emphasis on putting, then the complete switch and strengthening of the wind on Saturday had an undoubted effect. Without in any way begrudging Watson and Newton their prominence, the historical stature of the Championship would have been enhanced had Nicklaus or Miller, or both, been involved in the play-off. Personally, I was sorry that Cole was not.

The Championship was notable more for errors than great strokes and Cole, Nicklaus, and Miller particularly will recall it as one of lost opportunities. Cole could have played the last five holes, all down wind except the seventeenth, in one over par and won. The fourteenth was very short but Cole missed this green and the next with shortish irons.

The moving of the winds to the west during the preceding night had transformed the course, a merciful change from its monotonously easy state. Very few knew the course against the wind going out; a readjustment of distance was essential and, rightly, several pin positions were severe. Although Nicklaus was four strokes behind I felt that his massive experience would compensate, particularly as those ahead of him, except Miller, would probably be vulnerable to the pressure over the closing holes.

Tom Watson beat Jack Newton of Australia by a shot in the 1975 Carnoustie play-off to win the Open at his first attempt.

As it happened, Nicklaus missed a short putt on the sixth and failed to make his four at the seventh, now very difficult into the wind. He came home in 34 but was never in sight of a birdie on the closing holes except at the eighteenth, where his little chip shot almost disappeared. And so his incomparable record of marginal failures continues. Apart from his two victories he has been second four times, three times third, and only twice outside the first six in 14 years.

For Miller, too, it was a cruelly disappointing day. For the most part he played finely controlled par golf and seemed likely to win or at least tie if he could play the last three holes in par. The sixteenth, still a threateningly narrow target even though the tee shot was two or three clubs short, defeated him as it did Cole, Watson, and Newton.

The finish produced the first real excitement of the Championship for the experienced watcher. After Nicklaus had finished on 280 Miller and Watson needed a birdie on the last two holes to beat him. Into the breeze the seventeenth needed two perfectly judged shots. Both made admirable fours, then Miller's drive just failed to draw away from the bunkers on the last fairway. As millions doubtless saw his sixth iron, as he perforce went for the green, did not emerge at the first attempt, but his little chip shot for a four, like that of Nicklaus, threatened the hole.

Then Watson, after a lovely pitch, holed his putt for a three and the possibility of a quadruple or even quintuple tie was averted. Many people discounted Watson after seeing him take three putts on the first three greens after the turn but apart from the sixteenth, where he tried to float a one iron from the tee, he played the last six holes better than all those about him.

The great stage, the stands packed with thousands, now belonged to Cole and Newton alone. Both were fortunate not to be in the Barry burn at the seventeenth. Newton, to the astonishment of those near the tee, took an iron, Cole a driver, but he pulled it slightly. Both shots finished on the bank of the burn, leaving awkward stances. Fives there meant that Newton needed a four to tie, and Cole a three. Newton hit a punched nine iron from the light rough, Cole only a wedge after a superb long drive, but sadly he misread the line of his putt. Newton, uncertain of his putt to win, understandably made a not great stab at it and left himself a beastly little one, which he referred to as a 'knickertwister'.

Fittingly, Coles and Oosterhuis headed the little British contingent. Neither was ever in the thick of the last battle but they tied for seventh, as did Oosterhuis in the US Open. Graham Marsh, with the lowest round of the leaders, played very solid golf without remarkable putting and deservedly finished sixth alone. Only 22 British and Irish players were in the 63 who qualified for the day, and only three finished in the first 18, a depressing reflection of the present state of professional tournament golf in these islands.

Play-off: hole by hole

	OUT			IN		
Par	444	445	434–36	445	354	344–36–72
Watson	434	455	434–36	445	334	444–35–71
Newton	445	444	434–36	444	444	345–36–72

When Tom Watson received the Open Championship trophy from the R. and A. captain, Sir John Carmichael, a few minutes after victory he found his name already engraved on the trophy, thanks to the speedy work of Alexander Harvey, of Perth, the official engraver for the R. and A.

'I was able to engrave the last two letters beforehand as both names finished with "on",' said Harvey. He got the name of the new champion right but the R. and A. captain did not. While publicly congratulating him he called him 'Tom Kite'.

The scores

Play-off – T. Watson (USA) 71 (£7,500); J. Newton (Australia) 72 (£6,000)

279: T. Watson (USA) 71, 67, 69, 72; J. Newton (Aust) 69, 71, 65, 74

280: J. Nicklaus (USA) 69, 71, 68, 72; J. Miller (USA) 71, 69, 66, 74; R. Cole (S Africa) 72, 66, 66, 76 (£3,866 each)

281: G.V. Marsh (Aust) 72, 67, 71, 71 (£3,000)

282: P.A. Oosterhuis (Pacific Harbour) 68, 70, 71, 73; N.C. Coles (Holiday Inns) 72, 69, 67, 74 (£2,700 each)

283: H. Irwin (USA) 69, 70, 69, 75 (£2,400)

284: G.F. Burns (USA) 71, 73, 69, 71; J.D. Mahaffey (USA) 71, 68, 69, 76 (£2,125 each)

1976

MILLER SEES THE GREEN LIGHT

By Pat Ward-Thomas at Royal Birkdale

Everyone was beginning to wonder when Johnny Miller would win a second major championship because three years had passed since his victory in the United States Open. His response at Royal Birkdale could not have been more emphatic. Palmer also triumphed by six strokes at Troon in 1962, but not since J.H. Taylor, who won by eight at Hoylake in 1913, has the margin been greater.

A final round of 66 – a score equalled only by Mark James in the Championship – gave Miller a total of 279 (72, 68, 73, 66) six ahead of Severiano Ballesteros and Jack Nicklaus. Ray Floyd was fourth, and the home counties were splendidly represented by Tommy Horton, Christy O'Connor jnr, and, remarkably, James with a share of fifth place.

Miller became the thirteenth golfer to win the Opens of the United States and Britain, an enduring mark of distinction which raises him into the category his shining talent deserves. More important, from his viewpoint, it was his second major victory. Several times in Britain and in the Masters he had come close and he was aware that to have missed the opportunity at Birkdale would have endangered his confidence and that of people in him.

He is much a golfer of moods. 'It is green light or red light, there is no in-between; I do not just play good tournaments like Nicklaus, but I am a heck of a front-runner.' This was an undeniable statement of fact, not a boast. When Miller is feeling right and senses that the tide is with him he becomes irresistible.

From the moment he arrived last Monday he said he was bubbling with enthusiasm and strength but – 'This was the most conservative tournament I have ever played.' To this end the one iron which, in the last round, he used from eight tees and 10 times in all, was the key club. He had decided that any score below par would win, and in the event a 71 would have sufficed. Apart from the one iron, his wedges, and putter, Miller's irons were graphite shafted, assembled for him shortly before he left America.

Although there was to be no stirring finish, the climax was alive with contrasting emotions. Admiration for Miller's beautiful, transcending golf was mingled with that for the courage and smiling charm of Ballesteros; the golf of James, whose 66 first set the pace, and the resolution with which Horton and O'Connor played to the very end.

It was a heartening day for British golf. That James, less than a year after turning professional, should finish so high was a great performance. Faldo, who had a 69, continues to gain in strength and his total was four strokes lower than those of Jacklin and Oosterhuis.

The memory of Ballesteros will live long. Far from being unnerved by having led for three days, he continued to attack. This was the happy nature of the man but it was expensive. He hit only three fairways from the tee, and as Miller said: 'He was so bold, but his driver killed him.'

Many a golfer, having shed early strokes, would have vanished without trace. That he came back so strongly was a tremendous feat and gave the huge crowds great entertainment. No continental golfer since van Donck in 1956 and 1959 in much weaker fields has been second. I hope the Spanish properly understand that he is a great player in the making.

Finally there was sympathy for Nicklaus, second for the fifth time in the only major championship he has not won more than twice. His son Jackie as caddy did his utmost for him. Without telling his parents, on the last day he wore the same clothes he had on when winning a junior tournament in America, hoping he might bring his father luck. It was not to be, but he shared the incomparable ovation that the Open accords its heroes – a rare experience for a boy.

The outline of the plot for the last day was simple. Could Miller's closest pursuers pressure him, and would the elements favour his golf? The breeze remained a helpful zephyr, but no more, for three of the last long holes. Nicklaus and Floyd were well aware than an early attack might unsettle Miller, but that if they gave him a few lengths they might never see him again.

Rarely can one point to a single early hole as being so crucial to the outcome. The sixth was so for Miller. Nicklaus and Floyd, two pairs ahead of him each made two birdies in the first five holes; then Nicklaus's tee shot to the sixth finished close to a bunker in the dunes crossing the fairway. He had 220 yards to go to the green but had to make sure that he got the ball up quickly to avoid the bunker and also to be sure of not hooking from an uphill lie.

In so attempting, Nicklaus blocked the shot, which vanished forever in willow scrub and he took six. Floyd had a five and when, soon afterwards, Miller holed from four yards for his four and Ballesteros tacked his way to a six, I was certain the pattern of affairs had been determined.

Masterfully though Nicklaus continued to play to the greens he could not, as on the previous day, hole the telling shortish puts. The reason, he said, was that when the greens are somewhat 'bristly' he was unable to get the ball rolling from his putter and the stroke suffered. He was condemned to continuing frustration. Floyd played wellnigh as solidly but after the sixth was never quite in sight of the essential low round.

The short twelfth was another key hole. The pin was set in the right corner of the bank – enclosed green with the breeze from the right. The shots of Nicklaus and Floyd hit the green but bounded away to the fringe from where they took three more. Miller's glorious four iron settled soft as a feather 10 ft from the flag and he holed for a two. The Championship then was almost decided because Ballesteros had heavily lost yet another encounter with the dunes on the eleventh and had taken seven.

When Miller chipped into the thirteenth hole for an eagle after missing the fairway from the tee – 'My only bad shot, I felt the tournament was mine and that I could relax and enjoy it.' but Ballesteros was far from finished. With wonderful spirit he continued to attack, holed long putts at the fourteenth and seventeenth, played a marvellous little pitch at the last, and drew level with Nicklaus. What more could any golfer of 19 hope to achieve?

Johnny Miller celebrates the Open title after a last round of sixty-six. It gave him a six-shot triumph over Nicklaus and a then little-known Severiano Ballesteros (right).

The scores

279: J. Miller (USA) 72, 68, 73, 66

285: J.W. Nicklaus (USA) 74, 70, 72, 69; S. Ballesteros (Spain) 69, 69, 73, 74

286: R. Floyd (USA) 76, 67, 73, 70

288: M. James (Burghley Park) 76, 72, 74, 66; H. Green (USA) 72, 70, 78, 68; T. Kite Jnr (USA) 70, 74, 73, 71; C. O'Connor Jnr (Shannon) 69, 73, 75, 71; T. Horton (R Jersey) 74, 69, 72, 73

289: V. Fernandez (Argentina) 79, 71, 69, 70; P.J. Butler (unattached) 74, 72, 73, 70; N. Suzuki (Japan) 69, 75, 75, 70; G. Burns III (USA) 75, 69, 75, 70

THE NICE PART OF BEING BEATEN

By Frank Keating

The nice guys finish second, they say. And so it was at the end of the Birkdale Desert Classic on Saturday. But in golf nice guys finish first as well. To me, one of the most enduring memories of a memorable Championship was the way Miller nursed and encouraged his closest rival, young Ballesteros, through the final holes.

The astonishing Spanish teenager who had so charged the tournament with refreshing devil-may-care, seemed on the point of cracking about six holes from home. But with handshake and backpat, Miller caressed the boy back from the brink of what could have been, for him and all others, a suicidal anti-climax.

After the eleventh, the likelihood of Ballesteros dropping off the largest leaderboard like a brick out of a biplane was very real. Miller soothingly piloted him through the disaster area and the boy gave up biting his lip and was cheerily ready to play dare again to the extent of thrilling birdies at the thirteenth and fourteenth, a rampaging eagle at the seventeenth and a celebration birdie for all the world in the vast arena of the eighteenth. The champion traditionally makes the last putt. But this time Miller put his in and then stood back to let Ballesteros sign off the Championship.

And afterwards Miller ('praise the Lord and pass my No. 1') was still thinking of the kid. 'Don't get me wrong, but I think it's a real good thing for Sevvy that he didn't win. Day in day out he wouldn't yet be able to back it up. He might have been swamped by the resulting pressures. Now lots of lovely things can happen to him because he's come second. Just like me: best thing that happened to me was not winning the Masters in 1971, but coming second. It gave me just that bit more time to prepare myself for winning a big one.'

The finale as ever was a plush curtain to draw to a close a week's outstanding memories. The week that started with our own Pat Ward-Thomas winning the star-studded Press Golf Society's tournament at Hesketh (it took till Friday to explain how he did it and then only thanks to a combination of Tom Weiskopf's gracious gift of wine and the fact that the US Open champion, poor Pate, had taken seven shots more than our celebrated hyphen to get round a golf course).

It continued through such events as jolly Jack Newton saying that he liked playing a round with Miller, but he always remembered never to talk to him about booze or birds; Miller himself saying that if he broke his No. 1 iron (which he used 21 times in the final 36 holes) it would be like a death in the family; coming across S. Ballesteros in the locker room, pulling on his Johnny Miller Patent Slacks, conspiratorially and enviously examining the other pros' equipment; coming across him again in deep trouble at the fifteenth, but before examining his awful lie, taking time off to smell the scent of a flowering bush of yellow bracken; to hear the same dark-eyed Severiano discuss with his brother the merits of two busty local groupies outside a Southport disco. To faithfully but vainly raise a glass each night and pray that Jacklin and Oosterhuis pull themselves together for Queen and Country, but then to exalt at the spunky play of Barnes, his best pal Horton – and at the last the trenchant flag-carrying of young James and Faldo.

But the pleasure of the week to a tyro in the press tent (who realised that big time sport, and one in which pay cheques are highest, still has room for graciousness and fair play and where gamesmanship is ever expelled) was to shake hands and sit briefly at the feet of the man who still carries the public banner for all the game's enduring virtues. Jack Nicklaus. A long-ago paragraph by Alistair Cooke about Bobby Jones sits well on Nicklaus: '. . . The best performer in the world who was also the hero as human being, the gentle, chivalrous, wholly self-sufficient male. Jefferson's lost paragon: the wise innocent.' And when soon the time comes for Nicklaus to hand over the banner, a Jolly Miller will be there to hold it as high. Or, for that matter, so would just about anyone else. Professional golfers are a credit to professional sport.

1977

WATSON IS HEIR TO THE KINGDOM

Pat Ward-Thomas on Nicklaus's successor

Records galore as Watson (right) beat Nicklaus by a stroke in a head-to-head battle. Watson lowered the record aggregate by eight shots and Nicklaus by seven. Mark Hayes' sixty-three was the lowest round in any Open and the crowd total of 92,200 the biggest ever in Scotland. Total prize money was £100,000 with Watson taking £10,000.

In all the history of the Open Championship there can never have been a contest to surpass the one at Turnberry in which Tom Watson, for the second time this season, faced and overcame formidable opposition from Jack Nicklaus. One never thought to see the day when the champion would have to play the final 36 holes in 130 strokes and finish with a birdie for a total of 268 to win by a single shot; nor that the Open's record would be beaten by eight.

That Hubert Green in third place was eleven strokes behind Watson emphasised the immense superiority of the two leaders not only at Turnberry but in the world. For sustained attack and counter on such a pitch of scoring right down to the wire it was an epic that may not be approached for generations. Let no one think that the course was all that short. For his shots to the greens in the last round Watson twice used wood, twice a long iron and seven times medium irons. Nicklaus's clubbing was similar.

The capacity of Nicklaus for momentous conquest has long been famous; now Watson has done so twice and proved that he has full measure of the qualities for lasting greatness. His courage, resilience and golfing perception are remarkable. His technique has matured to a very high degree in swing, power without strain, rhythm and shot making.

And withal Watson is an uncommonly intelligent man. Britain could have no more fitting champion. If the reign of Nicklaus as a winner of great titles is drawing to a close Watson is the perfect successor, but I doubt that Nicklaus will relinquish his kingdom lightly. Even for the most successful golfer of all time defeat was acutely disappointing. This was the sixth time he has been second and a third victory would have rounded off an almost impregnable tally in major championships.

The match, because match it was, with no one else involved, revealed Watson's resource and unyielding character. When Nicklaus made a birdie at the second, and holed for two at the fourth he was three ahead but Watson struck back immediately. After a perfect five iron to the fifth he holed for a three and then came a crucial hole.

Watson was bunkered by the green but got down in two, as he did on two other occasions during the round, and avoided being three behind again. As if to celebrate he hit a wonderful driver shot of some 250 yards from a tight lie to the seventh, while Nicklaus from the rough could not get home. As on the fifth and eighth, where Watson made another birdie, Nicklaus's drives had not made matching them likely.

Neither played the ninth, with its blind drive from the rocks, well but Nicklaus holed and Watson missed putts of similar length. Again Nicklaus went ahead on the 12th but again Watson countered with a birdie and then came the shot that, conceivably, won him the Championship. Ironically it was probably his worst of the round but led to the most telling thrust. His four iron to the 15th was pulled some twenty yards left of the flag and was fortunate not to be bunkered. Nicklaus had every reason to expect that Watson would take two or even three more but he putted through the light rough straight into the hole. This was a cruel blow for Nicklaus.

The match was even again and the two great men were quite alone since Crenshaw's remote challenge had evaporated. So absorbed were the huge crowds that whenever a shot was about to be played you could feel the tension in the deep silence broken only by the whisper of the breeze.

Both hit long drives into the valley of the 17th. Watson's perfect three-iron shot backed down the green and Nicklaus knew it must be fairly close. His second shot was pushed into light rough; he played a splendid chip but finally missed from four feet.

Watson finished like the great champion he is, hitting what was at such a moment a marvellous approach with a seven iron to within a yard of the last hole. The huge amphitheatre thundered its approval but Nicklaus, whose drive was lucky by inches not to finish unplayable in gorse, never yielded and was not about to make victory easy for Watson. His recovery with an eight iron found the green, he holed his long putt and made Watson hole his to survive a truly extraordinary contest, magnificent in its skills and character. As Nicklaus smiled his congratulations and walked from the green, his arm about Watson's shoulders, we knew that this day would remain in the memory for ever more.

All else was in a minor, almost inaudible key. Green did splendidly after his unhappy third round, everyone was sad for Crenshaw but delighted for Palmer, whose last two rounds were 67 and 69, enabling him to finish seventh. The pride of the great champions rarely fails when the Open comes around. The first eight places were occupied by Americans, and Horton, who shared ninth place with three more, was the leading British player. This was a reasonable expression of the present state of affairs. By every count, of which I am aware, the Championship was a great success. The crowds were the largest ever in Scotland, the organisation was equal to its demanding tasks and so Turnberry richly justified its choice as an Open course and so doubtless the Championship will return there.

The scores

(US unless stated)

268: T. Watson 68, 70, 65, 65 (£10,000)

269: J. Nicklaus 68, 70, 65, 66 (£8,000)

279: H.M. Green 72, 66, 74, 67 (£6,000)

280: L. Trevino 68, 70, 72, 70 (£5,000)

281: G. Burns 70, 70, 72, 69; B. Crenshaw 71, 69, 66, 75 (£4,250 each)

282: A. Palmer 73, 73, 67, 69 (£3,750)

283: R. Floyd 70, 73, 68, 72 (£3,500)

284: J. Schroeder 66, 74, 73, 71; M. Hayes 76, 63, 72, 73; J. Miller 69, 74, 67, 74; T. Horton (Ryl Jersey) 70, 74, 65, 75 (£2,875 each)

Turnberry celebrated its first Open with a classic shoot-out and Scotland's largest crowds. Press photographers delighted in the visual attractions of the ninth tee.

1978

NICKLAUS AT NEW THRESHOLD WITHOUT THE OLD POWER

John Samuel reports from St Andrews

The Scottish Constabulary take full care of Jack Nicklaus, the only golfer to win the British and US Open Championships, the Masters, and the US PGA three times.

Jack Nicklaus, with a victory as mature in attitude as it was in technique, arrived at a new threshold for modern golfers with his third Open Championship at St Andrews on Saturday. No golfer in history has three times won every major championship – the British and US Opens, the Masters and the US PGA – but it is totally the order of the man that afterwards he claimed no unsurpassing virtues.

'Sure, there'll be someone else along, 6ft 4in, knocking it up to the hole, birdying his putts like crazy, who'll see off Jack Nicklaus's records. It's the same all over in sport. No one is unbeatable for ever.'

Nicklaus at 38 won because he believes he is now a better player and wiser than he has ever been. Not because he hits it as far as the great golden bear of youth. He no longer overpowers a course as once he did: St Andrews was not there to be floored with a few cuffs of a mighty paw.

When he saw Simon Owen, the 27-year-old New Zealander, effectively the finalist with him, taking his driver to the inward holes, he was quietly pleased. The back nine with the wind behind, as suddenly it became after five days in completely the reverse direction, are not to be attacked with the bludgeon. Sooner or later, Nicklaus felt, Owen had to be in trouble. It was a long time coming. Owen, with his pitch from 20 yards, just off the fifteenth green, rattling into the hole, at this point had shot five threes in eight holes, three birdies among them.

'He didn't back off the Old Course,' said Nicklaus with typical generosity. 'He charged it all the way.' Just as Ballesteros did, just as Palmer, for all his experience, tried to do. The respect that Nicklaus has for the nature of British golf, the cathedral hush of the record crowds, the clapping which in these parts, anyway, breaks out only for a genuinely good piece of play, was never more reciprocated than the swelling applause as he walked, with pride but without arrogance, to the eighteenth.

He had not won at this point. But few doubted for a moment that the Open had chosen him for its winner. Owen could have chipped up and putted for a birdie three; Nicklaus, with a seven-iron chip to the back of the green, could have three putted. That thought occurred to Nicklaus for the first time as he walked up the shelf of the green which he knew could have left any chicken-hearted shot contemptuously at its foot. He putted the 35-footer stone dead, and we all knew he would.

The crises of the round came at the fourth and the sixteenth. At the 463-yard fourth, the Ginger Beer, his drive found a poor lie. A seven iron left him 70 yards short, but a sand wedge to six feet and a single putt saved his par. At the sixteenth, Owen, winner of only one major tournament, the 1974 German Open, stood to the tee after his extraordinary chip into the fifteenth hole, seven under to Nicklaus's six. Both drives were good. Owen, all fired up, was longer than the mighty Nicklaus, as often these days the young and unwary are.

Nicklaus now employed yet more of that wisdom which makes him, still, the most formidable player in the world. His nine iron was precisely played to six feet short of the pin of the plateau green with a tricky hollow beyond. Owen, still mightily charged, took a sand wedge for a shot no more than 80 yards, and hit it all of 120. He remarked afterwards that never had he hit a wedge so far. 'I really don't know what happened.' Anyway, it was in the hollow with a serpent-like set of bumps and curves to negotiate to the flag.

Surprisingly, in view of the chip before, he took his putter, but left himself badly short. Two more putts, with Nicklaus sinking his own putt for a birdie, and the lead had abruptly changed hands. It was a blow to heart and mind. Up at the hotel by the seventeenth, immediately ahead, eight chefs, all in a row, were etched against the sky-line on the top floor. Owen's goose, one felt, could not have been more completely cooked.

The seventeenth's fangs were drawn in the following wind. Nicklaus played it almost meekly to the front of the green, and two-putted over the crest – his first four there of the Championship. Owen was over the road and chipping back for a five.

So to a climax of enduring memory. Nicklaus has promised he will be back, God willing. He has many challengers, as this great event showed. Faldo, of Britain, not yet 21, was ninth, only four shots behind the mighty man, and must surely represent an exciting home challenge. Oosterhuis, one shot better, must rue his three putts on the thirteenth which effectively ended his hopes, but a consistent performance it was. Floyd, like Nicklaus, arrived early for practice while the wind was in the west, as on Saturday, and profited with a fine round of 68, with six birdies in the home nine.

Not least encouraging for Britain's huge array of amateur golfers, McEvoy finished on 293, only a shot adrift of Player, Palmer, Barnes, Cullen and Brown. Three other amateurs – Brodie, Miller and Godwin – made the final cut.

The final words ought to rest with Nicklaus. 'I am very proud of myself to have done what I had to do so well. You get unhappy at times. Three years without a major win makes you think, "Am I ever going to win again?" I had been playing lousy and winning on

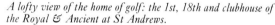

A lofty view of the home of golf: the 1st, 18th and clubhouse of the Royal & Ancient at St Andrews.

the tour. This was different. Next year, I'll maybe cut my schedule a little more, but I'll continue to play as long as I enjoy it.'

MUTUAL RESPECT MAKES SUCCESS SO MUCH SWEETER

By Pat Ward-Thomas

Once again, St Andrews has been the place of destiny for Jack Nicklaus. His victory was as if the gods, as in 1970, having made him do penance for three lean years, relented and rewarded him in the golfing place closest to his heart. Not since James Braid in 1910 has any golfer won the Open twice on the Old Course.

As if to emphasise his massive superiority over the past decade and more, his 15th major victory as a professional came just over 16 years after his first. If this triumph proves to be his last, then it could not have happened in more splendid fashion. Nicklaus has now won all four major championships at least three times, a tally that may remain unapproached for generations to come.

For one who has failed so often in the Open, usually by the narrowest margins, it was entirely suitable that he should win again but, far more than that, his victory was just reward for one whose presence over so many years has been of incalculable benefit to the Championship. Had he, as the supreme golfer of his time, decided not to compete, other Americans might have followed suit and the Open would have declined as it did in the fifties.

That Nicklaus has played every year since 1962 is partly because from youth he has had a deep respect for the tradition of the game. Very soon he came to love and respect the whims and variables of British seaside golf, and aside from any question of winning, or money, positively enjoys the challenge to his mind and technique that they afford.

Bobby Jones was his earliest hero – probably his only one in golf – and I am sure that Nicklaus's admirable father ensured that his son would profit from the example of Jones. I am sure, too, that had Jones been at his beloved St Andrews on Saturday, he would have been proud indeed.

This victory has set aside the doubts, which I was beginning to share, that his formidable mental powers as a competitor were waning somewhat. There was no conceivable sign of it here because, as he said, he did what he had to do when it mattered most. There was nothing amiss with his nerve and concentration.

To say that I was anxious for him to win needs no excusing. Obviously, a British victory would be welcome, but not until a golfer of fitting class emerges, and there has not been one since Jacklin. I felt that another victory at St Andrews for Nicklaus was essential not only to round off, although not necessarily complete, a championship-winning career, but as the most fitting accolade to a prodigious talent and to one whose example in all the ways of golf has been a great benefit to the game.

I first saw Nicklaus play in 1957 and down all the years since have come to know him well, as a golfer and a domestic person, a side of his life that means a great deal to him and which has helped him to achieve a wonderfully balanced outlook. Balance, I am certain, has been one of the main keys to his continuing success. Another is that although he is a superb professional golfer, he has always approached the game in a spirit that is basically amateur in the grace with which he has accepted defeat and triumph alike.

Nicklaus is an uncommon human being and golf has been blessed that he should remain its foremost figure for so long. When in the lovely evening sunshine the vast throng gathered around the timeless setting, thundered their applause for his triumph, they were acclaiming not only a great champion but a man they had taken to their hearts.

The scores

281: J. Nicklaus (US) 71, 72, 69, 69

283: R. Floyd (US) 69, 75, 71, 68; T. Kite (US) 72, 69, 72, 70; B. Crenshaw (US) 70, 69, 73, 71; S.M. Owen (NZ) 70, 75, 67, 71

284: P. Oosterhuis (Mission Hills) 72, 70, 69, 73

285: R. Shearer (Aus) 71, 69, 74, 71; J. Schroeder (US) 74, 69, 70, 72; N. Faldo (unatt) 71, 72, 70, 72; I. Aoki (Japan) 68, 71, 73, 73

1979 Lytham St Annes, 23rd July

FORTISSIMO IN THE FINAL MOVEMENT

Peter Dobereiner at the Open Championship

Seve Ballesteros wins the 1979 Open at Lytham, the first by a continental European since Arnaud Massy in 1907. Everyone who had watched him knew his destiny was a sporting Valhalla.

It is rather early for reflections in tranquillity on the 108th Open Championship at Lytham because, after that final storming day with Severiano Ballesteros's triumph, tranquillity is a long time returning.

The winner of a major championship – and the Open must be the major championship par excellence – automatically assumes the status of a demigod within the game, and nearly everyone who has ever watched Ballesteros in action must have recognised his destiny in this sporting Valhalla.

What came as a shock and delight was the way he kicked down the doors, elbowed the mighty Jack Nicklaus, Hale Irwin, and Tom Watson aside, and plonked himself down in the seat of honour.

The dust of that brutal assault has not yet settled. Debris continues to fall. It will take a while for the spectators of the violence to recover; we are dazed like witnesses to a nearby explosion . . . not a scratch on us, but the medics know that we are candidates for a cup of sweet, strong tea and a quiet lie down. Tranquillity will come later.

What can be said is that the day's events produced a clear pattern. Ballesteros, two strokes behind Irwin at the start, went into the decisive fourth round in a cautious frame of mind. He sank a good birdie putt at the first hole, which was heartening, as he showed with the most incandescent grin in golf, but it was no reason to cause him to change his tactics.

Out came the No. 1 iron, symbol of prudence, on the next tee and he clipped a modest one safely up the fairway no more than 290 yards.

As the round progressed the opposition cracked. Some, like Watson, went quickly. Some, notably Nicklaus, Mark James, and the tenacious Ben Crenshaw, faltered just enough to stimulate the devil in Ballesteros. The Australian Rodger Davis and Isao Aoki of Japan, actually edged briefly into the lead before they disappeared.

Ballesteros detected the trend and reacted in typical style. Those watching him for the first time may have though it was desperation which prompted him to start going for broke. Old Ballesteros-watchers knew differently; it was the Spaniard's essential nature coming out. He hates to pussyfoot around. His way is to bludgeon the course into submission and, in the process, accelerate the downfall of the demoralised opposition.

His fortissimo golf was a sight to behold. I swear he has never hit the ball harder. When he let fly with his driver he had to improvise an Arnold Palmer twiddle with the club on the follow-through to prevent himself from falling over.

It is to be hoped that his orthopaedic specialist was not watching after advising him to give his back more consideration. The medical ban on long air flights may prevent Ballesteros from cashing in fully on his win.

America is where the endorsement plums are fattest, and it is sad for us that such a player may not be able to represent Europe in the Ryder Cup match.

According to the pundits, Ballesteros's type of abandoned fury is a sure way of finding the rough. Of course it is; Ballesteros was seldom out of it. And when he avoided the rough he found sand. It made no difference to him. In the rough he simply hit the ball harder than ever, and from bunkers he displayed the touch of an artist.

That same touch brought him putts just when they were needed. A long one from the fringe at the thirteenth for a birdie was met with a roar which must have rattled the teeth of Crenshaw playing up ahead. The American dragged his approach to the seventeenth into the direst rough and took six.

By all the sacred canons of golf, Ballesteros ought to have put up the shutters and pit-patted his way safely home. Instead, he became even more aggressive if anything, blasting his ball via car park and rough and himself into the record books for a closing round of 70 and victory by three shots.

In the process he became the youngest golfer, at 22, to win the Open since young Tom Morris back in the 19th century, and the first continental European champion since Arnaud Massey of France in 1907.

It would be a gross overstatement to say that by this victory Ballesteros has broken the American domination of world golf. At best it should be seen as a refreshing interruption and a well-deserved accolade for a remarkable individual.

What we may dare to hope is that this result may inspire a renaissance of European golf, in the way that Tony Jacklin's victory at Lytham 10 years ago ushered in a new era in British professional golf.

An even more appealing prospect is the possibility that Ballesteros's success could stimulate a vogue for his swashbuckling philosophy and bring to an end the day of the calculating technician and his dreary method golf. This game was always meant to be an exercise in imagination, flair, and emotion, and these elements have been largely disappearing from the tournament scene.

The scores

283: S. Ballesteros (Spain) 73, 65, 75, 70 (£15,000)

286: B. Crenshaw (US) 72, 71, 72, 71; J. Nicklaus (US) 72, 69, 73, 72 (£11,250 each)

287: M. James (Burghley Park) 76, 69, 69, 73 (£7,500)

288: R. Davis (Aust) 75, 70, 70, 73, (£5,500)

289: H. Irwin (US) 68, 68, 75, 78 (£6,000)

291: G. Marsh (Aust) 74, 68, 75, 74; R. Byman (US) 73, 70, 72, 76; I. Aoki (Japan) 70, 74, 72, 75 (£5,000 each)

292: M. Ozaki (Japan) 75, 69, 75, 73; R. Charles (NZ) 78, 72, 70, 72; G. Norman (Aust) 73, 71, 72, 76 (£4,000 each)

1980

WATSON WIZARDRY MAKES IT PURE AND SIMPLE

The 109th Open Championship: Peter Dobereiner reports from Muirfield

Muirfield 1980: Tom Watson's third Open victory, again in Scotland, included a sixty-four representing the lowest ever round by a champion. It was the first Open to end on a Sunday.

With Tom Watson, the best golfer in the world today, taking a four-stroke lead into the last round at Muirfield there was always the strongest likelihood that he would win his third Open Championship. As the round progressed under grey but mercifully dry skies that probability turned to inevitability. Watson's lead stretched briefly to six strokes, was never less than three and his score of 69 for a total of 271 gave him victory by four strokes from Lee Trevino, who also finished with a round of 69.

Ben Crenshaw, likewise with a 69, was third but Ken Brown, who had held second place for two rounds, fell away with a closing 76 and was displaced as the leading British competitor by Carl Mason (69).

At the age of 30 Watson, winner of 21 American PGA tournaments since 1974 and leading American money winner for the past three years, now has four major championships in his record – 3 Opens and a Masters.

With the wind blowing from the north, chilly and just strong enough to restore some of the traditional values of links golf, Watson started with enough of a lead to know that a par round should see him safely home.

Both he and Brown saw the wind push their drives off the flight path over the tight corridor of fairway at the first hole and into the left rough. As soon as he hit his second shot Brown turned away in disgust because he knew that his ball had flown off the club face with too little backspin. His ball streaked across the green to the back fringe and he three-putted. Watson's approach suffered a similar fate and he chipped back to save his par and savour a stroke added to his lead.

At the third hole Watson dragged his approach shot to the collar of light rough bordering the green. He did well with his chip, running the ball 6ft past the flag but failed with the putt. Brown missed a tiny putt at the fourth and was thus displaced from his second position by Crenshaw; Trevino who started level with Brown, had also dropped two strokes.

That stroke which Watson gave back to his rivals opened the door a chink but only Crenshaw was making any progress and his long birdie putt on the eighth reduced the lead to three strokes.

Watson is a golfer much in the mould of Ben Hogan in that he is motivated almost entirely by an uncomplicated ambition to achieve absolute control over the golf ball. Purity of striking rather than dreams of wealth (of which he had plenty before he became a professional golfer) or glory is his inspiration.

Even his perfectionist spirit must have glowed with satisfaction at the long iron he struck to the partially obscured sixth green. The shot was almost inch-perfect, the ball nearly hitting the flag-stick and rolling to a stop 10ft away. The putt clipped the side of the hole but at the short seventh he had the length and line exactly right with the putter on his 25-footer for a birdie which put him back on that level par target.

Brown also holed a good birdie putt on the seventh but now, with Crenshaw losing a stroke up ahead and the holes running out, Watson's grip on this 109th Championship was strengthening by the minute and his growing confidence was evident in his play and bearing.

Card of the course

Hole	Yards	Par	Hole	Yards	Par
1	449	4	10	475	4
2	349	4	11	386	4
3	379	4	12	381	4
4	181	3	13	153	3
5	558	5	14	447	4
6	471	4	15	396	4
7	185	3	16	188	3
8	444	4	17	542	5
9	495	5	18	447	4
Out	3,511	36	In	3,415	35

Total 6,926 yds: Par 71

Another masterly iron shot into the eighth green left him a 9ft putt which he duly despatched for his second birdie of the day. By now he was fireproof. Thanks to his third-round 64, one of the finest performances of his career and indeed one of the great rounds of the modern era of golf, he was now in a position from which he could afford to drop a few strokes without a tremor. He was therefore playing golf with the nerve removed, a very different game from the one the others were engaged in.

At this stage a change came over Trevino. On the first nine holes he had been grim and taciturn. As the reality of the situation took the pressure off him, he relaxed and his natural ebullience took over and the putts began to drop for him.

Brown, of course, never relaxes on the golf course. His grinding determination and fierce self-criticism make him appear a morose character, which is far from the case; without a club in his hand he is one of the most cheerful and engaging young players in British golf. His last glimmer of hope disappeared when he dropped strokes at the tenth and eleventh, the tension seeming to be throwing his swing off line. At the eleventh even his short game, normally in the Aoki class, let him down and it is a long time since I have seen him hit such a poor pitch.

Watson, playing exhibition golf, over-hit his pitch into the tenth green to drop a stroke but, if his challengers took comfort from that lapse, the leader soon turned it into bleak despair by rolling in birdie putts at the eleventh and twelfth. At the fourteenth he hit what he judged to be his finest shot of the Championship, a five iron into the wind which finished four feet from the hole for another birdie.

By now all the rest was a sideshow. In the case of Crenshaw and Trevino it was a highly diverting sideshow for they played some masterly golf. Crenshaw, faintly reminiscent of Rupert Bear in his check trousers, has long been recognised as a player of championship calibre and he desperately wanted to win this one. Once more he had to settle for a near miss after his second place at Lytham last year. He had driven the ball better than ever before in an important tournament, he said, but he had never quite had the confidence with his irons.

As Trevino and Crenshaw came up the eighteenth fairway they were given a thunderous ovation by the crowds massed in the amphitheatre of grandstands around the green. That was the last chance for some considerable time that the spectators had to clap the chill from their fingers for Watson and Brown had fallen three holes behind.

Watson played out the formality of these closing holes in par figures to take the title he first won at Carnoustie in 1975 after a play-off with Jack Newton and which he regained in the greatest Open of them all, at Turnberry in 1977, when he and Jack Nicklaus battled head to head over the last 36 holes.

Brown's finish was a disappointment but this week he has surely made significant progress as a golfer

The defending champion, Seve Ballesteros, driving off the 5th but this was not one of his years.

and won many friends. His success is a reward for the real effort he has applied to his game and for his new mature attitude and determination to put behind him his youthful indiscretions which from time to time had brought him into conflict with authority. His hopes of having his 12-month disqualification from international team matches lifted surely deserve sympathetic consideration.

Trevino's second place was his best finish in the Open since his victory here in 1972. At the start of the Championship he set himself the target score of 276 and in fact improved on that mark by one stroke. He was thus fairly satisfied with his week. It was no disgrace, he said, to finish second to the greatest golfer in the world today.

'It was my bad finish in the third round which knocked me out of the box,' he said and that conclusion might well be extended to summarise the story of this championship. Its climax and destiny were decided in the third rather than the final round.

After the presentation, Watson revealed that he had woken early and then fallen into another three hours of nightmare sleep. He dreamt he was playing golf in a hotel corridor with all the doors shut; trying to steer his ball through the narrowest fairways one could imagine. He awoke in a sweat and was nervous all morning waiting for his starting time, and had felt nervous, though confident, on the course. It was not until he hit his tee shot to the sixteenth green that he felt the title was secure. He must have been the only person at Muirfield who felt the outcome was still in doubt at that late stage.

The last round, hole by hole

Watson 69 (271)
Out: 4-4-5-3-5-4-2-3-4 – (34) In: 5-3-3-4-4-4-3-5-4 – (35)

Trevino 69 (275)
Out: 5-4-4-4-5-4-3-3-4 – (36) In: 4-4-4-3-3-3-3-5-4 – (33)

Crenshaw 69 (277)
Out: 3-4-4-3-5-4-3-3-5 – (34) In: 5-4-3-3-4-4-4-4-4 – (35)

Nicklaus 69 (280)
Out: 4-3-4-3-5-4-3-5-4 – (35) In: 4-4-4-3-4-4-3-5-3 – (34)

Mason 69 (280)
Out: 4-4-4-2-5-3-3-4-5 – (34) In: 5-4-5-3-3-3-3-5-4 – (35)

Brown 76 (282)
Out: 5-4-4-4-5-4-2-4-5 – (37) In: 5-5-4-3-5-4-3-5-5 – (39)

Green 72 (282)
Out: 3-5-4-3-6-4-3-4-5 – (37) In: 5-4-4-3-4-4-2-5-4 – (35)

Bean 72 (282)
Out: 3-5-4-4-5-4-3-4-4 – (36) In: 4-4-3-3-4-5-3-6-4 – (36)

Stadler 71 (282)
Out: 4-4-3-3-4-5-3-4-5 – (35) In: 5-4-3-3-4-5-3-5-4 – (36)

The scores

271: T. Watson (US) 68, 70, 64, 69 (£25,000)

275: L. Trevino (US) 68, 67, 71, 69 (£17,500)

277: B. Crenshaw (US) 70, 70, 68, 69 (£13,500)

280: J. Nicklaus (US) 73, 67, 71, 69; C. Mason (unatt) 72, 69, 70, 69 (£9,250 each)

282: C. Stadler (US) 72, 70, 69, 71; A. Bean (US) 71, 69, 70, 72; H. Green (US) 77, 69, 64, 72; K. Brown (Ridge Engineering) 70, 68, 68, 76 (£7,250 each)

283: J. Newton (Australia) 69, 71, 73, 70; G. Morgan (US) 70, 70, 71, 72 (£5,750 each)

THE LOW ROAD TO VICTORY

By Pat Ward-Thomas

Although low scores have a powerful appeal Saturday was disappointing for those who believe that an Open course should be a demanding test. It proved nonetheless to be the key to the championship, giving Watson his chance to establish supremacy.

In breathless calm with hardly a murmur of breeze and greens holding any range of approach Muirfield was as harmless as it could possibly be. Never was there a clearer instance of the truth that British links must have a measure of wind and/or firm fast greens. Provided the deep rough and the bunkers were avoided there was no technical reason why first-class golfers should not score in the middle sixties.

Aoki is famous for his genius round the greens. In his 63 he had only 24 putts but the quality of his iron play was the foundation of his eight birdies. Watson took similarly ruthless advantage with a remarkable exhibition of target golf. His homeward half of 30 included five birdies in the last eight holes.

Watson used a three iron for the approach to the fourteenth and two drivers to the seventeenth green but holed only two putts of any appreciable length.

Watson's one poor shot of the day was a six iron into a bunker at the eighteenth but he made his four. His gesture had been made, a great round in the circumstance that he was playing but with only one thought in his mind – to win.

As if repenting their failing the weather gods produced a breeze from the north for the final day, the sky was grey and the air bitter but the quality of the golf was restored. The wind no longer helped the fifth, well out of range, or the 17th. Many were short with two woods to the tenth and the last short holes with the wind from the left were more of a problem.

If the contest was hardly enthralling and there was little of the atmosphere of tension and surging excitement one has come to expect from the Open, the fault was that of Watson's masterly golf and the failure of his pursuers to sustain a challenge. Only Crenshaw and Trevino were ever as close as three strokes behind and then only for a moment but there was much to admire among several rewarded with substantial prizes.

Carl Mason can never have played as finely and consistently on a great occasion. His last three rounds of 69, 70, 69 were a rare tribute to his composure and control of a fine swing. He learnt the virtue of keeping going in the knowledge that he could finish high while others, such as Lyle, Brown and the huge figure of Bean, were falling away.

Overall the showing of the British, which included good final rounds by Faldo and Oosterhuis, was encouraging. A handful of the world's finest golfers is now necessary to beat the British. A few years ago that was far from true.

For those watchers anxious to learn there were several perfect examples of the beauty and poise that can be expressed in golf swings. That of Nelson is the very image of Littler's; Morgan and Pate also swing with rare balance and elegance and as ever there was Nicklaus.

To Nicklaus, more than any other golfer, does the Championship owe its present stature and prosperity. His chance of winning diminished early on Saturday but not his resolution. Although his game was not at its sharpest, notably on the greens, he still summoned a 69 with the final birdie that so often has been his gesture to the massed stands that give him so tremendous a welcome. Once again he finished in the first four and Mason could be proud indeed of sharing his eminence.

The first two days may have been Palmer's farewell to competing in the Open. He looked so fit and alert that I could hardly believe 20 years had passed since he played so great a part in starting the modern golden era of championship golf.

Among those that sadly failed to qualify for the last act were Player and Miller, who four years ago conquered all with the beauty and excellence of his golf. It was unfortunate that Player should fail on the course where in 1959 his great career began to unfold but that was one of the hazards of the third day when low scoring was readily within the power of any good golfer.

ROGERS DOES PRECISELY AS HE PLEASES

Peter Dobereiner at Royal St George's

The return of Sandwich after thirty-two years brought victory for the Texan, Bill Rogers, with Bernhard Langer of Germany runner-up six shots away. Freakishly, there were three holes in one at the 165-yard 16th.

In the end the 110th Open Championship came down to formality. Bill Rogers played Royal St George's in 71 to win by four strokes and his progress developed into more of a lap of honour than a competitive round of golf. The Championship had been won with his third round of 67, which left him five strokes clear, just as Tom Watson won last year's Open at Muirfield with a third round of 64.

Before this ritual performance by the 29-year-old Texan there was plenty of speculation about whether he could be caught. It took some recondite analysis to discover stray shreds of evidence to suggest that there might be any other winner.

Perhaps if gales howled with real venom then Rogers would not be able to reach the par fours. Perhaps his record of only two victories on the US tour since 1975 meant that he was psychologically frail in coping with the unique pressures which accompany victory. All that was grasping at straws. The day dawned fine, with a breeze from the West. For Rogers that was perfect.

As for his temperament, he had solid victories to his credit in Japan and the World Match Play Championship at Wentworth. He was no choker, as he soon confirmed. In any case nothing loosens the collar like a stockpile of five strokes, and nine or ten in hand over the men he would most fear to have on his heels, such as Lee Trevino and Watson.

The reality of his position was that he could score a two-over-par 72 in the confidence that nobody would remotely threaten his vision of holding aloft that old silver claret jug in triumph. The others had to take all the risks of flirting with the penal rough in their attempts to hit the ball close to the flag. He could steer clear of danger and play for the fat of every green. It could be golf with the nerve removed.

It did not work out quite like that because golf never strictly follows the logical line nor ceases to throw up surprises. These, though exciting enough at the time for the large crowd to tingle with doubt over the outcome, were of a temporary nature.

At the fifth hole Rogers hit his drive to the right side of the fairway which left him a blind approach over a sand dune. He missed the green and dropped one of his nest-egg of strokes – nothing too serious in that.

At the seventh he selected an iron for safety when a fairway wood might have got him home. The ball finished in a sandy lie on the banks of a bunker and he was much too strong with his pitch, clear over the green and wide. For the first time in this Championship he looked shaken and he fluffed his pitch-shot short of the green. A chip and two putts gave him a seven and, with Bernhard Langer getting a birdie at this hole, the five-strike lead was down to one.

Now Rogers showed the qualities of a true champion with a run of superb golf, hitting his approaches dead for three birdies in four holes. His lead was back to comfortable proportions and interest switched to secondary issues.

Sam Torrance, for example, produced the third hole-in-one of the Championship at the sixteenth for a round of 70 and a finish in fifth place which put him straight into the Ryder Cup team. And a valuable man the fighting Scot will be against the Americans at Walton Heath in September.

Mark James, starting the last round in equal second place with Langer, also guaranteed his place in the side with a last round of 73 for joint third place with Raymond Floyd. As such he was the leading Briton, a distinction he also enjoyed in 1976. Howard Clark was another of the young British players to do himself a power of good with a 68 for joint eighth place. That will put him too into the team.

Geoff Godwin wobbled over the last three holes, dropping five strokes and handing the silver medal for leading amateur to Hal Sutton of America. As the only other amateur to survive to the fourth round Godwin had to be content with bronze.

Langer, the revelation of the Championship to the Americans, who will surely get to know the mettle of the man on their circuit in the coming years, held his game together wonderfully well for a 70 and his fifth finish of the season in second place. His cheque for £17,000 put him on top of the European order of merit table.

But the day belonged to the slightly-built Rogers in what he described as easily the biggest thrill of his life. Thank God, he said, that he had enjoyed the best of the weather on all four days. It was not the luck of the weather, though, which won the title. It was a precision swing, a deft short game and the fortitude to keep them going over 72 holes.

● Open history was made when Torrance yesterday holed in one at the sixteenth. Three holes-in-one had never before been scored at one hole in the Championship. Gordon Brand did it on the first round, Robin Chapman on the third. The hole is 165 yards.

● Rogers had a fright before he started his last round. Having come within 30 seconds of being disqualified from the first round for being late on the tee, he was delayed for nearly half an hour on his way to the course when his car was held up by level crossing gates a mile away.

● Four past champions finished in joint twenty-third place: Jack Nicklaus, Tom Watson, Arnold Palmer, and Tony Jacklin.

Leaders' rounds hole by hole

Rogers 71 (276)
Out: 4-4-3-4-5-3-7-4-3 – (37) In: 3-4-3-4-5-4-3-4-4 – (34)

Langer 70 (280)
Out: 4-3-4-4-4-3-4-4-4 – (34) In: 4-4-4-4-4-5-2-5-4 – (36)

Floyd 70 (283)
Out: 5-3-3-4-4-2-4-3-5 – (33) In: 5-3-4-5-4-4-3-5-4 – (37)

James 73 (283)
Out: 4-4-4-4-5-3-5-4-3 – (36) In: 4-3-6-4-4-5-3-4-4 – (37)

Torrance 70 (284)
Out: 5-4-3-3-4-3-4-5-4 – (35) In: 4-3-5-4-4-4-1-4-6 – (35)

Lietzke 69 (285)
Out: 3-4-4-4-3-3-4-5-4 – (34) In: 3-3-4-5-5-4-3-4-4 – (35)

Pinero 70 (285)
Out: 4-4-4-4-3-3-6-4-4 – (36) In: 4-3-4-5-4-4-3-3-4 – (34)

The scores

276: W. Rogers (US) 72, 66, 67, 71 (£25,000)

280: B. Langer (W Ger) 73, 67, 70, 70 (£17,500)

283: R. Floyd (US) 74, 70, 69, 70; M. James (Otley) 72, 70, 68, 73 (£11,750 each)

284: S. Torrance (Caledonian Hot) 72, 69, 73, 70 (£8,500)

285: B. Lietzke (US) 76, 69, 71, 69; M. Pinero (Spa) 73, 74, 68, 70 (£7,750 each)

286: H. Clark (Moor Allerton) 72, 76, 70, 68; B. Jones (Aus) 73, 76, 66, 71; B. Crenshaw (US) 72, 67, 76, 71 (£6,500 each)

1982

WATSON RIDES AGAIN ON OPEN ROAD

Peter Dobereiner on the Open Championship at Royal Troon

Tom Watson won the 111th Open Championship, riding the comet of his success in the US Open a month ago in his own words, with a final round of 70 which gave him victory by a stroke over Peter Oosterhuis and Nick Price of South Africa.

So Watson took his fourth Open Championship in Scotland out of five attempts and joined the illustrious band of Willie Park, old and young Tom Morris, Bobby Locke and Walter Hagen as quadruple winners of the old claret jug whose possession for a year is reward enough in itself; although these days they give you a cheque for £32,000 to go with it.

It all worked out exactly the way his wife Linda had predicted as they relaxed in their hotel room before the final round when she said: 'Tom is going to do a Nicklaus, only this time there won't be anyone to chip in at the 17th.'

She was referring to Pebble Beach in June, when her husband settled the US Open with a delicate chip into the hole as Jack Nicklaus stood by the final green with his score safely on the board and waited for his rivals to destroy themselves in their attempts to match it.

After Bobby Clampett's collapse in the third round with a 78 which utterly shattered his morale, the Championship was wide open, a handful of shots covering a dozen or so players. If anyone of them could put in a strong round the Championship would be his.

Conditions were perfect: a glorious shirtsleeve day with just enough breeze to stir the national flags above the packed grandstands around the amphitheatre 18th green. An early 67 by Raymond Floyd of America showed the possibilities.

For once the home countries were well represented among the contenders for the greatest prize in golf; Des Smyth of Ireland, Sandy Lyle of Scotland, Nick Faldo and Peter Oosterhuis of England. All of them had proved themselves fine strikers but technique alone is not enough for the last round of the Open, as Clampett now demonstrated.

The pattern, as always, would be for those contenders to drop away one by one and Clampett was

Watson's appetite for Scottish courses was unabated at Troon in 1982. His fourth title linked him with Willie Park, old and young Tom Morris, Bobby Locke and Walter Hagen.

the first to go. The slim Californian, who believes that golf can be reduced to mechanics, showed that the emotional battering of his horrendous third round had taken a severe toll.

The precision he had shown in the winds of the opening rounds to take him to within a stroke of the Championship 36-hole record had been destroyed in Royal Troon's rough and bunkers on Saturday. He was out in 40 and out of the hunt.

Card of the course

Hole	Yards	Par	Hole	Yards	Par
1	362	4	10	437	4
2	391	4	11	481	5
3	381	4	12	432	4
4	556	5	13	468	4
5	210	3	14	180	3
6	572	5	15	457	4
7	400	4	16	542	5
8	126	3	17	223	3
9	419	4	18	425	4
Out	3,422	368	In	3,645	36

Total 7,067 yds: Par 72

It had not been totally out of the question for either Jack Nicklaus or Severiano Ballesteros to win from their three-round totals of 219 but it would take an early charge and a 66 or so to rattle those ahead. They were paired together but could not get it going over the rich birdie territory of the opening holes and had to settle for the second biggest ovation of the day at the last green. Nicklaus had 69, Ballesteros 71.

As the leading group approached the finish it became clear with each passing hole that a British charge was not going to materialise. Lyle, Oosterhuis, Smyth and Faldo kept going well enough but in every case it was unconvincing, scrambling golf, rather than the commanding play of a champion.

Of course Oosterhuis has made unconvincing scrambling golf a way of life, and very successfully too, and his 70 for joint second place was due reward for the stoutest heart and most patient temperament that British golf had produced in the modern era. His 70 was a fine round, as was Faldo's 69, but both had been just too far back at the start of the day.

It all came down to Price and Watson and these two had it between them for most of the tense afternoon. For much of the day the running was made by the modest 25-year-old South African.

He had said that he did not fancy leading the Open Championship after two solid rounds of 69 had put him right into contention. However, he did not look at all put out when he caught Clampett on the first hole and then chipped in at the second to take over the lead.

Standing proudly and upright to the ball and swinging the club in his markedly vertical plane, he briefly lost his lead to Clampett but the American gave it away and Price's birdie at the seventh gave him three strokes in hand.

That was rather too early in the round to shoulder such a burden. Price has had little experience of winning: only the Swiss Open and the South African Masters have been of any consequence. He had a chance to take the Dutch Open last year but fizzled out in the last round for second place.

In fact he hung on well enough, wobbling as he came to the turn for an outward 36 but then making a strong bid with three birdies in a row. Watson was playing four groups ahead and not exactly setting Royal Troon on fire. What he was doing was safely making par and advancing steadily without dropping shots.

A birdie at the fourth to be out in 35 and then a superb eagle at the 11th, the railway hole, where his approach shot pitched and rolled exactly on line to finish four feet from the cup, changed the picture.

The effect of that two-stroke jump went back through the field like an electric shock. Watson was on the move. Price still held a two-stroke lead at this point and it was not exactly a disaster when he dropped a stroke at the 13th, a difficult enough hole in the most benign of conditions.

However, at the long par-four 15th of 457 yards Price began to lose the battle with his nerves. Before this round Watson had remarked that nothing brings out the guts in a player more than links golf, and that challenge is increased tenfold during the pressures of the last few holes of an Open Championship.

That is not to say that Price lacks guts. What he lacks is experience, the vital schooling which allows a golfer to learn about pressure and how to deploy his fortitude in subduing it.

Watson dropped a stroke at the 15th and then finished out with straight pars to set the target score at 284, four under par. So Price had two strokes in hand again and five to play. His drive at the 15th was wild, his second shot worse, both strokes showing the tell-tale signs of a quickening swing and an anxious raising of the head. His two-stroke lead vanished there and his vision of victory had changed to a question of whether he could hang on to force a play off.

It was not to be. His long iron to the 223-yard 17th found the fringe and three putts later his world had collapsed. Only one stroke separated the scores of Watson and Price at the end but that single digit represented a wide gulf of experience.

● Watson's win made him only the fifth man to win US and British Opens in the same year. He follows Bobby Jones (1926 and 1930), Gene Sarazen (1932), Ben Hogan (1953) and Lee Trevino (1971).

● This year's Open was the second best attended in history, falling 1,202 short of the record at Royal Lytham three years ago. The total for the week was 133,299, yesterday's crowd being 27,849.

Last rounds hole by hole

Watson 70
Out: 4-4-4-4-3-5-4-3-4 – (35) In: 4-3-4-4-3-5-5-3-4 – (35)

Oosterhuis 70
Out: 4-4-4-5-4-4-4-2-4 – (35) In: 4-6-4-4-2-4-5-3-3 – (35)

Price 73
Out: 3-3-4-6-3-5-3-4-5 – (36) In: 3-4-3-5-3-6-5-4-4 – (37)

Purtzer 69
Out: 4-4-4-4-3-4-4-3-4 – (34) In: 4-4-4-4-3-5-5-2-4 – (35)

Faldo 69
Out: 3-4-5-3-2-5-4-3-5 – (34) In: 4-4-5-4-3-4-5-2-4 – (35)

Kuramoto 71
Out: 5-3-4-5-3-4-4-3-4 – (35) In: 4-4-4-4-4-4-5-3-4 – (36)

Smyth 73
Out: 4-4-4-6-3-5-3-3-4 – (36) In: 4-4-5-4-4-4-5-3-4 – (37)

Zoeller 70
Out: 4-4-3-5-3-5-4-3-4 – (35) In: 4-4-4-5-2-4-5-3-4 – (35)

Lyle 74
Out: 4-4-4-5-4-5-4-4-5 – (39) In: 5-3-3-4-4-4-5-3-4 – (35)

The scores

284: T. Watson (US) 69, 71, 74, 70 (£32,000)

285: P. Oosterhuis (GB) 74, 67, 74, 70; N. Price (SA) 69, 69, 74, 73 (£19,300 each)

286: N. Faldo (Glynwood) 73, 73, 71, 69; T. Purtzer (US) 76, 66, 75, 69; M. Kuramoto (Japan) 71, 73, 71, 71; D. Smyth (EAL Tubes) 70, 69, 74, 73 (£11,000 each)

287: F. Zoeller (US) 73, 71, 73, 70; S. Lyle (Hawkestone Park) 74, 66, 73, 74, (£8,750 each)

288: B. Clampett (US) 67, 66, 78, 77; J. Nicklaus (US) 77, 70, 72, 69 (£7,350 each)

1983

Birkdale, 18th July

WATSON JOINS THE ELITE WITH A FIVE-STAR SHOW

Peter Dobereiner on the climax to the Championship

Tom Watson yesterday won his fifth Open Championship, stepping on to the pedestal alongside James Braid, J.H. Taylor and Peter Thomson and now just one championship short of matching Harry Vardon's record six titles.

Watson will surely take another because every win makes the next one easier and with his five wins coming in only nine attempts, he has emerged as the greatest Open Championship specialist of the modern era.

Watson had a final round of 70 for a nine-under-par total of 275, to win by a stroke from Hale Irwin and Andy Bean. It was Watson's eighth major championship, to set alongside last year's US Open Championship and two Masters titles.

The boyish 34-year-old Kansan was probably the calmest man at Royal Birkdale on a day of swiftly changing fortunes when as many as 10 players made and lost their chances of victory in the world's premier golf tournament.

Another hot and sultry day with only a light breeze threatened to turn the climax of this Championship into a putting contest. Links courses need wind to complete them as true examinations in the arts of golf and in the absence of a good blow the putter was dominant.

Over the first nine holes all the contenders of the leading group holed putt after putt of extraordinary length, a tribute to their talents and to the skill of Birkdale's greenkeeper. It was magnificent but it was only half of golf.

One exception to that pattern was Graham Marsh of Australia who again demonstrated that he is a golfer of the highest class with a round of exceptional virtuosity. Marsh's round contained only one small blemish, when his ball luckily scrambled over a bunker at the sixth. For the rest it constituted what he called a dream round of 64, equalling Craig Stadler's record of the first day, in keeping with his three previous rounds, with not a single putt longer than 15 feet.

Marsh's total of 277 set the target and, with the leaders still with another two hours of golf to play, the flags above the grandstands (including Norway's for some inscrutable reason) began to tug at their halyards as the wind freshened. That was much better.

Another more subtle but extremely pertinent change also took place at this time. Nobody knows more about championship golf than Jack Nicklaus and he has described the last nine holes of a major tournament as almost a different game because it is now that the tension becomes dominant.

The swing has to be switched to instinct as the player shifts the focus of his concentration to controlling his emotions. Flipping the lid is now a bigger danger than the rough or the bunkers.

Stadler, who had led the Championship for the first 53 holes, was the first to succumb to the nervous pressure. The putting stroke which had brought him to the fore now left him and he dropped five strokes in seven holes. Exit the walrus.

Nick Faldo, who had kept the record crowds at fever pitch from the start at the prospect of a home victory, especially when he went into the lead with three birdies in a row from the second, began to miss the short ones, a tell-tale sign of inner commotion.

On the run to the finishing post you need hard cases, men who have experienced the heat of the kitchen, and they were the ones who held their games together. The veteran from South Africa, Harold Henning, moved up.

Irwin, winner of two US Open Championships, profited from his long experience and his 67 beat Marsh's total by one. So did the 67 of Andy Bean, a tough nut if ever there was one, who has the reputation of wrestling with golf balls and biting alligators in half, or some such macho diversions.

Card of the course

Hole	Yards	Par	Hole	Yards	Par
1	450	4	10	384	4
2	423	4	11	411	4
3	410	4	12	184	3
4	206	3	13	505	5
5	343	4	14	108	3
6	468	4	15	542	5
7	150	3	16	415	4
8	470	4	17	526	5
9	410	4	18	473	4
Out:	3,330	34	In:	3,638	37

Total: 6,968 yds. Par 71

Lee Trevino made his inevitable move until he tangled with the Birkdale shrubbery towards the end. Trevino can match his will and his skill with any living golfer but no mortal can prevail against buckthorn.

Severiano Ballesteros finally remembered what made him a world-class golfer and abandoned his policy of playing it safe. Impatience has always been a virtue in Ballesteros's philosophy and he let rip as of yore. His 68 gave him sixth place but he had left himself too much to do and the shiver of fear which his charges normally induce in his rivals was momentary and muted.

All the while Watson kept cool and played his normal game, which happens to be better than anyone else's at the moment. He wanted to make up for losing the US Open at Oakmont last month with a poor last nine holes, and was determined this time he would play a good homeward stretch. The key to his round, he felt, was the 12-foot birdie putt at the 11th to put him back into the lead.

Finally, after looking odds-on for a play-off for most of the day, it came down to what Nicklaus describes as the ultimate thrill and challenge a golfer can face: three holes to play in the Open Championship and needing a birdie to win. The wind conveniently abated and Watson got that birdie under his

Watson's fifth victory – at Birkdale – joined him with James Braid, J.H. Taylor and Peter Thomson and proved he could win in England, too.

The 6th green, damaged by protestors from the 'Free Kelly' campaign, undergoes emergency repairs on the Saturday morning.

belt right away, holing his best putt of the tournament across 20 feet of the 16th green.

He saved his par after a stray drive at the 17th and played the difficult last hole with the confidence of a man who brought the trophy over with him from America and told the Royal and Ancient officials that they could keep it for the week until it was time for him to go home again.

A controlled drive shaped on the breeze left him 213 yards from the flag and he hit what he called the best two-iron shot of his life into the green. He had the luxury of two putts for the Championship and took them, savouring the roars from the massed tiers of appreciative spectators.

● The final day's attendance of 26,666 set an Open record. The total audience of 142,894 beat the previous best at Lytham in 1979 by 8,393.

● Taiwan's Yu-Shu Hsieh registered the highest single hole scored in the final round of the Open. Hsieh had played the first 16 holes in level par before taking a six-over 11 at the 17th. He was on a sandbank just short of the green in three shots, but needed five more to get clear, chipped onto the green and two-putted. He finished with a 78 – seven over par – for a final total of 295.

Leaders' rounds hole by hole

Watson 70 (275)
Out: 4-4-4-4-4-4-3-4-5 – (36) In: 4-3-3-4-3-5-3-5-4 – (34)

Irwin 67 (276)
Out: 5-3-3-3-4-4-2-4-4 – (32) In: 4-4-3-4-3-5-4-4-4 – (35)

Bean 67 (276)
Out: 4-4-3-3-4-4-2-4-4 – (32) In: 5-4-3-4-2-5-4-4-4 – (35)

Marsh 64 (277)
Out: 4-4-4-3-3-3-3-4-4 – (32) In: 3-3-3-4-2-5-4-4-4 – (32)

Trevino 70 (278)
Out: 5-4-4-2-4-4-3-4-4 – (34) In: 3-5-4-3-3-4-4-5-5 – (36)

Henning 69 (279)
Out: 4-4-4-2-4-4-2-4-3 – (31) In: 5-4-4-4-2-5-4-5-5 – (38)

Ballesteros 68 (279)
Out: 4-4-3-3-4-5-3-4-4 – (34) In: 4-4-2-4-3-5-4-4-4 – (34)

Faldo 73 (280)
Out: 5-3-3-2-4-5-3-4-4 – (33) In: 4-4-4-5-4-5-5-5-4 – (40)

O'Connor 68 (280)
Out: 4-4-3-3-4-4-2-4-4 – (32) In: 4-4-3-5-3-5-4-3-5 – (36)

Rogers 68 (280)
Out: 4-4-4-4-3-4-2-4-4 – (33) In: 5-4-2-4-4-4-4-4-5 – (36)

Durnian 67 (280)
Out: 4-4-5-3-3-4-2-4-4 – (33) In: 4-4-2-4-3-5-4-4-4 – (34)

The scores

(GB and Ireland if not stated)

275: T. Watson (US) 67, 68, 70, 70 (wins £40,000)

276: H. Irwin (US) 69, 68, 72, 67; A. Bean (US) 70, 69, 70, 67 (£23,000 each)

277: G. Marsh (Aus) 69, 70, 74, 64 (£15,000)

278: L. Trevino (US) 69, 66, 73, 70 (£13,600)

279: S. Ballesteros (Spa) 71, 71, 69, 68; H. Henning (SA) 71, 69, 70, 69 (£12,250 each)

280: D. Durnian 73, 66, 74, 67; C. O'Connor Jnr, 72, 69, 71, 68; B. Rogers (US) 67, 71, 73, 69; N. Faldo, 68, 68, 71, 73 (£9,625 each)

1984

St Andrews, 23rd July

BALLESTEROS BURST CASTS OFF WATSON

David Davies at St Andrews on the last day of the Open

The suspicion had been growing all week, and yesterday it became a certainty; Severiano Ballesteros – a renewed, resurgent Ballesteros – won the Open Championship over the Old Course at St Andrews.

His 12-under-par total of 276 beat Tom Watson and, glory be, another European, Bernhard Langer, by two shots and those three players utterly dominated the last day.

In fact, Watson and Ballesteros, indisputably the greatest golfer in the world today, fought out the final holes alone. Watson, who has trodden successfully in the Nicklaus bearprints in the past, was now stalking one hole behind the Spanish panther.

Watson had the advantage of knowing what he had to do, Ballesteros the advantage of having the opportunity to set the mark. But at the 17th, the hole that has been such a crucial factor all week, the hunted finally shook off the hunter.

Both men stood on that tee 11 under par and Ballesteros, as has been his wont all week, drew his drive into the left rough. He stood in practically his usual spot at that hole, knowing that he must do what he had not achieved in any of the earlier rounds: hit the green and make a par.

He took the same club that he had taken on two of the three previous occasions, the six iron, and hit the most telling shot of his week. He found the green for the first time in the regulation figures, got his par and marched on to the 18th tee, jaw jutting.

After hitting his drive to the final hole he looked back. He saw Watson's ball in the perfect position on

Watson drops a shot at the infamous Road Hole of St Andrews, hitting his two iron to within two feet of the wall. It lets in Ballesteros for a birdie and his second Open title.

the 17th fairway and, as he told us later, he said to himself: 'Well, Watson is on the fairway and Watson is Watson. He is going to make a par and he can make a birdie at any time.'

Such were the thoughts of the hunted, but the hunter was far from confident. He stood over his ball knowing that he had 210 yards to the hole and that he needed to carry 190 yards of them.

'I had the perfect angle to attack the pin,' said the American, 'but I was not sure of the club I needed. At first I thought it was a three iron, then I went for the two iron, but I pushed it. I knew as soon as I hit it that it was a bad shot.'

And it was. It was not only misdirected, but there was too much adrenalin behind it. The ball bounced once at the very back of the green, careered over the road, cannoned into the wall and came to rest about two feet from it. Watson had been faced with a real championship-or-not shot, and for once in his glorious career had made a mess of it.

At the time we thought that the great cheer that came up from the 18th green ahead of him may have affected his thoughts. Ballesteros, determined to close all the doors, hit an approach to 15 feet and then, to a roar that would have drowned a flight of jets from nearby RAF Leuchars, holed the birdie putt.

But Watson, another in a long line of true sportsmen among the great golfers, denied that it caused him any problems. 'I knew already what I had to do, in spades,' he said.

Having retrieved a good five out of his situation on the 17th, he refused to give up. At the 18th he hit a drive almost 300 yards and stood there with his wedge, some 93 yards from the hole. He prospected the entire route he proposed to take, but the very moment he hit the ball he knew that the eagle he needed was not about to be landed.

In winning his second Open in six years Ballesteros brought his total winnings from this event to £100,000, while Watson, who was denied a whole clutch of records, has amassed £155,000 in 10 years from the Open, including five wins and now his first runner-up spot.

Earlier in the year Watson told me that he thought he had no realistic chance of catching Jack Nicklaus in the matter of major championships, and certainly in order to do so he would have to win every time an opportunity presented itself.

Yesterday he credited Ballesteros with having applied all the pressure that was necessary, giving him no chance to take the merest of breathers. He knew he had to keep on playing at his best and he knew that what he called 'a baulky putter' would probably deny him that chance.

He had spent long hours on the practice green on Saturday night but was not satisfied with the results, and it showed over the first few holes. He had three-

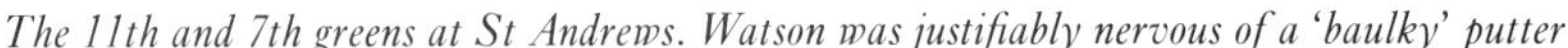
The 11th and 7th greens at St Andrews. Watson was justifiably nervous of a 'baulky' putter

putted three times by the time he reached the sixth tee, which, as he said, prevented him from 'putting any length between me and the field.'

The rebirth of Ballesteros coincides with his return from America. He relies on flair and inspiration, qualities nullified by the repetitious boredom of the US tournament circuit, so even though he had vowed to play there until he won, he decided to come back. He took three weeks off after the US Open, played at The Belfry where the cobwebs cloyed his swing, and then came here for the championship that means more to him than any other.

'I can't tell you,' he said in his broken English, 'just what it means to win at St Andrews.' His evident joy told it all.

He made his first move at the long fifth, where he holed a 13ft putt for a birdie four. A little later Watson hit the green in two but then three-putted – the first of a number of important swings.

At the short eighth Ballesteros put some pressure on his playing partner Langer when he holed from six feet for a birdie, having seen the West German miss from six and a half feet.

There was a hiccup at the 10th when the Spaniard three-putted after driving the green at this par four hole, and a bigger one at the short 11th where he missed the green and dropped a shot.

It was at that moment that Watson regained the lead, for he too drove the 10th green and got down in two more, but Ballesteros made an important move at the long 14th. He took the dangerous, direct route down the right-hand side and was rewarded with a pitch to 16 feet and a birdie putt to go 11 under.

That left the two leaders tied on that mark and they remained so until the 17th and the drama of the closing holes. Both men had the privilege of walking up the 18th into a sporting arena that has no equal elsewhere, but it was Ballesteros who was able to savour the jubilant sounds of success.

Bernhard Langer, having chased unsuccessfully for most of the afternoon, fought hard to the finish and finally holed a putt of some 6½ft for a birdie on the 18th green to ensure joint second place with Watson.

Langer, who had probably played the best golf of the three challengers up to the green, had suffered as he frequently does from a putter that refused to behave itself. In the first 14 holes he missed half a dozen putts of 10 feet and under and of the type that both Ballesteros and Watson regard as near certainties. But the West German is accustomed to such indignities and it is to his credit that he has continued to produce golf of outstanding quality both off the tee and with his irons to the green.

● Ben Crenshaw, the US Masters champion, had a hole in one at the 178-yard eight hole during his final round. The five-iron shot pulled him back to level par and he finished on 286, richer by £8,360.

● A record crowd of 187,753 watched the championship at St Andrews, with yesterday's final round attracting 35,686. The aggregate was up by some 45,000 on last year's record at Birkdale.

Leaders' rounds hole by hole

Ballesteros 69 (276)
Out: 4-4-4-4-4-4-4-2-4 – (34) In: 4-4-4-4-4-4-4-4-3 – (35)

Watson 73 (278)
Out: 4-5-3-5-5-4-4-3-4 – (37) In: 3-3-5-3-5-4-4-5-4 – (36)

Langer 71 (278)
Out: 3-4-5-4-6-4-4-3-4 – (37) In: 3-3-4-4-5-4-4-4-3 – (34)

Wadkins 69 (281)
Out: 3-4-4-4-4-3-4-3-4 – (33) In: 3-3-4-4-6-4-4-5-3 – (36)

Couples 68 (281)
Out: 4-4-4-5-4-3-4-3-3 – (34) In: 5-2-4-4-5-3-4-4-3 – (34)

Faldo 69 (282)
Out: 4-3-4-4-4-4-4-3-4 – (34) In: 4-3-3-6-4-4-3-4-4 – (35)

Norman 67 (282)
Out: 4-4-4-3-4-3-4-2-4 – (32) In: 4-3-3-4-5-4-3-5-4 – (35)

The scores

GB and Ireland if not stated

276: S. Ballesteros (Sp) 69, 68, 70, 69 (£55,000)

278: T. Watson (US) 71, 68, 66, 73; B. Langer (W Ger) 71, 68, 68, 71 (£31,900 each)

281: F. Couples (US) 70, 69, 74, 68; L. Wadkins (US) 70, 69, 73, 69 (£19,800 each)

282: G. Norman (Aus) 67, 74, 74, 67; N. Faldo 69, 68, 76, 69 (£16,390 each)

283: M. McCumber (US) 74, 67, 72, 70 (£14,300)

284: G. Marsh (Aus) 70, 74, 73, 67; S. Torrance 74, 74, 66, 70; R. Rafferty 74, 72, 67, 71; H. Baiocchi (SA) 72, 70, 70, 72; I. Baker-Finch (Aus) 68, 66, 71, 79 (£11,264 each)

1985

LYLE BANISHES ALL DOUBTS AND RIVALS

David Davies reports from Royal St George's

Sandy Lyle becomes the first Britain to win the Open since Jacklin in 1969, shooting a level-par seventy for an aggregate 282.

Sandy Lyle won the 1985 Open Championship at Royal St George's yesterday and in so doing proved wrong one of the oldest of all sporting adages. Nice guys, can, and just did, win.

Lyle, 27, will be the most popular, the most loved, if you like, champion that anyone can remember. He is the first Briton since Tony Jacklin in 1969 to win and in brisk breezes, studded by sunshine, he played the steadiest golf of all the challengers. He emerged with a level par 70 for a two-over total of 282 and won by one shot from Payne Stewart of the USA.

The men who had dogged him all the way and had been the overnight leaders, David Graham and Bernhard Langer, fell away at the last, leaving an emotional Lyle and his family in tears by the 18th green.

After a win that was almost hysterically received by the throngs around the final green, Lyle admitted that he had been 'pretty nervous' but mostly at the start of the Championship. For the first two days he had wondered about the state of his game, but, on finding it to be in good shape, played with increasing confidence.

Before the start, he told me that if there was a course on the Open rota on which he could win the Championship, he felt that it would be Royal St George's. He said: 'You have to drive the ball well, and you need to play long irons successfully.' He proved himself eminently capable of doing that with the first two rounds of 68 and 71.

On Saturday he needed 73 but he remained unworried. Yesterday morning, while waiting for his 2.40 p.m. start, he played Lego with his son, Stuart, and found the hands surprisingly steady. The Championship fluctuated throughout the afternoon but Lyle, having holed a long putt at the 14th for an unlikely birdie, then holed a 12-footer at the 15th to spring right back into contention. He said: 'At that point I nearly burst into tears – it was so exciting to be in there with the Open Championship at stake.

'I never got jumpy, there were no shakes and in fact I was thrilled to bits with the way I swung at the ball over the closing holes.' Asked if he felt any pressure at all, he said: 'Obviously you feel something but last November I played in a tournament where the first prize was £125,000 and I won it. The memories of that came back and I got a lot of comfort from knowing that I could win when there was a lot at stake.'

There could be £1 million and more at stake for Lyle now. The game in Europe has never been so prosperous and Lyle, who was always in demand by sponsors before all this, will now be at the top of their shopping lists.

For much of the day, the battle had seemed to be between Langer and Graham, both of whom had started at one under par. But neither could find his best form with Langer going to the turn in 39 while Graham took 37. Lyle was out in 35, and, at that point, was one behind Graham but one ahead of Langer. Then, as the heavyweights were watchfully sparring with each other, Tom Kite nipped in on the blind side, went out in 32, and stole a two-stroke lead over the field, then he ran into a haymaker, delivered by the 10th hole, where he needed to hole a five-foot putt for a double bogey six and that wrecked his confidence. He came home in 40 to disappear from sight.

Meanwhile, Graham was playing the kind of sustained golf of which we know he is capable, but Langer seemed to be struggling. During the course of his round, he was in seven bunkers, and it may be that his chance finally disappeared when he failed to birdie the long 14th. He did hole a nine-foot putt at the 15th for a birdie but promptly dissipated that by bunkering his tee shot at the short 16th to be back to three over par.

Lyle, two groups ahead, had dropped a shot at the 13th when, after bunkering his drive, he missed the green with his recovery and then missed the green with his chip. But he responded in spectacular fashion with a 35-foot birdie putt at the 14th and then a 12-footer at the 15th. When he arrived at the 18th he felt that he needed a four to win the Championship, but when his second trickled off the left edge of the green into the semi-rough he had problems. He elected, however, to go for a delicate, difficult shot, aiming to get the ball to trickle over the crest of a ridge so that it could run down to the pin. The ball got to the crest all right but turned away and ran back down, and Lyle, in the most emotional display I have seen from him in 16 years of watching him play competitively, sank to his knees and buried his head in the grass. He recovered quickly and ran a difficult 20ft putt 18 inches from the hole.

All this time, Graham and Langer had been having their own problems and, when they reached the 18th they needed a birdie to force Lyle into a play-off. Graham bunkered his second. Langer ran through the green, and although the latter's chip ran over the edge of the hole – neither man could prevent Lyle's triumph.

The scores

GB and Ireland if not stated

282: S. Lyle 68, 71, 73, 70 (£65,000)

283: P. Stewart (US) 70, 75, 70, 68 (£43,000)

284: J. Rivers (Spa) 74, 72, 70, 68; C. O'Connor Jnr 64, 76, 72, 72; M. O'Meara (US) 70, 72, 70, 72; B. Langer (W Ger) 72, 69, 68, 75; D. Graham (Aust) 68, 71, 70, 75 (£23,600 each)

285: A. Forsbrand (Swe) 70, 76, 69, 70; D. Jeihrine (US) 69, 71, 74, 71; T. Kite (US) 73, 73, 67, 72 (£15,566 each)

Lyle watches his putt roll up the 17th green.

THE PRODIGIOUS SHROPSHIRE LAD COMES OF AGE

By David Davies

Eleven years ago I sat in Alex Lyle's living room talking to his son Sandy. The lad was as big then as he is now, 6ft 1in and 13½ stones, and probably as good a striker of the ball as he is now.

'What,' I asked him, 'will you want to have achieved in ten years time?' His reply was almost casual. 'Oh,' he said, 'I think I'd like to have won the Open Championship.' Now, one year outside his schedule, he has.

The extraordinary talent he has displayed since he first hit a golf ball at the age of three – and sent it 80 yards – has finally come to full fruition, to the undisguised delight of most of Britain – and to the bafflement of a few.

Lyle has been a prodigy all his golfing life. Helped by a physique that demanded size 11 shoes at the age of 11, by the fact of a golf professional father, by living on a golf course, he has dominated every level of competition that he has ever encountered.

He was a boy international at 15 and for each of the next three years. He won the Carris Trophy, the Midland Open against the best local professionals, and in 1975 won the Brabazon Trophy against the best British amateurs of the time.

One of them was Nick Faldo, with whom he was frequently to compete over the years. But that same precocious talent was to frustrate some of the Lyle watchers who espied in him a lack of drive, an absence of the overweening ambition that is said to be necessary.

Most of them, indeed us, ascribed the fact of his ability to earn over £100,000 without really trying, to the other related fact, of his failure to win a Championship. But Lyle always denied that.

'No one,' he told me in an interview for the *Guardian* earlier this year, 'knows how much I want to win the Open. They say I don't practise, but they don't know where I go to do my work.

'I like to get away from the tournament course and go somewhere nearby and work from there. They say my chin goes on my chest but that's just not true. I've never given up on a golf course in my life.'

That remained true until June of this year, when he walked out of the Carroll's Irish Open after a series of horrors left him needing to hole a full one iron to break 90. He decided against the attempt and was duly disqualified. Afterwards his caddie, Dave Musgrove, said: 'I'm sure he was ashamed of the way he played – but I don't think he was angry.'

Most professional golfers would not just have been angry, they would have been livid. But the phelgmatic approach that most people thought would always hold Sandy Lyle back has now stood him in good stead.

It would have been easy to panic when his ball rolled back to him at the 18th green. Instead he collected himself to win a Championship he had been threatening to take since 1969. In that year, he sat in the stands on the left of the final green, cheering himself hoarse as Tony Jacklin won.

In his moment of triumph, Jacklin turned and threw his ball high into the crowd, where Lyle missed catching it by a few feet. But then, as he remarked yesterday: 'I've grown a few inches since then.'

The post-war British winners: 1947 Hoylake – E. Daly; 1948 Muirfield – T.H. Cotton; 1951 Portrush – M. Faulkner; 1969 Royal Lytham and St Annes – A. Jacklin.

THE MAN WHO CAME TO DINNER

By John Samuel

Sandy Lyle's victory is a celebration for so many of us in different ways. David Davies, as golf correspondent of the *Birmingham Post* before The *Guardian*, has followed his career from boyhood and even now would preserve a discretion that Lyle was our *Guardian* guest at Sandwich Guildhall on the eve of this Championship.

One of the speakers remarked: 'Under this roof most certainly sits the 1985 Open Champion. The question is who?' It was the man sitting opposite me,

Royal St George's from the air.

whose game we knew had the power to match any American, but whose temperament, many thought, lacked the disciplined excitability to raise itself to the pitch of triumph.

He sat like a Hardy character, chest so broad that the slender modern lapels looked the merest tucks on the swathe of sturdy flannel. The hand that propels a one iron 280 yards, a distance never excelled by Jack Nicklaus, stretched out for a comfortable few glasses of red wine.

He told us he did not think of himself as a Scot, in spite of his name, ancestry and participation for Scotland in the World Cup. He was born in Shrewsbury and his first representative appearance was for England Boys at 14. No doubt he was most things to most Britons, Scots included of course, early yesterday evening.

The late Pat Ward-Thomas believed that when a British player was again to win the Open it would be Lyle or Faldo. Lyle's method is so unfussy; he is through his shot before the slower cameramen can line him up. The short swing, it was said, was a product of the British climate, the reason why the British could never again win their own Open, why sun-soaked Americans hitting through the big ball would always beat us

Lyle was indeed the first player since Jacklin to sweep through the big ball, and with the shoulders and chest of a quarterback. In retrospect, why were there many doubters, especially on a classic British links course, of a man who could win the 1983 European Open at 25 with a finishing 65 and five birdies in six holes? David, you deserve to have landed your 50-1 wager. It was more than an act of faith.

1986

DAY THE SHARK SHOWED HIS TEETH

David Davies at Turnberry on the climax to the 115th Open Championship

Greg Norman of Australia is a delighted winner of his first major title, by five shots.

Greg Norman won the Open Championship at Turnberry yesterday taking, at last, the major title his talent has long deserved. On four previous occasions, in championships around the world, including the US Masters and the US Open this year, he had threatened and fallen back.

Now, the Great White Shark showed that he is more than just a dorsal fin, winning by a margin of five shots from Gordon Brand Snr and by six from Ian Woosnam and Bernhard Langer.

It was the biggest winning margin since Royal Birkdale, 1976, the year Severiano Ballesteros announced himself by finishing second to Johnny Miller, albeit by six shots.

In the process Norman silenced, thankfully, the sometimes strident doubters, not least the New Yorkers who, only five weeks ago at Shinnecock Hills, openly accused him of choking. Norman grabbed one by the shirt collar in order to refute the point; yesterday he took Turnberry by the throat with a closing round of 69 and was, at the end, the only man to equal par with his score of 280.

Yesterday, over a Turnberry that at last relented and presented calm and sunny conditions, the golfers were able to play a recognisable game again but no one, neither Nakajima nor Woosnam, Faldo nor Graham, could put any pressure on the man who, overnight led by one shot. That was the extent of his lead in the Masters and the Open at the same stage, but this time Norman truly had learned. He told himself to treat it like an ordinary tournament, just like any of the dozens he has won around the world; and, but for a lapse at the 17th, he succeeded. He managed, as Tony Jacklin so perceptively remarked 'to keep his mind in the present' and not to allow it to wander ahead to the fulfilment of ambition.

That he played without anyone applying immediate pressure or that the only real pacemaker was Ballesteros who posted a comfortable clubhouse mark of eight over, should not detract from the merits of Norman's win. He started the event as one of the favourites; he played the entire Championship in or around the lead and the whole of the last round knowing that, if he lost again, the critics would be seen to be increasingly justified.

Not that he thought about Shinnecock. 'All I want to say about that,' he said, 'is that it is a pleasure to play in front of people who want you to win.' He confessed that he woke up nervous and that he could not eat a full breakfast.

But that, he thought, was good. At Shinnecock he had woken feeling flat and could not get himself excited for the final round. This time he nursed his nerves, with some inspired help from his caddy, Pete Bender. He it was, after Norman had hit an awful duck hook at the seventh, who spotted that his boss was beginning to get a little quick.

That did the trick. Norman got his par from a dreadful place in the rough and then hit a good drive and an even better four iron, second to the eighth. From that moment Norman felt in control. 'I said to myself "well, guys, I'm playing too good for you this time",' and so it proved.

There had been an earlier indication that this was to be Norman's day. Not only had Tommy Nakajima three-putted from six feet at the first to immediately fall three behind; Norman had himself holed a bunker shot at the third for a birdie to go four clear.

As if recognising that the fates were with him. Norman began to attack the flag with his second shots. At the 12th he flew a six iron into the heart of the green, and at the 13th an eight iron carried straight on to the top tier. Then at the 14th, from a drive in the rough, he hit a seven iron which actually hit the pin from 198 yards out. It settled three feet away, and when Norman holed it, his lead was extended to six with only four holes to play. 'I was hitting the ball so well that even I was impressed with some of the shots,' he said later.

A two-iron tee-shot saw him safely on the green at the 15th, and a one iron at the 16th off the tee was followed by a magnificently played three iron from a place that the spectators had trampled flat. Norman deliberately cut the ball into the green, totally ignoring Wilson burn which lies in wait for the slightest mis hit.

At the 17th another drive escaped into the rough, and he had to use a sand wedge to get out. But then he crashed a six iron only four feet from the hole, at which point he suffered something of a crisis. He said to his caddy: 'My mind has gone dead. I can't even see the hole. You tell me what the line is and how hard to hit it.' But Bender miscalculated somewhere, for Norman ran the ball three feet past and had to hole that for his par.

By now it was all over. 'I knew the Championship was mine,' said Norman; and all he had to survive was the traditional rushing crowd down the 18th. 'You've got to experience that to believe it,' said Norman. 'Trying to win your first major championship is like having a monkey on your back. But, now it's off, I'd like to try and win 10 or 15 or even twenty of them before I finish.'

Norman: 'I was hitting the ball so well even I was impressed with some of the shots.' He comes out of this bunker well from a less-than-perfect approach.

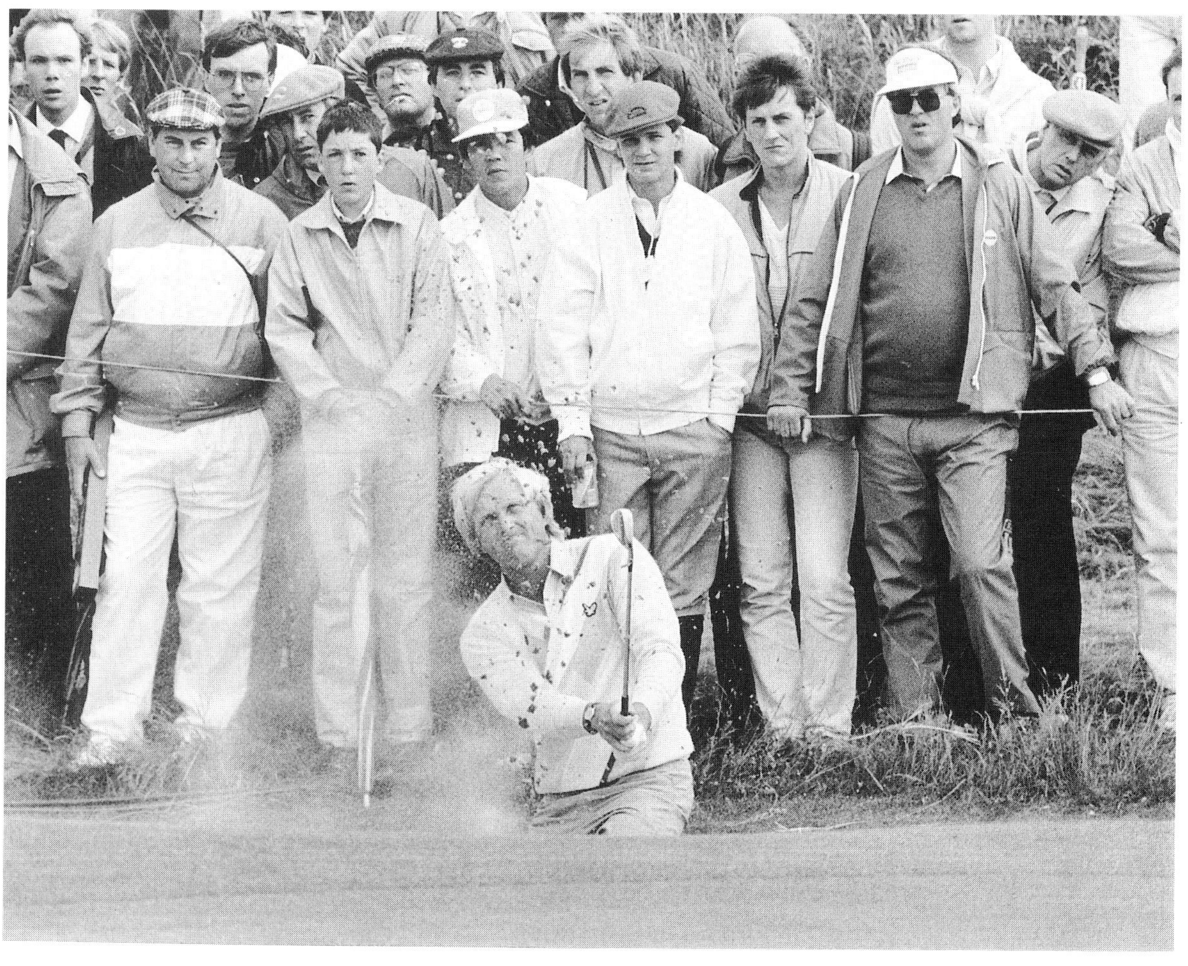

For Gordon Brand this was the biggest day in his golfing life. There was never any danger of him winning the title nor even of mounting a realistic challenge. For most of the day he was between three and eight shots behind, but an eagle at the 17th edged him ahead of Woosnam with whom he was playing and earned him a cheque for £50,000. Woosnam, with Langer, won £35,000 and Nick Faldo, with a level par final round of 70, made it five Europeans in the top five.

There were only two Americans, Gary Koch and Fozzy Zoeller, in the top 10, a remarkable change since 1977 when there was only one European, Tommy Horton, in the top 12. Sandy Lyle finished at 15 over par, and for him it was the end of a wonderful year in office. For Greg Norman, who has now taken his winnings this year to a stunning £433,000, it is all still to come and yesterday was, as he said 'a real sweet thing.'

The scores

GB and Ireland if not stated

280: G. Norman (Aus) 74, 63, 74, 69

285: G.J. Brand Jr 71, 68, 75, 71

286: B. Langer (W Ger) 72, 70, 76, 68; I. Woosnam 70, 74, 70, 72

287: N. Faldo 71, 70, 76, 70

288: S. Ballesteros (Spa) 76, 75, 73, 64; G. Koch (USA) 73, 72, 72, 71

289: F. Zoeller (USA) 75, 73, 72, 69; B. Marchbank 78, 70, 72, 69; Tsuneyuki Nakajima 74, 67, 71, 77

1987

Muirfield, 20th July

FALDO SWINGS TITLE AT LAST

David Davies reports from Muirfield on a dramatic British victory in the 116th Open

Nick Faldo wins at Muirfield, 1987. Better, even, than a first prize of £75,000 was the rebuttal of critics questioning his change of swing.

In surreal surroundings, with golfers materialising through swirling mists, Nick Faldo emerged as a truly substantial champion when he won the 116th Open, at Muirfield yesterday.

He became the second British champion in three years, following Sandy Lyle's win at Royal St George's in 1985, and he beat Paul Azinger with one of the most remarkable championship rounds in Open history. He had 18 straight pars, a round of 71, and the only time he led was when Azinger missed a 30-foot putt on the final green.

It was, literally, a round *par excellence*, and it won for him the first prize of £75,000. His five-under-par total of 279 was one better than Azinger and Rodger Davis, who, with Ben Crenshaw, was the only one of the leaders to play a sub-par final round.

Better than that for Faldo, though, was the rebuttal of his critics, including this one, who have questioned the need for him to spend the better part of three years rebuilding his swing. His game has not, in fact, changed that much, as he showed with some masterly scrambling yesterday. But the intense hard work he put in to gain a full grasp of David Leadbetter's dictates, gave him the belief he needed to play his game when it really counted.

There were many moments in yesterday's ghostly Open as the Scottish *haar* enveloped the course when Faldo could have taken fright. That he did not, and that he turned back the challenge of the man who has won three events in America this year and almost $500,000 in prize-money, is an immensely creditable achievement.

It is one that Faldo believes could not have happened without the help of Leadbetter. The decision to change the Briton's swing came after the 1983 Open at Royal Birkdale when Faldo led twice on the final day but found that he could not handle the pressure.

Yesterday he said: 'I went to Dave because I believed that my game was not good enough to play 18 holes with an Open Championship at stake. But when it came to it today – and here's a crazy quote – I knew I'd do it. I knew I'd do it this week. I had a good feeling all week but I had to keep it to myself because you really look a fool if things go wrong.

'I don't think I've ever had a round like that last one, and to do it on the last day of an Open, well, it's fantastic.

'I never looked at the leader board all day. I had to play my own game. There was no point in looking, I can't alter anything out there. I did not want to put any extra pressure on myself by thinking "I'm winning the Open" if that happened.'

But the only time it did was on that last green. The drama of the day, as always, concentrated itself on the last few holes as Azinger, who at the 5th and 8th holes had led by three shots, strove to retain something of that advantage.

The American had, in fact, dropped shots at the 10th and 11th holes, and from that point to the 17th, had only a one-shot lead. At the 10th he had bunkered his second, at the 11th cut his drive into rough, but just when it looked as if he might disintegrate he began to hit a stream of good shots, and in fact had more chances to stretch the margin.

But good putts at the 12th, 14th and 16th all refused, and with Faldo already on the 18th in the match in front, Azinger began to show signs of distress. His drive to the long and, in an east-north-easterly wind, devilishly difficult 17th, caught a fairway bunker and he could only come out at an angle of 45 degrees.

That meant not only that he could not get up in the regulation three shots, he would also have a considerable distance to go with his fourth. In fact he needed a seven iron, got the ball to 15 feet but missed the putt.

Up ahead Faldo was playing a superbly judged 18th. A magnificent tee shot gave him a second shot that was between clubs, and it is an enormous tribute to his clarity of thinking that although it was four-iron distance, he knew that with the adrenalin coursing it would be better to take the five iron. 'I just said "stand up there and hit it" to myself,' and the ball flew on to the green.

It was still, however, some 35 feet below the hole and Faldo's partner, Craig Stadler, was making considerable inroads into Faldo's nerve with his play of the hole. He hit his second against a crowd barrier, had to take a drop then only just got the ball onto the green. It all took ages and Faldo could only stand there, licking his lips nervously and unconsciously hitching up his right sleeve with his left hand. His sweater, incidentally, had a pattern that resembled the blueprint for some complicated electronic circuitry and I daresay he would have welcomed a robot to take the putt for him.

But the moment eventually came when he had to hit it himself, and to an indrawn breath of horror, he hit it five feet past the hole. This was the moment, of course, and no amount of practice prepares any golfer for it. 'As a boy I had had lots of putts for the Open,' said Faldo afterwards, echoing everyone who has ever, in adult life, actually holed one. 'I just said to myself "don't dribble it, hit it firm",' and he did, and it went in.

The roar echoed back to Azinger, who now had to make a par four on what Jack Nicklaus has called the most difficult finishing hole of any major championship course. It is 448 yards of bunker bestrewn terror and Azinger chose to hit an iron off the tee to take the fairway bunkers out of play. That bit was successful, but he now had more than 200 yards to go with his next, to a green guarded by sufficient sand to contain the entire Championship field.

The American could not manage it. His ball trickled into the sand on the left and the huge crowd roared their approval. It is a moot point as to whether in these circumstances they were cheering the mistake or the advantage that accrued to the favourite, but it is an unfortunate fact of golfing life that it takes place.

Azinger had to stand partially outside the bunker to play his shot, and while he is the best in America at this department of the game, he could not hope to get this one close. Nor did he, and Faldo, barely able to watch the television in an R & A tent, must have known that only a fluke of Larry Mize/Bob Tway proportions could rob him of his first major championship. Azinger is also a good putter, but no one is that good, and a few moments later Tony Jacklin's Ryder Cup team had another title to add to its honours list.

Faldo said afterwards: 'I knew I may never get another chance and I told myself that at least I must try 100 per cent, otherwise I would not be able to forgive myself. I've had chances in the past and I didn't want to think, when the time came to hang up my hat, that I'd come close and not succeeded.'

What does the Open mean to him? In material terms: 'I'll get into every major for the next few years, and that's what we work for. And now I've done it once I can do it again.'

But the story in the greenside tent was slightly different. As he sat waiting for the award ceremony, he was overcome by emotion and had to be comforted by his wife, Jill. 'You deserve every bit of it,' she said. 'You've worked so hard.'

● Azinger said he 'made a couple of bad decisions,' hitting a two iron instead of a one iron at the 10th and using his driver at the 17th, but, he added, 'I think I proved to myself and a lot of people that I can be a contender over here. I don't want anybody to feel sorry for me'.

The scores

GB and Ireland if not stated

279: N. Faldo 68, 69, 71, 71 (£75,000)

280: R. Davis (Aust) 64, 73, 74, 69; P. Azinger (US) 68, 68, 71, 73 (£49,500 each)

281: B. Crenshaw (US) 73, 68, 72, 68; P. Stewart (US) 71, 66, 72, 72 (£31,000 each)

282: D. Frost (SA) 70, 68, 70, 74 (£26,000)

283: T. Watson (US) 69, 69, 71, 74 (£23,000)

284: I. Woosnam 71, 69, 72, 72; N. Price (SA) 68, 71, 72, 73; C. Stadler (US) 69, 69, 71, 75 (£18,666 each)

Card of the course

Hole	Yds	Par	Hole	Yds	Par
1	447	4	10	475	4
2	351	4	11	385	4
3	379	4	12	381	4
4	180	3	13	152	3
5	559	5	14	449	4
6	469	4	15	417	4
7	185	3	16	188	3
8	444	4	17	550	5
9	504	5	18	448	4
Out	3,518	36	In	3,445	35

Total yds 6,963: Par 71

WELWYN CONTENTION...

By Frank Keating

His mum wanted him to be a male model. He'll have every chance now.

His father, George, worked for ICI Plastics at Welwyn Garden City and was a dab hand at the amateur dramatics; early on he had ambitions for the boy to take to the stage professionally. But his mother, Joyce, a pattern cutter and drafter for Cresta Silks, was the driving force.

She took him first to dancing and elocution lessons and once said, 'Even before his 11-plus Nick had smashing legs and I really though he might be a model one day.' She even dragged him along to fashion shows at Harrods and at Oxford Street.

At school he was a stunningly good sportsman – but always the loner, never team games, always concentrating on his swimming, or cycling, or athletics.

In the spring of 1971, just after the first colour TV had been delivered to the semi in Knella Road, Welwyn, Nick stayed up late to watch the ITV transmission which featured Jack Nicklaus playing the Masters at Augusta. He was transfixed and a few days later, when Easter holidays began Joyce booked him one lesson at the local golf club.

By the beginning of the summer holidays, his 14th birthday present on 18th July was a half-set of clubs costing £36. The obsession was off and away.

Within four years, on 26th July 1975, remarkably, he was English Amateur Champion at Royal Lytham. A year later he shot 69 in the final round of the Open itself at Royal Birkdale to finish level with Player, Coles and Sanders, at 29th in the whole wide world. He was not yet 19.

For 10 full years on the big, wide circuit they knew him to be always thereabouts – but the name was gaining ground, El Foldo. Not any more. And the contracts await for a new star in the modelling world.

PRAISE THE LORD AND PASS THE WATERPROOFS

By Dai Davies

More than 25,000 people attended the third day's play of the Open Championship on Saturday. This either indicates a mass outbreak of temporary insanity in the East Lothian area, or a severe lack of anything else to do.

Muirfield was vile. A north-easterly wind of 30 mph and gusting was accompanied by squally rain. The clothing to keep out the consequent chill has yet to be invented.

The players resorted to mittens and hand-warmers, to double seaters and waterproofs, plus a variety of headgear. Jack Nicklaus came close to looking cuddly in a floppy, while Greg Norman looked as if he had escaped from the local production of the Pirates of Penzance.

Norman complained that being subjected to such vicious weather (which duly abated in late afternoon) was unfair and that the Royal and Ancient should adopt the standard tour procedure of two-tee starting. This, he said, would mean that fewer players were exposed to the extremes of the weather.

He is quite right. The R and A should really go all the way and play the whole affair in a giant, hermetically-sealed balloon and ensure that no one suffers from anything. Perhaps Richard Branson could be called in.

Norman had a 74, playing nine holes in reasonable weather. Sandy Lyle had a 71, playing his whole round in totally unreasonable weather.

Playing at the same time, the US Open champion, Scott Simpson, began to fear that he might not break 90, so severe was the effect on his hands and his grip. But he got round in 82, and gave thanks.

As a member of the US tour's Bible-study group he might well have reflected that in golf, and in matters of being under par, to them that hath red numbers, it shall be given, and to them that hath not, even that which they hath shall be taken away.

1988 Lytham St Annes, 18th and 19th July

RAIN PRECIPITATES FLOOD OF PROBLEMS

By David Davies

18th July

Four years of foul and frustrating weather for the period of the Open Championship have given rise to a number of expensive problems that the Royal & Ancient will have to face.

Almost 22 hours of heavy rain washed out the third day's play of this year's event at Royal Lytham and St Annes, drenching over 35,000 spectators but, remarkably, not quenching their enthusiasm for what has now become an enormous attraction in its own right.

That being so, it seems imperative that something is done about the difficulties that have been emphasised by this week's weather – the vast crowds, lack of bad-weather equipment, stewarding problems and slow play.

The R & A have always resisted the temptation to go all-ticket, because of the obvious black-market problems. But that would be the easiest way to control the crowds which are now getting unwieldy, although not, thankfully, unruly. It is now almost impossible to watch, in any comfort, the best groups, with the fairways lined by spectators five or six deep.

When it rains, the umbrellas make it totally impossible and, with the ground wet underfoot, dangerous as well. In the last two weeks, at Gleneagles and at Lytham, there have been eight broken legs, not to mention five heart attacks.

The bad-weather equipment which would have coped with Saturday's deluge has not yet been invented, but the sight of greenkeepers using inverted rakes to shove water roughly off greens rightly annoyed Ian Woosnam and should not have been necessary. A fleet of Water Hog machines is.

A corps of well-trained marshals is becoming a necessity. Volunteers from local clubs are always going to make up the bulk of the stewarding force but they have to be better directed by people who know, from years of experience, what they are doing.

Their presence would help kill the fallacy that swarming crowds are the sole reason for slow play by the professionals. They cause the occasional slight hold-up but the players who are mostly affected by the crowds are those behind the top players, as spectators rush all over the place to get a vantage point.

Authorities around the world make noises about dealing with slow play and then, to a man, take the easy option and refuse to impose penalties. The lead has to come from the top and the R & A, in the Open, to a proven offender, no matter how big a name, must provide that example.

BALLESTEROS CREATES A MASTERPIECE

By David Davies

19th July

He finished it as he had begun. With one of the great championship rounds in Open history Severiano Ballesteros won his fifth major title, his third Open and his second at Royal Lytham and St Annes.

With an almost unbelievable display of golfing virtuosity Ballesteros conjured up a 65 six under par, for an 11-under-par total of 273 to beat Nick Price by two shots and the defending champion Nick Faldo, by six.

The 65 equalled the lowest winning round in an Open, compiled by Tom Watson in what was perhaps the greatest Open of them all, the '77 version at Turnberry between Watson and Jack Nicklaus.

And so, in the end, sheer flair overcame the pragmatic mixture of power and putting that had kept Price going for the week. The Durban-born Zimbabwean with a Welsh mother and an English father had played the finest golf of his career and he was truly unfortunate to have to combat a man who, in yesterday's mood, is the finest player in the world.

For most of the day it was between Ballesteros and Price, the panther versus the springbok, and for long periods the latter was sufficiently spring-heeled to avoid a mauling.

In fact he went round in 69, an excellent score which in other years might have brought him his first Championship.

In doing so he carried out his game plan. 'He told me,' said his caddie, Dave McNeilly, 'let's just go out and shoot a 69 and not worry about anyone else.'

But the inspiration that fuelled Ballesteros on day one, when he birdied the first three holes and wrested a 67 out of awful conditions, returned yesterday to burn more brightly than ever.

This was Ballesteros at his most fantastic. He was, as McNeilly remarked, 'on the rampage' and in an incredible spell starting at the sixth he played the next eight holes in six under par, with five birdies, an eagle and a bogey. Price played those same holes in five under par, and lost a shot to the man who by then was his only rival.

Faldo's challenge had, by now, to be written off with the faint praise of 'a good defence'. He was as

1988: A chip dead to the 72nd flag at Lytham and Ballesteros is celebrating one of the great Open rounds – a six-under-par sixty-five – and his third title.

tentative with his putter as he had been in the final stages of the US Open, was never better than joint second, and after the seventh was effectively out of touch. Yesterday was his 31st birthday and hardly a happy one.

There was a significant omen in this major triumph for Ballesteros. In 1979, when he won the first of his Opens, at Lytham of course, he took a driver off the 16th tee, landed in a car park miles to the right, got a free drop and birdied the hole.

This time, older and wiser by nine years, he hit a one iron into the middle of the fairway, then a nine iron 135 yards and almost into the hole, finishing two inches away.

With that birdie he went one ahead and, as Price later observed, established a vital advantage. 'That was sheer class,' said Price, 'it was a perfect golf shot.'

The birdie coincidence did not go unnoticed by the Spaniard either. 'There were no cars out there on the fairway for me to bounce off,' he grinned. 'Most of you will agree that it was a good shot this time.'

It was Hale Irwin who called Seve the 'parking lot champion' all those years ago, and the implication that he was lucky has rankled ever since. But if ever a round of golf completely killed off any such criticism, this was it.

He was asked most of the banal questions that we writers contrive for him, but one of them – 'How important is this win for you?' – produced an unexpectedly revealing answer.

'Ever since 1986, when I hit my second shot into the water at the 15th at Augusta, my confidence has been a little bit down. From where I was I would have been the winner eight times out of ten. Then the next year I missed a short putt in the play-off and I started to wonder if my time was, well, you know . . .'

Ballesteros has always felt that he needs all the help he can get on the golf course and yesterday he went out armed with a talisman or two. He was wearing the same trousers and sweater that he had worn here nine years ago, and was also carrying the same driver, three wood, sand wedge and putter with which he had won in '79.

There was another important and largely unnoticed addition. To help ease the traditional golfer's bad back, he had a warm pad inserted in the shirt in the area of the small of his back. That, plus the late arrival of some semblance of summer, helped keep him fluent.

There was one other major factor. Half a dozen tournaments ago, on the recommendation of Vicente Fernandez, he hired Ian Wright, a 40-year-old caddie from Redcar regularly employed on the European Tour.

Wright is one of the more placid characters among the caddies and precisely the kind of person that many people had long urged Ballesteros to adopt. It

Nick Price, a Durban-born Zimbabwean with a Welsh mother and English father, pursued Ballesteros to the last hole with a pragmatic mixture of power and putting.

is all too easy for brother to abuse brother, as frequently happened, both ways, when brother Vicente carried for Seve.

'I think I am a lot calmer than his brother,' said Wright afterwards. 'Having family caddie for you must be a bit like trying to teach the wife to drive. I know when to keep quiet.'

He also knew when to speak up. When the time came to hit that shot to the 16th, Ballesteros enquired as to whether it really was a nine iron. A lot of caddies would have found an excuse to be tying their shoelaces at that moment, but Wright told him to go ahead and hit it.

The excitement, on what was to become an almost unbearably tense day, began at the long sixth, which both players birdied. The long seventh followed, Price hitting his second first. It bumbled and bumped its way to four feet, a clear eagle chance.

Ballesteros followed with a near-perfect shot which had his supporters screaming 'Go in'. But it ran 12 feet past before Ballesteros, realising that he had to hole the putt, did so. Price duly holed his and there followed some superb putting from the Spaniard.

In it went from 15 feet at the eighth to make him joint leader, a big move at exactly the right time with the hard holes coming up. He holed from 20 feet at the 10th, again knowing that Price, only six feet away, was likely to get a birdie.

Then he holed from 18 feet at the 11th, coming out of the shadows of the trees at the back like a predator bearing down on an innocent victim. That was five under for six holes and, for the first time, he led.

He faltered at the next. A wrong club, a four iron instead of the required three- or even two iron, left him 25 yards short of the green and meant a dropped shot.

Matters took a turn for the worse at the next, as far as Ballesteros was concerned. Price hit his second to two inches for a certain birdie and perhaps the lead. But the Spaniard hit his second to 13 feet and, to enormous acclaim, holed out.

'At that point,' said Price afterwards, 'we were each waiting for each other to make a mistake, and I made it at the 14th.'

Ballesteros was to drop a shot after missing, not drastically, the fairway and the green. But Price, with a four-footer for the lead, missed it and strode from the green with his arms hanging down, loosely shaking his hands as if to try to unjangle the nerves.

But he played the 15th badly, needing a good chip to five feet to rescue par, and the feeling began to grow that his time was running out. Perhaps Ballesteros sensed it, for his shot to the 16th was a Tysonesque blow delivered with perfect timing.

Price hit a wild, right-sliding drive at the 17th and got a free drop because the ball landed in 'unusual ground conditions' – a good phrase for us all to remember at the weekends.

He manufactured a four out of it, but Ballesteros got his the conventional way and now had a one-stroke lead with one to play.

There were anxious moments as his drive drifted towards the shrubbery off the 18th tee, but it was safe by about five yards and even though he missed the green on the left with his next, it was, as he and Price knew, the safe side from which he was always liable to get down in a pitch and putt.

In fact he almost holed the pitch, which would have been an appropriate ending to such a round. It left Price needing to sink his 50-foot putt, which he ran eight feet past and he missed the academic one back.

One of the truly great Championships was over and there was only time for Ballesteros to clap his arm round his protagonist and tell him, sincerely, 'If you go on like this, you will certainly win an Open Championship.'

The leaders' hole by hole

Ballesteros 65 (273)
Out: 3-4-4-4-3-4-3-3-3 – (31) In: 3-4-4-3-5-4-3-4-4 – (34)

Price 69 (275)
Out: 3-5-4-4-3-4-3-4-3 – (33) In: 3-5-3-3-5-4-4-4-5 – (36)

Faldo 71 (279)
Out: 3-5-3-4-3-4-5-4-3 – (34) In: 5-5-2-4-4-5-4-4-4 – (37)

The scores

GB and Ireland unless stated

273: S. Ballesteros (Sp) 67, 71, 70, 65 (£80,000)

275: N. Price (Zimb) 70, 67, 69, 69 (£60,000)

279: N. Faldo 71, 69, 68, 71 (£47,000)

281: F. Couples (US) 73, 69, 71, 68; G. Koch (US) 71, 72, 70, 68 (£33,500 each)

282: P. Senior (Aus) 70, 73, 70, 69 (£27,000)

283: P. Stewart (US) 73, 75, 68, 67; I. Aoki (Jap) 72, 71, 73, 67; D. Frost (SA) 71, 75, 69, 68; S. Lyle 73, 69, 67, 74 (£22,000 each)

WIDE OPEN SPACES BECKON BROADHURST AND HIS HERO

By Ian Ridley

The first Monday in 117 Open Championships was almost eerie. Whereas more than 40,000 people had swarmed over the links of Royal Lytham and St Annes for the second and third rounds, little more than 14,000 were scattered across them yesterday.

The tented village containing every conceivable item of golf equipment was closed as the exhibitors packed and left, unable to extend their arrangements. One felt sorry for the Japanese television crew with a yen to spend their money on the latest graphite-shafted, metal-headed, turbo-charged caddie car. Eddie Birchenough's professional shop was the only substitute.

Of course the real people to be pitied were the 36,000 who came on Saturday and were washed away. It brings no pleasure to tell them – like those pains on holiday who mention, as you huddle under your umbrella, that you should have come last week – that yesterday was the finest of the tournament.

The wind, naturally, still blew off the Fylde coast but the sun came out too. The two young men who wore T-shirts – one reading Shape Up or Wimp Up – and Bermuda shorts on chilly Sunday would have been less incongruous.

At one point Jack Nicklaus looked up to the skies, more in disbelief at seeing sunshine again than to give thanks for the three consecutive birdies he had just put together.

The was another enjoyable aspect to the day: you could actually get to within a few feet of Nicklaus rather than a few hundred yards.

You could also see the leaders play some of their shots and, remarkably, find a seat in the stands at the 18th green without having to queue at 7 a.m.

Nicklaus could probably pull a crowd in the Gobi desert and yesterday he received his customary warm welcome. He also made the day unforgettable for one of his playing partners, Paul Broadhurst, who was on the winners' podium with the silver medal for leading amateur.

Broadhurst signed for Nicklaus's 68 and was not embarrassed by his own 76. 'I just didn't want to make any cock-ups on his card or shoot an 85 myself,' he said before dashing off to be photographed by his parents with the great man.'

Playing with Nicklaus, Broadhurst added, had made him realise that he 'doesn't have enough shots in the bag'. So today it is more practice, starting with a club match for Atherstone against Nuneaton, which may feel just a little more eerie than yesterday.

Deliberately, he set out to play not Nick Price but the course. 'I holed a good putt at seven, a six-footer, and it got me started. It gave me the confidence for the the rest of the round.'

Price tried to do the same, but by the 13th it was match play for him.

Ballesteros around the turn was mesmeric, with six birdies in eight holes. But Price, so self-critical of his collapse against Watson at Troon in 1982, stuck to his task with pride.

The 542-yard eleventh, the first test going back against the wind, saw both play high irons to 20 feet. With exquisite timing, Ballesteros holed his; Price hit the back of the cup and lipped out. That put the Spaniard ahead for the first time.

A poorish four iron and a missed five-footer meant a bogey for Ballesteros at the awkward par-three 12th, where Price had a birdie. Then Price counter-attacked once more, with a superb sand wedge to two inches, but the Spaniard answered birdie with birdie.

The 14th, in Price's own view, cost him the Open. Ballesteros cut his drive and could only get down in five. Price badly sliced his approach but his recovery left a four-footer to regain the lead. He missed it.

Ballesteros paid him a handsome compliment at the finish; and Price later said: 'I think here we've seen a new Seve. Much more relaxed.'

The Spaniard smiled impishly. 'I wear the same clothes as nine years ago. It's the same everything . . . driver, three wood, putter, sand wedge. All the same. The difference is I am nine years older. It's not so difficult to look happy when you are making putts. I made some good ones this week.'

If the Armada had been to some extent avenged, Seve was not showing it. 'Without all the support I had from Lytham, I would not be champion,' were his final, smiling, grace-notes.

THE ROUND OF A LIFETIME

By John Samuel

There is a saying in Spain, said Seve Ballesteros, that there is never two without three, 'This is my third Open Championship title, and I will remember it for a round that happens only once in 40 or 50 years. I will remember it a lifetime.'

1989

CALCAVECCHIA REPELS THE NORMAN INVASION

David Davies sees an American victorious, without a European near, after the first three-way play-off in the history of the tournament

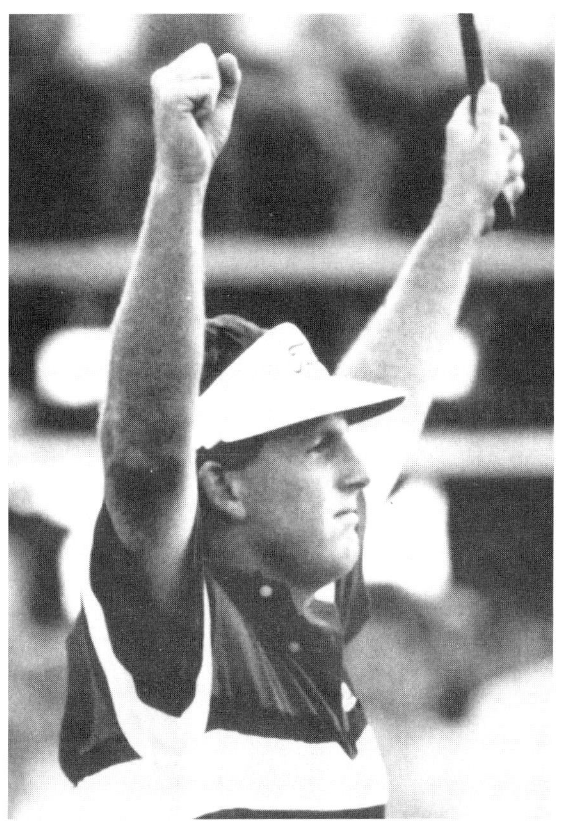

Mark Calcavecchia, a Rocky Marciano reborn, celebrates victory after the first four-hole aggregate play-off. The American qualified with two Australians, Wayne Grady and Greg Norman, all with totals of 275, Norman after a record-breaking last round of sixty-four.

Mark Calcavecchia won, and in a cruel sporting moment Greg Norman lost, the Open Championship at Royal Troon yesterday. For the first time in the history of the Championship there was a four-hole aggregate play-off: for the third time in his history Norman was beaten over extra holes for a major title.

Three men had qualified for the play-off – for the first time in the Open – over the 1st, 2nd, 17th and 18th holes: Calcavecchia, Norman and Wayne Grady, all with totals of 275, 13 under par. At the end of it the American with Italian forbears, who had birdied the 18th to get into the play-off, did it again to win the Championship.

As he rolled home a five-foot putt Norman stood disconsolately by, his third shot to that final hole having disappeared out of bounds. There was nothing that this magnificent sportsman could do but smile, shake Calcavecchia warmly by the hand, pat his back and offer sincere congratulations.

Twice in the past, in the 1986 US PGA and in the 1987 US Masters, he had been beaten by fluke shots. Tway holed from a bunker in '86, Mize a 140-foot chip in '87. But in the 1984 US Open, Fuzzy Zoeller beat him over 18 holes with a round of 67 to Norman's 75. This time defeat was administered by Norman's own hand.

Having taken the lead with successive birdies on the 1st and 2nd holes, he bogeyed the 17th by mishitting a chip. Then he hit a huge drive down the 18th. But he had failed to take account of the adrenalin that flows in such situations and he found, with some force, a bunker on the right, which, in the words of a magazine hole-by-hole account, 'cannot normally be reached'. Norman said: 'It's 352 yards to that trap; it never entered my mind.'

But these were not normal circumstances and the ball rolled through the sand, hit the revetted face of the bunker and stopped close to it. He had no realistic chance of reaching the green but, as he surveyed his shot, Calcavecchia, who had carved his drive miles, but safely right, hit a superb recovery. Norman knew by the crescendo of noise that not only was his opponent on the green, he was close, and he knew he had to go for a miracle shot.

But no player in the world could have reached the green from where he was and all he did reach was another bunker. Knowing that he now had to get the ball really close and hope Calcavecchia missed, he thinned the shot and was told that it was out of bounds at the back of the green, and the sickening realisation that he had been so close, and yet remained so far from a second major championship, dawned.

Earlier Norman had said, as he waited for the field to finish having shot a record-breaking last round of 64: 'I've had them taken away from me. I would just love to sit here and have one given to me.'

But the world of golf is not like that, and particularly not the aggressive, strong, bouncy and confident Calcavecchia. As a prize fighter he would be Rocky Marciano reborn, and when Sandy Lyle won the Masters, and he was second, he took it almost personally.

When he then won in Los Angeles this year, beating Lyle into second place, he said that, while it had given him great satisfaction, he would rather help win the Ryder Cup for his country. He will have that chance shortly.

He had ridden a rollercoaster round earlier. A nine-under start became 11 under by the fourth but was back to 10 under by the 12th tee. It seemed certain to go back to nine under when he carved his second way left, on to a sandy brown platform where there had been a thousand or more spectators ducking for cover moments earlier. He had a level stance but was 15 feet above the hole, with no green to work with. Five seemed certain, six a possibility. But Calcavecchia flew the ball high in the air, straight at the pin, and it dived into the hole on the fly. Things like that win Opens – eventually.

He also birdied the long 16th, routine on a day of little wind, and, to wrap matters up, hit an eight iron at the last to three feet to get into the play-off. He wins £80,000, the claret jug and the championship belt, plus a place in history.

The record-breaking 64 was played not by Norman but by Greg Norman Incorporated. On Saturday night the phone hardly stopped ringing as friends rang him to offer advice. First on the line was Jack Nicklaus, who, ignoring the odds at which Norman was being offered, 25–1, recognised that the Australian had a real chance to win.

'You'll have to play with your brain, rather than your game,' he said, which in the context of that particular conversation meant that Norman had to be

The second green, where Norman holed a 15-footer to stoke his great charge.

aggressive. Ray Floyd was next, advising that he 'let go of the reins', which meant much the same as Nicklaus, and then Tom Weiskopf came on the line and advised some finesse.

'Those are three very dear friends of mine,' said Norman afterwards, 'and when you have guys you play against every week pulling for you, it makes you feel great.'

So Norman, with a seven-shot deficit to make up, decided to go for everything, and took his driver at every opportunity. He was just 20 yards short of the 1st green, and holed from seven feet for a birdie three. A 15-footer went in at the 2nd and he wedged to two feet at the 3rd. 'You know,' said the Australian reflectively afterwards, 'I dreamed I would start with three threes.' But not many would have dreamed that he could start with six, which was the way it went.

He was on the green of the long 4th with a four-iron second, and the first of several good breaks came at the short 5th where he holed a monster of 45 feet. He missed the green with a three wood at the 577-yard 6th, leaving him with a nightmare pitch. 'I hit it as well as anything in my life,' he said, and that was six on the trot.

But he parred the 7th, then found the sand at the 8th, the Postage Stamp.

Even that was a good break, for he pitched in the mound on the left and had he stayed there he would have a job to hold the green with his second. As it was he came out of the bunker to 20 feet and missed.

The momentum was temporarily stilled. It took to the long 11th to regain it, where Norman 'chipped' a five-iron second on to the green and two-putted to go 11 under. That became 12 at the 12th where another big putt, this time 33 feet, ran home, and now the early threats were beginning to be actualities. The pressure that Norman was exerting was beginning to be felt by the remainder of the field.

At the long 16th yet another of the best shots of his life got its reward. Norman, 277 yards from the green in one, hit a driver from the fairway that carried the profusion of bunkers around the green and finished 18 feet away.

Now he knew he had a real chance; knew too that a further birdie would almost certainly win, for the leaders had all the hard holes still to play. Instead, he struggled for par.

'I hit a two iron real poor, real fat, off the 17th,' he said, and he failed to reach the green of this 223-yard hole. Nor was the saving pitch much better, running just off the green. A four would have been entirely respectable from there but Norman, with the modern shot that the pros play so well, the bladed wedge, holed out. The ball is addressed halfway up its circumference, hit with the leading edge of the wedge, pops up an inch or two out of its immediate environment, then runs like a putt. It ran 30 feet into the hole. 'That was vital, that was so important,' said Norman afterwards.

He still had the 18th to go, though, and after their drives, he saw his playing partner Scott Simpson hit his second out of bounds, through the green. 'I had to walk away. I had to put it out of my mind,' he said, and he did, although his second did run to the back of the green. He got safely down in two, for a score that beat by one the marks set by Jack Nicklaus in 1973 and Payne Stewart on Saturday.

The scores

GB and Ireland unless stated

275: G. Norman (Aus) 69, 70, 72, 64; M. Calcavecchia (US) 71, 68, 68, 68; W. Grady (Aus) 68, 67, 69, 71
Play-off: Calcavecchia won over four holes.

277: T. Watson (US) 69, 68, 68, 72

278: J. Mudd (US) 73, 67, 68, 70

279: D. Feherty 71, 67, 69, 72; F. Couples (US) 68, 71, 68, 72

280: E. Romero (Arg) 68, 70, 75, 67; P. Azinger (US) 68, 73, 67, 72; P. Stewart (US) 72, 65, 69, 74

AN EXPECTANT FATHER DELIVERS

By John Samuel

There were times when no man had his mind less on golf than Mark Calcavecchia. Back home in West Palm Beach, his wife Sheryl is expecting their first baby any moment.

'He's phoned her two or three times every day,' said his caddie and business partner, Drake Oddy. 'If the contractions had started, he would have been up and gone from here.'

Calcavecchia appeared at his celebratory press conference still wiping the tears from his eyes after talking to his wife. 'She was crying here eyes out. I was praying I wouldn't have to miss this. Important as this is, it's a golf tournament, not life.'

Oddy and Calcavecchia have been buddies since university so there were no bad feelings about the

14-stone, six footer's tantrums when he missed a short putt at the 7th.

'He just lost his brain for a couple of minutes,' said Oddy. 'He got himself together again straight off but on the 11th green with a 40-footer for par and four shots off the leaders I guess it looked pretty bad.'

Bad? Calcavecchia rated it disaster as he duck-sliced into gunge, slammed a three iron into a hump concealing the flag, hit the ball out of a thorn bush, and with punctured hands ran the ball 40 feet past the pin with an eight iron. 'I got my wits back to hit the best putt I could hit.'

His five iron to the 12th hit someone and finished in a hole on a shelf overlooking the green. His next shot, straight down the flag into the hole, simply embarrassed him. 'How lucky can you get?' he said. 'That shot changed everything. It was a miracle.'

Did they learn as they went along over the four days? 'We got to learn there are places you don't want to be,' Oddy said, 'but he and Greg Norman know they hit the ball a whole lot further than the others. This place is like Phoenix, just desert, so why throw your advantage away staying back with everyone else?'

Birdies on 16 and 18, which took him to 13 under and the play-off shoot-out with Norman, were typical howitzer blasts: one iron from the tee 270 yards to a grassy lie, fairway driver 290 yards.

No man can be as long as that without finding sand or rough round the green. Calcavecchia's recoveries had some of the finesse of Ballesteros at his best.

All the same he wondered whether the three balls left in his bag would be enough for the play-off. As Tom Watson, who used the same brand, walked off the green, Calcavecchia did what the average hacker might do at Troon. He asked if he could borrow some balls. Watson, ever the gentleman, obliged.

HOPES HIGH BUT SCORES LIKEWISE

By John Samuel

Sandy Lyle forecast that it would be someone coming from behind; Fred Couples that it would be whoever got off to the best start.

Some of the nearly men could blame bad beginnings, but for others it was the pressures of the closing holes as Calcavecchia soldiered on to his desert victory.

David Feherty had a last round of 72 to finish equal sixth, nine under, the best performance from a home player. He began with a birdie, holing from five feet, and at the 2nd hit the hole from 20 feet only to lip out. He made another birdie at the par-five 6th from eight feet and another at the 11th from four feet, but bogeys at 12, 14 and 15 did for him.

'I proved to myself that I can hole out under pressure,' said the Northern Irishman, 'and I can hold my head up. My putting was extremely good.'

The American Jodie Mudd, a touch ironically, was also the man for the conditions. He got off to a birdie-birdie start, and birdied again at the 6th.

Another birdie at the 11th put him 12 under par and in serious contention, but at the 179-yard 14th he was bunkered and then two-putted from 20 feet.

The closing short holes cost Mudd dear. Another bogey at 17, when he missed the green right, and his challenge was finished.

Couples never really got going, justifying his own prediction, to finish nine under and equal sixth with Feherty.

The defending champion, Seve Ballesteros, tailed off tamely into a practice round of 78. 'I never felt I was really going to get going,' he said. Saddest of all was Bernhard Langer, so often a militant challenger, this time a miserable 82.

Russell Claydon, with a 75 and a total of 293, took the Amateur Medal. 'I'm just not thinking about turning professional,' said the man who finished second in the Australian Masters. 'I'm playing in the St George's Challenge Cup at Sandwich next Saturday. That's what I'm looking forward to.'

Nick Faldo offered a postscript after his three-under 69. 'I've had enough. I've got my flight and I'm going fishing.'

1990

St Andrews, 23rd July

FALDO RULES WITH GRANDMASTER TOUCH

David Davies on a supreme exhibition by the Englishman who has become – by any rational assessment – the best player in the world

Faldo rules with a grandmaster's touch. His 270 is the finest score in Open Championship history, eighteen under par compared with Tom Watson's thirteen under in 1980. His caddie, Fanny Sunesson, shares in the delight.

Nick Faldo, with the finest score in Open Championship history, yesterday won his fourth major championship, over the Old Course at St Andrews. Faldo, playing golf like a Grandmaster, moving through a sandy minefield with complete precision, completed his four rounds in 270, which was 18 under par.

The previous record of 13 under, by Tom Watson at Muirfield in 1980, was destroyed by Faldo's 67, 65, 67, 71 and the man whose golfing bite is far worse than his bark won by five shots from Payne Stewart and Mark McNulty. He also won £85,000, plus the old Claret Jug and yet, with the imbecility that causes them to be called the Phoney, rather than the Sony Rankings, he remains second in the world to Greg Norman.

This despite having won two major championships this year, the US Masters being the other – the first man since Tom Watson in 1982 to do so. As Faldo also ran a 10ft putt fractionally by the hole in the US Open at Medinah to join the play-off, he could by now be heading for the US PGA facing the prospect of the unthinkable, the Grand Slam. As it is, he has to content himself with the knowledge that since he won the Open last, in 1987, he has compiled an overall record that has only ever been equalled by the likes of Jack Nicklaus, or maybe Ben Hogan. From July 1987 his major record reads: 1, 28, 30, 2, 3, 4, 1, 18, 11, 9, 1, 3, 1.

Perhaps it was ignorance of that record that dictated the odds on Faldo before the off. Whatever, some £2 million will be paid out by the bookies as a result of Faldo's win, and he may never be long odds again.

Faldo won in the Kingdom of Fife, at the very place where, two years ago in a Dunhill Cup match, he was booed by the locals for not playing a shot, in a swirling mist, when they thought he should. That has rankled with him, but yesterday, quite remarkably, he was given a rapturous reception right from the first tee. And on his return, as he walked into the enormous amphitheatre created around the 18th green, there were somehow crammed into that space some 40,000 people all cheering another European winner of a major championship. The Kingdom had a new Ruler.

He will prove to be a benevolent one if his early proclamations are to be typical. 'I've been very fortunate,' he said, 'to win a Green Jacket at Augusta. But to win an Open at St Andrews, in this fabulous town, is really quite special. Half an hour after that US Open I had decided that I would make up for it by winning the Open and since then I've had some crazy dreams. I've dreamed that I would be leading after three rounds by five, and I've dreamed that I would come to the last four in the lead. It's scary really.'

He also had some frightening moments, he admitted, on the course. 'In general my iron play has been so good that I only missed two greens all week, apart from places like the 17th where I deliberately played short at times. But when my lead dropped down to two at the 12th that was a real worry because there are some tough holes with some really deep bunkers out there. Then I had a putt on 12 for a birdie and I thought: "If I make this, it's mine." But I missed it and fortunately Payne Stewart was dropping one at the same time up ahead. Then I hit a great six iron into the 15th and I said to myself: "I need this putt, I need this putt, I've got to make it," and I did. That was a key moment for me.'

Faldo also admitted to human frailties. 'This morning I was really nervous. I started thinking that it's so easy to lose a five-shot lead, just go in one pothole. I was praying to get on to the golf course and I really had to force down lunch because I knew I should eat. I was all churned up inside and my mind is only really happy when it's on a golf course; outside it starts running wild. But everything was okay once I had started.

'There were no three-putts all week, only one bunker and my driving was good too. That was the key improvement on Medinah where I had to take irons off the tee because I'd lost my driving.'

Faldo played in the last pair – with Ian Baker-Finch, cruelly known, since he took 79 in the last round after leading after three, as Baker-Flinch. But there was to be no backing away over the early holes this time, and the two of them went at it heel-to-heel and toe-to-toe, going to the turn in matching 35s. They were accompanied by a huge entourage, both inside and outside the ropes, with no one able to see very much at all.

This was hardly surprising since inside the ropes were one scorer, two men from the rules committee, a bunker raker, two 'Quiet Please' sign holders, three buggies for radio and television, four backpacked men with aerials, a team of scurrying Japanese tellymen, five policemen, hordes of men in yellow armbands – the press – and hordes more in green bibs, the photographers.

There was also Faldo, going quietly and impressively about his business and it surely helped that he was able to hit a nine iron into the first green to no more than two feet for a birdie that would help dispel the nerves.

The 4th, though, took away a shot. Faldo drove miles left on the ultra-safe line and that left him an exceedingly dangerous second, which he duly deposited in a bunker. He had to hit a really good shot just to get out, but there was never a chance of a par-saving putt. Thankfully for Faldo, Baker-Finch had driven into a bunker on the right, caught the lip as he came out, and also took five.

With no one in the sub-plot making a serious move, Faldo was able to stay on cruise-control. As no one else was able to press the accelerator, he had no need to, and there is no one better in the world of golf at grinding out the pars than the man Mark Calcavecchia calls Mr Hang Around Faldo. Well old HA himself was doing the job he does best extremely well and the final tally of three birdies, two bogeys – one of which was all but deliberate at the 17th – told a hugely successful tale.

Stewart was Faldo's biggest threat for most of the day and when he hit a blind second shot to eight feet at the 12th and then holed for a birdie to close the gap to two, there was momentary panic in the European camp. But Stewart relieved the pressure immediately by driving into a bunker at the 13th, to make the margin three again.

In the end Stewart failed to cope not only with the 17th, where he was over the road, but also with the 18th, where he finished in the Valley of Sin and took five. Peter Jacobsen tangled with the Road Hole bunker too, but not before he had got tangled up in the rough to the left of this hole. It took him five blows to find the sand, at which point this immensely likeable man held up both hands high in the air in surrender. He took eight, for a 41 home.

Ian Woosnam presented a flickering challenge, particularly when he drove the 10th green and then birdied the 11th for three birdies in a row. That took him to 14 under, only four behind at the time, but there was nothing left. Woosnam drove so far left at the 14th that he could only go even further left with his second and that left him an impossible third. He took a bogey six, as did Jose-Maria Olazabal at the same hole, and both these luminous talents had, in the end, a poor Open by their standards.

So, by his standards of 18 months ago, did Sandy Lyle, but to finish seven under par, joint 16th and win £11,150 was by the standards that have obtained of late, entirely satisfactory.

The scores

GB and Ireland unless stated

270: N. Faldo 67, 65, 67, 71 (£85,000)

275: M. McNulty (Zim) 74, 68, 68, 65; P. Stewart (US) 68, 68, 68, 71 (£60,000 each)

276: J. Mudd (US) 72, 66, 72, 66; I. Woosnam 68, 69, 70, 69 (£40,000 each)

277: G. Norman (Aus) 66, 66, 76, 69; I. Baker-Finch (Aus) 68, 72, 64, 73 (£28,500 each)

279: D. Graham (Aus) 72, 71, 70, 66; D. Hammond (US) 70, 71, 68, 70; S. Pate (US) 70, 68, 72, 69; C. Pavin (US) 71, 69, 68, 71 (£22,000 each)

THE MAN BEHIND THE CHAMPION

By John Samuel

On the St Andrews eve-of-battle practice ground the tall, stooped figure of Dave Leadbetter loped from Ian Baker-Finch to Mike Hulbert to Sandy Lyle and finally to Nick Faldo.

The guru working his magic? Not David Leadbetter. 'I'm no man with his arms folded on a mountain,' said the Florida-based tutor, a confident American accent overlaying the original Sussex vowels.

He was never, he says, cut out to be a touring professional. As an analyst for top players' swing styles and rhythms he is now unsurpassed.

Faldo . . . Since he won the Open in 1987, his record in major events has been equalled only by Jack Nicklaus or Ben Hogan.

Leadbetter first began working with Faldo in 1985. But though he was already an established player, Faldo knew there were things amiss. He ballooned too many shots. His apparently clean, simple swing would not allow him to win majors on windy links.

Leadbetter reasoned that the 6ft 3in Faldo was standing too far away from the ball. Much time was spent building a more solid base, widening his stance, straightening his legs and raising his pelvis.

He had him move more of his weight to the balls of his feet and turned his right foot outwards for a better rotation.

'What I offer Faldo now,' he says, 'are little triggers. More width. Stand a little taller. More coil. No one is more aware of the sensations of the golf swing than Nick.'

Leadbetter talks animatedly, seeking concentration and understanding from his listener, prominent nose under the very American white peaked hat nodding, his long, slender fingers demonstrating grip, take-away and follow through.

'Faldo feels the parts of his body very acutely. He's not out there on the course thinking of nothing but striking the ball. He is feeling for the right swing sensations all the time. You see him at it before every shot.

'People say he's slow, but he moves quickly between shots. He won't set up until he's totally happy with his swing impression.'

Each day it may be a different trigger. 'Today it could be "a little more pressure on the inside of the left foot".

'Top golfers know that these days it's the majors that really count. That's where the big money is. That's when they have to peak. No one knows it better than Nick.'

On the practice ground they make an oddly contrasting pair, stork and eagle, with a third figure, the busy little Fanny Sunesson, starling-like, fussing around, cleaning club grips, standing them housewife-proud in ascending order, wedges first, round the bag.

Yesterday there were two sessions, one earlier in the morning, the other for 30 minutes or so before going out. Between times Faldo is relaxing with the children back at the hotel.

Sandy Lyle's Leadbetter session had a fourth presence, the Australian psychologist Noel Blundell. Leadbetter's advice dominates at this point.

'Sandy knows he still has work to do, but he's on much better terms with himself,' says Leadbetter. Lyle asks his caddie Dave Musgrave for the driver. 'A month ago I wouldn't be hitting a driver on the range,' says Lyle. No one has better recent experience of golfing mind and matter coming apart but, as this Championship has shown, he is distinctly on the mend.

Little wonder that suffering champions such as Ballesteros, Watson and Strange are now beating a path to the Leadbetter door at Lake Nona, Orlando.

TALL, DARK AND HYPHENATED STROLLS IT

David Davies at Royal Birkdale sees the Australian, who has come so close in the past, stay the course to defy the doubters

Ian Baker-Finch, 1991 Birkdale champion . . . Playing the 1990 final round with Faldo taught him toughness and focus.

In benign breezes Ian Baker-Finch, at the third time of asking, won the Open Championship at Royal Birkdale yesterday. Twice in the past the handsome 30-year-old Australian had been in the final group on the last day and failed spectacularly. Yesterday, when all the world was expecting brilliance from Severiano Ballesteros, Baker-Finch began with three birdies in the first four holes, five in the first seven, and finally gave the lie to one of the nastiest nicknames in sport; no longer is he Ian Baker-Flinch.

He stood on the 72nd tee with a three-stroke lead, produced a final round of 66, four under par, and won by two strokes from his fellow Australian Mike Harwood.

It is the first time Australians have finished one and two in a championship. Fred Couples and Mark O'Meara were jointly third, three behind, and Bob Tway, Jodie Mudd and Eamonn Darcy were joint fifth. In the top 11 there were four Australians, four Americans, an Irishman, a Spaniard and a German.

Baker-Finch, in winning his first major, won £90,000 in the short term. But this most marketable of men will make millions over the years from the kind of clothing endorsements he can now expect. Not that it worries him. 'I know that my lifestyle will change. But I can handle that. I'm a big boy now.'

The money flows in from his on-course activities, too. In his last three events, the Anheuser-Busch Classic, the New England Classic and now the Open, he has finished third, second and first. He has won almost £200,000 in that time alone. 'I've had about 11 seconds since I last won,' he said, 'but that doesn't matter any more.'

The nickname was born in 1984 after a plague of headlines concerning him that year. After opening up with rounds of 68, 66 this almost totally unknown, at that time, led by three. 'Ian Baker-Who?' screamed a tabloid.

After three rounds Baker-Finch was joint leader with Tom Watson, went out last, found the Swilean burn at the first hole, took 79 and finished ninth, and 'Ian Baker-Flinch' was inevitable.

Then last year Baker-Finch, although five behind Nick Faldo, was the man nearest to him and was alongside him in the last round. He took 73 and finished sixth. 'All I did was eat dust,' he said afterwards. 'Faldo taught me I needed to be tougher, to focus on what I am out there to do, rather than on what's going on around me.'

Yesterday, though, no man could have avenged himself more gloriously for those two failures. The way he destroyed the field with that opening burst called to mind the devastation that another hyphenated player once inflicted on a sports field.

It was Tony O'Reilly, the Irish rugby wing, who missed the tackle and complained: 'Horrocks went one way, Taylor went the other and I was left holding the hyphen.'

Yesterday no one saw which way Baker-Finch went after that superb start.

It was in part inspired by a message from the last Australian to win at Royal Birkdale, Peter Thomson in 1965. He rang an Australian journalist covering the event to ask him to pass on his best wishes, adding: 'I'll be watching every shot on the telly.'

The message was received gratefully and Baker-Finch said to its bearer: 'What you doin' tonight, mate? Wanna come to a barbie at my place?' There is relaxed for you. In contrast, perhaps, the buggies that shuttled the players to and from the practice ground were, at the time, taking the Ballesteros entourage to the 1st tee. As he rode by, waving royally, Ballesteros received the plaudits of an expectant crowd: 'It's all yours Seve.'

It was far from that. Ballesteros began bogey, par, bogey and, although each of his three Opens has been won from two shots behind, this was already not going to be another.

Baker-Finch, having parred the 1st, hit a drive and six iron to the 2nd, holing from 15 feet, and followed that with a 10-foot birdie putt at the 3rd. The good start was made better at the 4th, a short hole of 203 yards where Baker-Finch hit his best shot of the day, a three iron to seven feet, for a two.

For the first time in the week the players were able to go for the carry over the bunkers at the 6th and the Australian set up a six-foot birdie putt, which he holed, and he promptly holed another from 15 feet at the short 7th.

At that point he was five under for the round and five clear of any opposition. His thoughts? 'I said, "Jeez, I'd better not stuff up now or I'll really cop it".' He reached the turn in 29, one of only 10 men to break 30 for nine holes in an Open.

In a sense it was a dangerous start, for the Australian began to play a touch conservatively. He hit a defensive tee-shot at the 10th and came off it a little, and the ball ran into the horrible pot bunkers on the right, whence he could only chop it out. 'That stopped me playing cautiously,' he said. 'I've been playing such good golf recently I told myself to just carry on playing it.'

Baker-Finch arrives at the 72nd, the Open his for the taking.

He took his time, though. If things were not right he stepped away and waited until they were. From the 11th to the 16th he addressed the ball on the tee, only to stop and start again. Near-perfect tee-shots showed it was common sense operating and not nerves.

There were to be no more mistakes until the 18th where, with his three-shot cushion, he hit a wild drive that was to cost him an unimportant five. But the wild charge of the crowd to see the last green almost cost him more than that.

'Mark O'Meara was knocked to the ground and I got banged on the head, on the back and on the shoulders,' said Baker-Finch. 'It's the only tough thing in this championship, but someone may get really hurt some time. The pity of it was that with that big lead I didn't get time to smell the roses.'

After he won he wept. 'I cried for about an hour after that 79 in 1984,' he said. 'Then I forgot about it. This time I couldn't stop myself because this is the world championship, it's the most important of them all. I'd give everything I've ever won before for this old claret jug.'

The gentle breezes, the soft greens and the lack of direct pressure allowed some early dashes and Greg Norman, as is his wont, took the opportunity to do some stormin', opening up with three birdies in the first five holes to move to level par. But he played the next four in two over, to be out of contention again, a sadly familiar tale.

Jodie Mudd, however, broke the course record with his seven-under-par 63 which he called 'the greatest round of golf I have every played'. It contained eight threes, five of them in succession from the 10th, and took him to three under for the Championship.

The scores

GB and Ireland unless stated

272: I. Baker-Finch (Aus) 71, 71, 64, 66

274: M. Harwood (Aus) 68, 70, 69, 67

275: F. Couples (US) 72, 69, 70, 64; M. O'Meara (US) 71, 68, 67, 69

277: J. Mudd (US) 72, 70, 72, 63; B. Tway (US) 75, 66, 70, 66; E. Darcy 73, 68, 66, 70

278: C. Parry (Aus) 71, 70, 69, 68

279: G. Norman (Aus) 74, 68, 71, 66; B. Langer (Ger) 71, 71, 70, 67; S. Ballesteros (Sp) 66, 73, 69, 71

1992

FIGHTING FALDO AVERTS MAJOR DISASTER

David Davies sees the finest English player of the modern era survive a spirited late challenge and the intense pressure of the occasion to win his third Open championship.

Faldo, caught in one of the sharp showers that fell on Muirfield during the final round.

With a monumental display of courage and determination Nick Faldo recovered from being two behind with four to play and won the Open. It is his fifth major championship and his second at Muirfield. He won the 1987 Open here, the 1990 Open at St Andrews and the US Masters titles of 1989 and 1990. Yesterday he earned £95,000 and also the Sony world ranking of No. 1.

Faldo began the final round with a four-stroke lead and gradually frittered it away until, as he stood on the 15th tee, it seemed almost certain that the American John Cook would snatch the title. But at that point Faldo said to himself: 'You've simply got to play the best four holes of your life' and he did so. He birdied the 15th and 17th holes while Cook bogeyed the 18th and Faldo, with a 12-under-par total of 272, had won by one stroke.

As he sank the final putt, a one-foot tap-in, the Faldo façade of icy control finally cracked. His tears were plentiful as he celebrated reaching a plateau in the game no other modern British player has achieved.

Yet his final round – a two-over-par 73 with four bogeys and two birdies – bore no resemblance to his previous winning round here, when he had 18 consecutive pars. He bunkered his opening drive and went back to 13 under, but this error did not seem to shake the massive calm he brings to the task in hand these days. Nor did a sudden, sharp shower on the second fairway. He took his practice swings under a brolly held by his caddie, Fanny Sunesson, and took his par comfortably. He then had eight more, in succession if not in comfort. At the 5th, for instance, he took an age to determine his second shot while the huge scoreboard beside the green was signalling the unwelcome news that Cook, in the group in front, had eagled the hole and gone to 12 under, only one behind.

Faldo selected a five-iron, hit it hard and high, and saw it plummet into a greenside bunker. What he did not know was that the recent rain had given a crust to the sand. The ball had plugged and only a white spot, the size of an old sixpence, was visible. Faldo had to fold his left leg against the face of the bunker and just hit and hope, but he got the ball out to 50 feet and two-putted for a wearing, tearing par five.

The 8th was also nerve-racking, for this is a hole with a history for Faldo. When he won in 1987 he hit his second into the bunkers 30 yards short of the green. He then hit a wonderful recovery shot to four feet, holed the putt and later recalled the moment as crucial. This year he found the same bunker in the second round, came out to 20 feet and again holed for a par. Yesterday he avoided the sand by going a long way left and putting up to six feet. Now he had another crucial putt, and again in it went. So far, so solid.

But the adage is that the championship does not start until the last nine holes, and the adage is accurate. Faldo led by three at the turn, from Steve Pate and by four from Cook, but the unique pressures of championship golf began to bear down. He only had a nine-iron second to the 11th but, as he was to say, he was 'very negative' over the shot and dumped it in a bunker. His shoulders slumped and he stared in disbelief at such a basic error.

Worse was to follow at the short 13th where, although he found the green, he was in definite three-putt range. The first was rolled to three feet but the second was pushed and he departed muttering.

He was back to 11 under and within a minute or so Cook had joined him on that mark. The American, accumulating while Faldo had been fruitlessly speculating, holed a 10ft putt for his second birdie of the back nine. Faldo drove off the 14th into a bunker, and in the same instant Cook hit the green at the short 16th. For Faldo the bogey was automatic; for Cook the birdie putt from 25 feet was an amazing bonus. He was now two ahead.

The 17th offers a birdie to those wary of its bunkers, and had Cook availed himself of that opportunity he might have become Open champion. But behind him Faldo, who is never less than grimly determined, was now positively obsessed.

At the 15th he hit a superb drive and a simply magnificent second, which pitched short of the green and ran and ran, taking the contours of the green and trickling two feet from the hole. That was a birdie but even so he needed some help from the leader, Cook. It came on the 17th green, the same surface that had seen Tony Jacklin take three putts and lose the 1972 Open to Lee Trevino. From 20 feet Cook ran his first effort two feet past and lipped the next

The final curtain falls on the 1992 Open and Faldo celebrates his victory with a brief rendition of 'My Way'.

one back. A seemingly certain birdie, a championship-winning birdie, had become a possible title-losing par.

Behind him Faldo chipped superbly at the short, downwind 16th to save par, and then hit two wonderful shots to the 17th green. The eagle putt was left a foot short, the birdie was a formality and now the championship was reaching its climax.

Cook, off a good drive, shoved his second miles right, into the crowd, and while he managed a good recovery to 10 feet he could not manage the par putt, which slid by on the low side.

Now Faldo had a par for the championship. A good drive gave him a three-iron second. 'I told myself "Come on, it's your favourite club" and I hit it fantastic.' In fact the ball almost pitched in the hole, but then ran to the back fringe some 20 feet past the pin. 'I couldn't believe it had gone so far past,' said Faldo. 'It gave me a really difficult putt. But I trundled it down to a foot, and thank God it wasn't any more than that, because I might not have been able to handle it. My legs were shaking over that putt. I was absolutely gone, I was whacked.'

But in it went and Faldo was champion for the second time at Muirfield. He bent down to retrieve the ball and as he stood up the tears were already in his eyes. He was still overcome as he went into the recorder's hut to sign his card and said to his playing partner, Pate: 'Tell me what to do.'

Recovering a little, he said: 'I need a smack on the head to sort me out. Why do I make it so difficult? I thought I had blown it. But the pressure wears you to a frazzle.'

But Faldo had survived it all. In his words, he had gone 'from disaster to the ultimate' and afterwards, accepting the trophy, he took the opportunity to settle a few old scores. He thanked the television commentators 'for telling me how to practice' and he thanked the press 'from the bottom of my, er, well from the heart of my bottom'.

It was hardly gracious, but it may be understandable given his adversarial relationship with the media. He finished his speech with a brief rendition of Frank Sinatra's 'I did it my way'. Unlike the events of the last day of Muirfield 1992, it was hopelessly flat.

The scores

(GB and Ireland unless stated)

272: N Faldo 66, 64, 69, 73

273: J Cook (US) 66, 67, 70, 70

274: J-M Olazabal (Sp) 70, 67, 69, 68

276: S Pate (US) 64, 70, 69, 73

279: A Magee (US) 67, 72, 70, 70; R Karlsson (Swe) 70, 68, 70, 71; M Mackenzie 71, 67, 70, 71; I Woosnam 65, 73, 70, 71; G Brand Jnr 65, 68, 72, 74; D Hammond (US) 70, 65, 70, 74; E Els (SA) 66, 69, 70, 74

280: M O'Meara (US) 71, 68, 72, 69; J Spence 71, 68, 70, 71; R Floyd (US) 64, 71, 73, 72; S Lyle 68, 70, 70, 72; L Rinker (US) 69, 68, 70, 73; C Beck (US) 71, 68, 67, 74

PICTURE CREDITS

The publishers acknowledge the following sources of the photographs: page 4, Jean Ward-Thomas; page 6 (bis), *Guardian*; page 10, Hulton-Deutsch Collection; pages 11, 12, 13, 15 and 16, The Illustrated London News Picture Library; pages 18, 19, 22, 25, 28, 31 and 33, Hulton-Deutsch Collection; pages 34 and 35, The Illustrated London News Picture Library; pages 37, 39, 42, 44, 48, 50, 51 and 53, Hulton-Deutsch Collection; pages 56, 59, 61 and 65, The Illustrated London News Picture Library; pages 67, 69, 71, 73, 75, 76, 78, 80, 82 and 84, Hulton-Deutsch Collection; page 85, Phil Sheldon; pages 87 and 89, Press Association Ltd; pages 92 and 94, Hulton-Deutsch Collection; page 97, Press Association Ltd; pages 99 and 101, Hulton-Deutsch Collection; page 103, Press Association Ltd; pages 106, 108, and 111, Hulton-Deutsch Collection; page 112, Press Association Ltd; pages 113 and 115 Hulton-Deutsch Collection; page 117 (bis), Central Press Photos Ltd; *Guardian*; page 119 (bis), Hulton-Duetsch Collection; page 122, Press Association Ltd; page 124, Central Press Photos Ltd; page 126, Press Association Ltd; page 128, Hulton-Deutsch Collection; page 130, Don McPhee/*Guardian*; pages 133 and 136 *Guardian*; page 138, Phil Sheldon; page 139, Phil Sheldon; page 140, *Guardian*; page 141, Phil Sheldon; page 143, Don McPhee/*Guardian*; page 145, Kenneth Saunders/*Guardian*; page 146, Phil Sheldon; page 149, Kenneth Saunders/*Guardian*; page 151, Press Association Ltd; page 155 (bis), Phil Sheldon; Kenneth Saunders/*Guardian*; pages 156, 157 and 158 Phil Sheldon; page 160, Don McPhee/*Guardian*; page 161, Phil Sheldon; page 163, Phil Sheldon; pages 164, 165 and 167, Kenneth Saunders/*Guardian*; page 171 (bis) *Guardian*; Jan Traylen/Phil Sheldon; page 172, Press Association Ltd; page 175, Reuters; page 176, Phil Sheldon; page 179, uncredited; page 181, Frank Baron/*Guardian*; page 183, Peter Dazeley; page 184, Phil Sheldon; pages 186 and 187, Frank Baron/*Guardian*.

INDEX

Adams, James, 55–7, 62–3, 73, 75, 78–9, 86
Alliss, Percy, 17, 26, 32, 35, 36–7, 42–3, 45, 52, 57, 58, 66
Alliss, Peter, 83, 84, 86, 93, 102, 105, 116, 120
Anderson, J. S., 88
Andrade, Bill, 169
Aoki, Isao, 142, 143–4, 146, 147, 173
Armour, Tommy, 4, 37, 41–3, 58, 63, 101, 132
Ayerst, David, 3
Ayton, Laurie, 54, 69
Azinger, Paul, 166–7, 169, 178

Bachli, D. W., 84
Baiocchi, Hugh, 159
Baker-Finch, Ian, 6, 159, 181, 182, 183–5
Balding, A., 116, 118
Ball, Frank, 21–3
Ball, John, 38
Ballesteros, Severiano, 5, 6, 135, 137, 140, 143–4, 152, 155–6, 157–9, 164, 170–3, 174, 179, 182, 183, 184, 185
Barber, Miller, 120
Barber, Tom, 20, 27–9, 38–40
Barbieri, R., 88
Barnes, Brian, 101, 118, 127, 129, 137, 141
Barnes, Jim, 4, 9–11, 14, 15, 17, 23, 24–6, 35, 37, 40
Beamish, C. H., 79
Bean, Andy, 147–8, 154–6
Bell, R. K., 68
Bembridge, Maurice, 118
Bender, Pete, 164, 165
Bertolino, E., 90
Birchenough, Eddie, 173
Blair, D. A., 77, 100
Blundell, Noel, 182
Bonallack, Michael, 98, 118
Boomer, A., 23, 30–2, 35, 46
Bousfield, Ken, 88, 102
Boyer, A., 39–40, 47
Boyle, Hugh, 116
Bradshaw, Harry, 4, 73–5, 81, 94
Braid, James, 28, 33, 36, 71, 76, 92, 110, 142, 154
Branch, W. J., 53–4, 57, 58, 60
Brand Jr, Gordon, 150, 164–5
Brewer, Gay, 118, 129
Brews, S. F., 50–2, 62
Broadhurst, Paul, 173–4
Brown, Eric, 81, 82–3, 88, 93, 94–6, 100, 102
Brown, Ken, 141, 145–8
Bruen, Jimmy, 66
Buckle, G. R., 11
Bulla, Johnny, 4, 64–6, 67–8, 70, 72
Bullock, Fred, 63, 76–7, 81, 97–8
Burns, G. F., 134, 139
Burns, G. III, 137
Burton, Dick, 4, 61–2, 63, 64–6, 67, 70
Busson, J. J., 62–3
Butler, Peter, 129, 137
Byram, R., 144

Calcavecchia, Mark, 6, 176–9, 181
Cardus, Neville, 3
Carmichael, Sir John, 134
Carr, J. B. (Joe), 98, 100
Casera, 86
Casper, Billy, 117–18, 125
Caudin, J. W., 26
Cerda, Antonio, 78–9, 81, 82–3, 84, 86, 88, 91, 93, 97
Chapman, Robin, 150
Charles, Bob, 104–5, 106–7, 109, 117–18, 120, 129, 144
Chen, H. S., 124
Christmas, M. J., 102
Churio, M., 42–3
Clampett, Bobby, 151–3
Clark, Clive, 115–16
Clark, Howard, 150
Claydon, Russell, 179
Cole, Bobby, 131, 133–4
Coleman, Peter, 174–5
Coles, Neil, 102, 116, 118, 123, 128–9, 133–4
Compston, Archie, 11, 24–6, 29, 33–5, 38–40, 42, 45
Coody, Charles, 125
Cook, John, 186–8
Cooke, Alistair, 5, 137
Cotton, Henry, 3, 4, 30, 32, 40, 41–3, 45, 46–7, 49, 50–2, 53–4, 55–7, 58–60, 62–3, 66, 67–8, 69–70, 71–2, 80–1, 90–1, 93, 95–6, 119, 127, 132, 162
Couples, Fred, 159, 173, 178, 179, 183, 185
Cox, Bill, 62–3
Crampton, Bruce, 93
Crenshaw, Ben, 139, 142, 143–4, 145–8, 150, 159, 166–7
Cruickshank, R., 36–7
Cullen, Gary, 141

Dailey, A., 63
Dallemagne, M., 51–2, 57, 62
Daly, Fred, 4, 68, 69–70, 71–2, 76–7, 78–9, 80–1, 162
Darcy, Eamonn, 183, 185
Davis, David, 5–6
Davies, W. H., 26, 33, 35, 41–3, 45, 51
Davies, Rodger, 143–4, 166–7
De Foy, Craig, 124–5
Demaret, Jimmy, 86
Devlin, Bruce, 108–9, 111, 114, 116, 118
Dickinson, Jimmy, 127
Diegel, Leo, 36–7, 39–40, 46–7, 49
Dobereiner, Peter, 5, 6
Dudley, Ed, 46–7, 49, 59–60
Duncan, George, 3, 9–11, 14, 15, 17, 18, 19, 20, 21–3, 26, 28, 35
Durnian, Denis, 156
Dutra, Olin, 49

Easterbrook, S., 46–7, 49, 54
Ecila, J., 72
Edward, Prince of Wales, 41, 45
Edwards, Danny, 131
Enderby, K. E., 79

Faldo, Nick, 6, 135, 137, 141–2, 148, 151–3, 155, 156, 159, 162, 163, 164–5, 166–7, 168–9, 170–1, 173, 179, 180–1, 182, 183, 186–8
Fallon, Johnny, 62, 64, 66, 75, 87–8
Farrell, Johnny, 36–7, 42–3
Faulkner, Max, 4, 73, 75, 77, 78–9, 93, 96, 111, 162
Feherty, David, 178, 179
Ferguson, R., 89
Fernandez, Vicente, 137, 172
Fernie, Tom, 18, 20, 26
Floyd, Raymond, 135–7, 139, 142, 150, 151, 177
Forsbrand, Anders, 161
Fowler, W. Herbert, 3
French, Emmet, 29
Frost, David, 167, 169, 173

Gadd, B., 54, 63
Garaialde, Jean, 107
Garner, John, 131
Gaudin, H. A., 28
George VI, King, 127
Godwin, Geoff, 141, 150
Goggin, W., 81
Grady, Wayne, 176, 178
Graham, David, 160–1, 164, 181
Grappasonni, U., 79, 86
Green, Hubert, 131, 137, 138–9, 147
Green, T., 55–7
Greenhalgh, V., 62
Gregson, Malcolm, 116
Guardo, Jose, 116

Hagen, Walter, 3–4, 10, 14, 15–17, 18, 19, 20, 21–3, 27–9, 33–5, 36–7, 46–7, 57, 76, 87, 89, 92, 96, 101, 103, 130, 151
Haliburton, Tom, 93
Halsall, R., 86
Hammond, D., 181
Harvester, J., 72
Harvey, Alexander, 134
Harwood, Mike, 183, 185
Havers, Arthur, 3, 11, 14, 18, 19, 20, 31–2, 42–3, 44–5
Hayes, Mark, 139
Henning, Harold, 100, 102, 109, 116, 122–3, 129, 155–6
Herd, Sandy, 9, 11, 14, 18, 32
Hilton, H. H., 27, 30
Hitchcock, Jimmy, 98
Hodson, B., 30, 32, 52
Hogan, Ben, 4, 5, 74, 82–3, 89, 96, 97, 100, 101–2, 104, 112, 121, 124, 130, 132, 145, 152, 180
Holland, L., 9–11, 23
Hope, W. L., 44
Horne, Reg, 69–70
Horne, W. H., 11
Horton, Tommy, 115, 116, 123, 135, 137, 139, 165
Hsieh, Yu-shu, 156
Huggett, Brian, 103, 105, 110–11, 116
Hulbert, Mike, 182
Hunt, Bernard, 88, 100, 108–9, 110–11, 116
Hunt, Guy, 127
Hutchison, Jock, 3, 12–14, 15–17

Irwin, Hale, 5, 134, 143–4, 154–6, 171

Jack, R. R., 97–8, 100
Jacklin, Tony, 6, 115–16, 118, 119–20, 123, 124–5, 126–7, 128, 135, 137, 142, 144, 150, 160, 162, 164, 167, 175
Jackson, H., 123
Jacobs, John, 125
Jacobsen, Peter, 181
James, Mark, 135, 137, 143–4, 150
Jeihrine, D., 161
Jolly, H. C., 20, 39
Jones, B., 150
Jones, Bobby, 3–4, 27–9, 30–2, 38–40, 44, 57, 74, 76, 82, 87, 96, 101, 112, 121, 124, 137, 142, 152
Jowle, F., 88
Jurado, Joseph, 29, 33–5, 41–3, 79

Kenyon, E. W. H., 53–4, 66
Kerrigan, 14
King, B. L., 72
King, Sam, 66, 70, 71–2, 73, 75, 77, 81, 83, 86, 98
Kirkwood, J., 14, 19, 20, 30, 32, 46–7, 52, 68
Kite, Tom, 134, 137, 142, 161
Koch, Gary, 165, 173
Kuramoto, M., 153

Lacey, A. J., 43, 45, 57, 58, 60, 62
Lacey, C., 58, 60
Laidlaw, W., 60
Langer, Bernhard, 149, 157–9, 160–1, 164–5, 174–5, 179, 185
Leadbetter, David, 166, 182
Lee, Arthur Leonard (A. L. L.), 3–4
Lees, A., 69–70, 71, 75, 77, 81
Lema, Tony, 5, 108–9, 110–11, 132
Lester, E. G., 96
Lietzke, Bruce, 150
Lister, Hartley, 42
Little, Lawson, 68
Little, W. L., 53–4
Littler, Gene, 148
Locke, Bobby, 4, 5, 7, 57, 62–3, 66, 67–8, 73–5, 76–7, 78–9, 80–1, 82–3, 84–6, 87–8, 92–3, 94, 96, 100, 151
Longhurst, Henry, 4
Love, Davis Jnr, 120
Lu Liang Huan, 124–5, 131
Lucas, P. B. (Laddie), 53, 106
Lyle, Sandy, 6, 148, 151–3, 160–1, 162–3, 165, 168, 173, 177, 179, 181, 182

McCumber, Mark, 159
McEvoy, Peter, 141
Mackenzie, J., 20
McLean, J., 62
McLeod, Fred, 29
McNeilly, Dave, 171
McNulty, Mark, 180–1
Mahaffey, John, 134
Margaret, Princess, 127
Marr, Dave, 114
Marsh, Graham, 134, 144, 154–6, 159

Mason, Carl, 145, 147–8
Massey, Arnaud, 144
Mayo, Paul, 169
Melhorn, W., 27–9, 35
Middlecoff, Cary, 89, 93, 108
Miguel, Angel, 93, 109
Miguel, Sebastian, 107, 111, 114, 116
Miller, Johnny, 128–9, 131, 133–4, 135–7, 139, 141, 148, 164
Mitchell, Abe, 9–11, 14, 18, 20, 21, 24, 26, 27–9, 35, 36–7, 40, 45, 46–7, 49
Mize, Larry, 176
Monkhouse, A. N., 3
Montague, Evelyn, 3
Montague, Larry, 3, 5
Moore, E., 77
Morgan, Gil, 147–8
Morris, Old Tom, 151
Morris, Young Tom, 3, 144, 151
Mudd, Jodie, 178, 179, 181, 183, 185
Musgrove, Dave, 162, 182

Nagle, K. D. G., 6, 99–100, 102, 103–5, 107, 111, 114, 120, 125
Nakajima, Tommy, 164–5
Nelson, Byron, 60, 108, 132, 148
Newton, Jack, 132–3, 137, 146–7
Nicklaus, Jack, 5, 107, 108–9, 110, 112–14, 115–16. 117–18, 120, 121–3, 125, 126–7, 128–9, 130–1, 132–4, 135–7, 138–9, 140–2, 143–4, 146–8, 150, 151–3, 155–6, 157, 158, 163, 167, 168, 170, 173–4, 177, 178, 180
Nicklaus, Jackie, 135
Norman, Greg, 6, 144, 159, 164–5, 168–9, 176–9, 180–1, 185

O'Connor, Christy, 88, 91, 94, 96, 98, 102, 107, 109, 110–11, 116, 120, 129
O'Connor, Christy Jnr, 135, 137, 156, 161
Oddy, Drake, 178–9
Olazabal, Jose-Maria, 181
O'Meara, Mark, 161, 183, 185
Oosterhuis, Peter, 122–3, 130–1, 133–4, 135, 137, 141–2, 148, 151–3
O'Reilly, Tony, 6, 184
Owen, Simon, 140–2
Ozaki, Masashi, 144

Padgham, Alfred, 4, 45, 49, 50, 52, 53–4, 55–7, 59–60, 62–3, 71–2
Palmer, Arnold, 5, 6, 99–100, 101–2, 103–5, 107, 109, 110, 112–14, 117–18, 126–7, 128, 135, 139, 140, 143, 148, 150
Panton, John, 91, 98, 111, 123
Park, Willie, 3, 151
Parry, C., 185
Pate, Steve, 137, 148, 181, 187
Pavin, Cory, 181
Pennink, Frank, 63
Perkins, T. P., 30, 32, 33
Perry, Alf, 4, 53–4, 55, 62, 66, 69
Picard, H., 54, 60
Pinero, Manuel, 150
Player, Gary, 91, 96, 97–8, 105, 107, 109, 112, 114, 116, 117–18, 125, 127, 130–1, 132, 141, 148
Pose, M., 66
Price, Nick, 151–3, 167, 170–3, 174
Purtzer, Tom, 153

Rafferty, Ronan, 159
Ray, Ted, 9, 11, 20, 22, 24, 26, 101
Rees, D. J., 5, 66, 67–8, 76–7, 82–3, 84–6, 98, 100, 101–2
Rivers, J., 161
Robertson, 46
Robson, Fred, 30–2, 35, 38, 40, 45
Rodgers, P., 103–5, 106–7, 112–14
Rodgers, P. H., 31–2
Rogers, Bill, 149–50, 156
Romero, Eduardo, 178
Ruiz, L., 94, 96, 98

Sanders, Doug, 112–14, 121–2, 125, 127
Sarazen, Gene, 4, 33, 35, 37, 42–3, 44–5, 46–7, 49, 50, 53, 55–7, 81, 86, 95, 101, 112, 124, 152
Schroeder, Jody, 139, 142
Scott, Robert, 20
Scott, Syd, 81, 84, 86, 97–8, 100, 102, 105
Senior, Peter, 173
Seymour, 31
Shankland, Bill, 60, 66, 69–70, 79
Shearer, Bob, 142
Sherlock, J. G., 23
Shute, Densmore, 46–7, 48–9, 52, 59–60, 65, 132
Simpson, Scott, 168, 178
Smith, Horton, 38, 40, 42, 60
Smith, Macdonald, 18–20, 21–3, 24–6, 40, 42–3, 44–5, 52
Smith, W. D., 93
Smithers, W., 75
Smyth, Des, 151, 152–3
Snead, Sam, 4, 67–8, 105
Sota, Ramon, 107
Souchak, Mike, 91
Stadler, Craig, 147, 155, 167, 169
Stewart, Payne, 160–1, 167, 173, 178, 180–1
Storey, E. F., 63
Stranahan, Frank, 69–70, 72, 76–7, 78–9, 82–3
Strange, Curtis, 182
Sunesson, Fanny, 182, 186
Sutton, Hal, 150
Sutton, N., 62, 78–9
Suzuki, N., 137
Swaelens, Graham, 131

Taylor, J. H., 3, 15–17, 21–3, 26, 28, 35, 76, 92, 110, 135, 154
Thomas, Dave, 93, 94–6, 105, 112–14, 116, 121
Thomson, H., 57, 83
Thomson, Peter, 4, 5, 79, 80–1, 82–3, 84–6, 86–8, 89–91, 92–3, 94–6, 97, 98, 99–100, 102, 105, 107, 110–11, 114, 116, 120, 123, 125, 154, 184
Tolley, C. J. H., 20, 27, 46, 63
Toogood, P. A., 86

Torrance, Sam, 150, 159
Torrance, W. B., 32
Townsend, Peter, 131
Trevino, Lee, 123, 124–5, 126–7, 129, 139, 145–8, 149, 152. 155–6
Turnesa, Jimmy, 84, 86
Tway, Bob, 176, 183, 185

Van Donck, F., 71–2, 77, 81, 86, 88, 89–91, 93, 95–6, 97–8, 135
Vardon, Harry, 17, 28, 36, 76, 81, 92, 101, 110, 115, 130, 154
Vaughan, D. I., 127
Vicenzo, Roberto de, 4, 71–2, 75, 76–7, 82–3, 89–91, 99–100, 108–9, 111, 115–16, 118, 120, 125
Vickers, R., 32
Von Elm, G., 27, 29
Von Nida, Norman, 68, 69–70, 72, 81

Wadkins, Lanny, 129, 159
Ward, Charlie, 68, 70, 72, 73, 75, 78–9
Ward-Thomas, Pat, 4–5, 6, 7, 137, 163
Watrous, Al, 27–9, 37
Watson, Tom, 5, 132–4, 138–9, 143, 145–8, 149, 150, 151–3, 154–6, 157–9, 167, 170, 174, 178, 179, 180, 182, 183
Weetman, Harry, 78–9, 88, 91, 96, 100, 109
Weiskopf, Tom, 127, 128–9, 130–1, 137, 177
Wethered, Roger, 3, 12–14, 17, 31, 98
Whitcombe, C. A. (Charles), 15, 17, 18–20, 22, 26, 30, 32, 45, 52, 53–4, 59, 60, 63
Whitcombe, E. R. (Ernest), 21–3, 32, 52
Whitcombe, R. A. (Reg), 4, 42, 49, 57, 58–60, 61–3, 66, 69
Will, George, 116
Williamson, T., 14, 32, 35, 42
Wingate, S., 9, 11, 18, 26
Wolstenholme, Guy, 98, 100
Wood, Craig, 46–7, 48–9, 65
Woosnam, Ian, 164–5, 167, 170, 181
Wright, Ian, 172

Yancey, Bert, 125, 128–9

Zoeller, Fuzzy, 153, 165, 169, 176